The Great Anger

Ultra-Revolutionary Writing in France from the Atheist Priest to the Bonnot Gang

Edited and translated by
Mitchell Abidor

The Marxists Internet Archive
2009

Marxists Internet Archive
P.O. Box 1541; Pacifica, CA 94044; USA.

CC-SA (Creative Commons Attribution-Share Alike 3.0)
2009 by Marxists Internet Archive
Printed in Brooklyn by Long Dash Publishing.
Cover design by Joan Levinson.

Abidor, Mitchell
        The Great Anger: French history, anarchism, atheism

ISBN: 978-0-9805428-0-6

For Joan

For Pascal

Contents

Introduction 1
Jean Meslier (1678-1729) 7
Paul-Henry Thiry, Baron d'Holbach (1723-1789) 54
Jean-Paul Marat (1743-1793) 70
The Enragés and Jacques Hébert 87
Jacques Hébert (1757-1794) 89
Anacharsis Cloots (1755-1794) 104
Jacques Roux (d. 1794) 109
Gracchus Babeuf (1760-1797) 125
Sylvain Maréchal (1750-1803) 133
Louis Auguste Blanqui (1805-1881) 170
The Paris Commune (1871) 209
The Propagandists of the Deed (1890s) 241
Ravachol (1859-1892) 243
Emile Henry (1872-1894) 250
Zo d'Axa (1864-1930) 262
Albert Libertad (1875-1908) 276
Georges Palante (1862-1925) 292
Victor Serge (1890-1947) 309
Epilogue May 1968 331

Acknowledgements

I would first like to thank all the volunteers at the Marxists Internet Archive (www.marxists.org) where most of these texts initially appeared.

In particular, I want to thank:

Michael Schauerte, Sam Berner, and Liviu Jacob all helped in reviewing and editing my translations of the texts.

Stéphane Beau, keeper of the flame of Georges Palante's philosophy, was the source of many texts and leads.

Curtis Price was unfailingly helpful and generous in tracking down and providing hard-to-find texts from the anarchist individualist tradition.

The most indispensable partner in this endeavor was Andy Blunden of the Marxists Internet Archive. He was my initial contact at the Archive and has provided me with support, guidance, and encouragement. His friendship and insights are invaluable to me. *The Great Anger* would not exist without him.

And I have no words to express my gratitude to my wife, Joan Levinson.

Mitchell Abidor
September 2008

Introduction

Now that what passes for French political thought and philosophy has fallen before the onslaught of what the historian Tony Judt calls "the Higher Drivel," we need more than ever to remember that things were not always this way. France was once the scene of lively and unbridled political discourse, aimed not at a university elite, but at the people, the ones actually suffering under the existing order. The main voices of this tradition, which we can roughly trace from the early eighteenth to the early twentieth centuries, hated this world and its injustice, and their main emotion, the motivating force of their actions, was their Great Anger.

The phrase "the Great Anger" appears in the context of the pages of the most unrestrained journal of the French Revolution, the "Père Duchesne" (Old Man Duchesne) of Jacques Hébert. The title of each issue of Hébert's journal spelled out Père Duchesne's emotion at that moment. And so we had "the Great Anger of Old Man Duchesne against the fucking slanderers of the ladies of Les Halles and the flower sellers of the Palais Royal." But this phrase, the Great Anger, is also a description of a current in French revolutionary activity. In the nineteenth and twentieth centuries, France didn't lack for theoreticians of revolutionary action, but it also didn't lack what can perhaps be called theoreticians of no theory, anti-theoreticians who believed that revolutionary action was the truest expression of revolutionary theory.

In the early- to mid-nineteenth century, there were thinkers who constructed theories that would serve as the basis for a better future, men such as Charles Fourier and Etienne Cabet with their utopian designed communities. There were also writers and activists who were moved not by a hypothetical beautiful tomorrow, but by the reality of a hateful today, one that had to be attacked in all ways and at whatever the cost. This is not to say that their viewpoint had no intellectual underpinnings or that it lacked roots in France's past. The struggle against the existing order during this period passed through two mutually supporting areas of action: the fight against God and the fight against those in power, the principles of which were laid out in the seventeenth century by an obscure country priest. Atheism being at the very heart of the Great Anger, its history actually begins with the first masterpiece of atheism, Jean Meslier's *"Mémoire contre la religion."* This massive book, written in secret by the country priest, contained everything that was to follow: the contesting of God and of the social structure that depended on God as its ally and its support. The great nineteenth-century revolutionary conspirator Auguste Blanqui called one of his many journals *"Ni dieu ni maître,"* neither God nor master. And these twin evils had already been analyzed and theoretically demolished, and an alternative vision of the future was proposed by Jean Meslier. Meslier exerted a tremendous influence, one too frequently ignored, on the next generation of pre-Revolutionary thinkers, those of the Enlightenment. The philosophers of the Enlightenment were strongly influenced by the atheist priest, and they provided much of the intellectual armament for the coming generations of revolutionaries of the Great Anger.

The questioning of the old order by Rousseau, Voltaire, Diderot, d'Holbach, and others was essential in laying the foundation for the direct action of the people, who entered the scene with their attack on the Bastille, symbol of tyranny, on July 14, 1789. But the victory was taken from the people by various progressive factions of the nascent bourgeoisie, and it is at this point that the Great Anger makes its appearance as an active force. The *Enragés*, men such as Jacques Roux, Anacharsis Cloots, and Jean Varlet, fought the rampant speculation and starvation policies, which benefited the rich and harmed the laboring classes. After the liquidation of this group by the Jacobins, Jacques Hébert and his followers from the Cordelier Club, took up their fight. The *Enragés'* defense of popular interests, their opposition to religion, stood on no grand ideological foundation. Instead, theirs was a rage directed at those who had snatched the power won by the people's struggle. Their fight was to ensure themselves sustenance, to prevent the *nouveau riche* from starving them; and they expressed themselves, and their anger, in no uncertain terms.

The machine now set in motion rolled on for more than a hundred years. The fall of Robespierre in July of 1794, though initially applauded by some, was followed by opposition to the reactionary

Directory that replaced the Jacobins. The anger at the Directory took concrete form in the Conspiracy of Equals of Gracchus Babeuf and his followers in 1795. Here, in this early and abortive outbreak, we again see the confluence of the struggles against economic and political injustice with the struggle against God. Sylvain Maréchal, author of the Conspiracy's manifesto, had been—and would continue to be until his death—a militant advocate for a godless communist society, the same society called for by Jean Meslier whom he so admired.

Auguste Blanqui tied all of these strands together over the course of the three great French revolutions of the nineteenth century, those of 1830, 1848, and the Paris Commune of 1871. Blanqui was less concerned with laying out a strict plan for the future communist society than with the blueprints for the organization that would bring down the existing order. Decades in prison did nothing to still the rage of "*L'enfermé*," "the Imprisoned," a rage directed not only at those in power, but also against those who had betrayed the fight, those too weak to stay the course, those all too willing to compromise. Ever optimistic, Blanqui believed almost any year was equally propitious for the final conflict; for him, the revolution was always the Thursday after next.

The Paris Commune of 1871 began in a burst of anger, that of the Parisians who had been defeated by the Prussians in Napoleon III's war against Prussia. The workers of Paris refused to surrender their cannons to the republic of Adolphe Thiers, which had fled Paris for Versailles, replacing the fallen empire. The ensuing revolutionary seizure of power was proof that rage and humiliated pride can be the motivating forces for a true revolutionary struggle, one without any prepared plan or clear direction other than that of giving power to those who had been deprived of it. It was the genius of the French working class that led it to spontaneously find the forms for its power; but it was the same lack of a plan that prevented the Great Anger from maintaining its hold on that power. More importantly, it also poses the question of the viability of inchoate rage as a basis for the seizing of power. Later, Marxist theory and Leninist practice provided some answers to these questions.

The next decades saw the final explosion of the Great Anger, its apotheosis and collapse as a form of confrontation with the established order, its definitive superseding by organized movements for change.

The executions, deportations, and bannings that followed the Paris Commune gave way to a series of strong mass movements that ultimately dominated the French left. The Marxists Jules Guesde, Paul Lafargue, and later Jean Jaurès drew to themselves vast numbers of working-class militants and took a significant place in French government and union organizations. At the same time, union organizations grew ever stronger, while mass anarchist organizations took on greater importance than ever. Alongside this rise in mass action, international anarchist congresses and journals were publishing recipes for the construction of explosive devices, placing the means for action and liberation in the hands of individuals.

Throughout this period there also remained the snipers, the irreducible negators, men like Zo d'Axa, whose journal *"L'endehors"* (The Outsider) expressed an opposition to everything and support of… nothing. There was also Emile Pouget, whose "Père Peinard" was a direct descendant of Hèbert's "Père Duchesne," written by workers and for workers in working-class French and advocating rebellion as an everyday act. There was no need to be member of a group or union to indulge in workplace sabotage, the subject of Pouget's most famous pamphlet. The righteous anger of the individual worker at the injustice of his lot didn't require the regimentation of a party to lead to struggle; such anger created its own framework, its own justification.

All of this came to a conclusion in the decades from 1892 to 1911, in the paroxysm of anger that was propaganda by the deed and anarchist illegalism. If mass movements, despite their growth and penetration, were unable to shake the foundations of the establishment, then the propagandists of the deed, Ravachol, Auguste Vaillant, Emile Henry, Santo Caserio would take a different path and directly confront the class enemy, with gun, knife, or bomb in hand. There was no need for a defined program when the acts—the assassination of the French president Carnot by Santo Caserio in 1894, the bombing of the Chamber of Deputies by Auguste Vaillant in

1893, Emile Henry's attack on the Café Terminus—were in and of themselves expressions of a program. The bourgeoisie's contempt for the lives of workers, most glaringly demonstrated by the massacre of striking workers at Fourmies in 1891, was met by a corresponding contempt for bourgeois life as demonstrated by Henry's bombing of a café or Ravachol's grave robbing and murder.

This individualist current, never in a majority (and indeed could it be?), produced figures of a stunning originality and rectitude. Particularly significant were Albert Libertad and those in the circle around his paper "*l'anarchie*"—Victor Serge and Emile Armand. At the same time, the works of the provincial philosophy teacher George Palante, gave individualism a markedly pessimistic, anti-political, and misanthropic form.

Its final outburst was in the form of anarchist illegalism, with bandits like Marius Jacob providing a social and political justification for their crimes in texts such as "Why I was a Bandit," while supporters of the movement wrote articles in defense—or at least exculpation of—the movement. Its most notorious avatar was the Bonnot Gang, a group of anarchists who unleashed a crime wave whose end brought down the curtain on the Great Anger.

Jules Bonnot himself, the leader of the gang, in the years before his death had renounced work and dedicated himself to counterfeiting and theft, particularly of automobiles and motorcycles. This culminated in the (perhaps accidental) killing of an anarchist comrade and the (certainly intentional) theft of thousands of francs the latter had with him at the time of his death.

The crime wave of Bonnot and his gang then truly took off, resulting in the robbing of the *Société Générale* on December 12, 1911, the killing of a policeman who had stopped them two months later, and further robberies in March 1912. The police pursuit became more heated, and two of Bonnot's associates were arrested on March 30. Nearly a month later the security forces found Bonnot and, in a furious gun battle on April 24, the assistant director of the security forces was killed. Bonnot, however, managed to escape. His hideout was discovered just four days later—at the home of an auto mechanic in Choisy-le-Roi—and he was placed under siege. The building was dynamited but Bonnot fought till the end, when he was mortally wounded. On May 15 the last of his accomplices were themselves killed in another shoot-out. The Bonnot Gang, and with it the Great Anger, disappeared as a vital current of the French left.

The Great War was approaching, and despite the failure of French socialists to halt it, mass movements henceforth held center stage in the form of the Socialists, the Communists after the foundation of the French Communist Party in 1920, or the left-wing unions of the *Confédération général du travail* and the *Confédération général du travail unifié*. The strength of the mass movements, their ability to effect change and to express and defend the interests of the working class, covered over the individual voices of anger that continued to try to make themselves heard. Particularly in 1935-36, after the wave of demonstrations against French fascists in February 1934 and the strike wave and Popular Front victory of the spring of 1936, it seemed that the programs of these groups could be realized, that mass action could effect profound change. But they failed in their larger goals, those of achieving important ameliorations in the lot of the worker: paid vacations, greater job security, the French *état providence*—the welfare state. The remaking of society that had been the dream of countless thousands had died. The Great Anger which exploded again in May 1968 had, by the early years of the twenty-first century, mutated simply into the Great Indifference.

Jean Meslier (1678-1729)

History willed it that the first Frenchman to embody the central anarchist idea of *"ni dieu ni maître"*—neither God nor master—was to be a provincial priest, an atheist priest, born in the late seventeenth century. Jean Meslier kept the manuscript of his 1000-page masterpiece, the "Memoir Against Religion," hidden during his lifetime. It was later passed from hand to hand and published in truncated and travestied form, yet it remains the foundational document of modern atheism, a work of a breadth and depth seldom equaled since its completion in 1729. The present-day philosopher Michel Onfray, who gave Meslier pride of place in his "Traité d'Athéologie," (translated as "Atheist Manifesto") praised Meslier not only as an atheist, but a revolutionary communist, internationalist, materialist hedonist, and philosopher, echoing the title of Maurice Dommanget's 1965 biography: "The Curé Meslier—Atheist, Communist, and Revolutionary under Louis XIV."

All of this is rendered more remarkable by the fact that Jean Meslier spent his entire ecclesiastical career in the tiny village of Etripigny in the Ardennes, a village with a population of 65. He is thought to have made only two trips to Paris, and his small library, apart from Montaigne's essays, could not have given him the basis for the ideas that were to set him on his unique revolutionary road. However unpropitious his background and setting, Jean Meslier cast the foundation for everything revolutionary that was to follow in the coming centuries.

Meslier's work is the most uncompromising of attacks not only on religion—which would not necessarily make him an atheist—but on the very idea of God, on the Bible, on the illogic of belief in a Supreme Being, and on the unhealthy effects on humanity resulting from a belief in such a being. But what makes Meslier's accomplishment even more astounding is the fact that he, from the depths of the distant provinces, unambiguously extended his attack to the political and social system that was constructed on a religious foundation. In words that were to find an echo in the acts of the "propagandists of the deed" two centuries later, Meslier called for the "bringing down, the assassination of all those detestable monsters and enemies of humankind" who were the tyrants in place, as well as for the sharing of goods in common, the free education of all children, the freedom of marriage and divorce. All fetters on human freedom were attacked by Meslier.

Meslier's enormous achievement and importance were obscured by his book's fate. He hand wrote four copies which, in order to protect those near to him, he kept secret during his lifetime. Upon his death, it quickly became known to a few freethinkers of the Enlightenment. Abridgements of the "Memoir" were prepared, some more faithful to the original than others. The best known was that written by Voltaire (included in this collection solely because it is the best known), which softens Meslier's conclusions nearly to the point of betrayal. In later years the Baron d'Holbach prepared his own distillation of the "Memoir" (which for many years was mistakenly thought to be the work of the priest), and the *Babouviste* Sylvain Maréchal used Meslier's work as the basis for his own atheist catechism.

The ideological undermining of the *ancien régime*, long thought to have begun with Voltaire, Diderot, and Rousseau in the mid-eighteenth century, truly began with the unheralded work of Jean Meslier. One of the main battering rams used to bring down the Bastille was the 1000 pages of the "Memoir Against Religion."

Testament of Jean Meslier[*]

Jean Meslier, priest of Etripigny and of But in the Champagne region, a native of the village of Mazerni, a dependency of the Duchy of Mazarin, was the son of a worker in serge. Raised in the countryside, he nevertheless pursued his studies and arrived at the priesthood.

Living soberly at the seminary, he became a follower of the Cartesian system. His morality was irreproachable, and he often gave alms. He was otherwise extremely temperate, as much in his words as in his relations with women.

Messrs Voiry and Delavaux, the one the priest of Va and the other of Boutzicourt were his confessors, and the only people he frequented.

He was a firm partisan of justice, and at times pushed his zeal too far. The lord of his village, Sieur de Touilly, had mistreated some peasants, and he refused to pray for him while officiating. M. de Mailly, Archbishop of Reims, before whom the contestation was brought, condemned him. But the Sunday following this decision the priest rose to the pulpit and complained of the cardinal's sentence. "This," he said, "is the ordinary lot of a poor country priest. Archbishops, who are great lords, hold them in contempt and don't listen to them. Let us then recommend the lord of this place. We will pray to God for Antoine de Touilly, that He convert him and that he be gracious enough to not mistreat the poor and to cheat orphans." Being present at this mortifying recommendation, the lord brought new complaints before the same Archbishop, who made Sieur Meslier come to Donchery, where he was harshly rebuked.

There were hardly any other events later in his life, nor was there any other parish than that of Etrépigny.

His principal books were the Bible, a Moréri, a Montaigne, and a few Fathers. He derived his sentiments from the reading of the Bible and the Fathers. He made three copies in his own hand, one of which was given to the Guard of the Seals of France, from which the following excerpt is taken. His manuscript was addressed to M. le Roux, Procurator and advocate at the Parlement of Mézières.

---

[*] From *Testament de Jean Meslier*, nouvelle edition. Geneva, Cramer, 1762. There are several abridgments of Meslier's *Mémoire*. This, the most famous of them, was done by Voltaire.

The following was written on the reverse of a simple piece of gray paper that served as an envelope: "I saw and recognized the errors, the abuses, the vanities, the follies and the evilness of men. I hated and despised them, but I didn't dare speak of them during my lifetime. I will at least say them upon dying and after my death, and it is in order that they be known that I make and write the present "Memoir" so that it serve as evidence in support of truth to all those who will see and read it, if they deem it appropriate. "

Also found among the priest's papers was an edition of the treatises of M. Fenelon, the Archbishop of Cambrai, on the existence of God and on his attributes, and the "Reflections" of Father Tournemine, Jesuit, on atheism, on which treatises he made marginal notes signed with his hand.

He had written two letters to the priests of his area in order to make his sentiments known to them. He told them that he gave the court clerk of his parish* a copy of his writing in 366 in-octavo pages, but that he was afraid they'd be suppressed, in keeping with the ill usages established to prevent the simple from being instructed and learning the truth. It is said that the Grand Vicar of Reims took the third copy.

This priest worked in secret all his life attacking all opinions he believed to be false.

He died in 1733 [*sic;* Meslier dies in 1729] at the age of 55. It was believed that, disgusted with life, he expressly refused the necessary aliments, since he wanted to take nothing, not even a glass of wine.

In his will he gave all he possessed, which was little, to his parishioners, and he asked that he be buried in his garden.

Forward

My brothers, you know my disinterestedness. I do not sacrifice my beliefs to any low interest. If I embraced a profession so directly opposed to my sentiments it was not through cupidity: I obeyed my parents. If I could have done it with impunity, I would rather have enlightened you. You can testify to the truth of what I say. I did not degrade my ministry by asking for the remuneration attached to it.

I swear by the heavens that I also detested those who laughed at the simplicity of the blinded people, who piously furnished large sums for the

---

* Sainte Menoult

purchase of prayers. How horrible this monopoly is! I don't condemn the contempt demonstrated by those who grow fat on your sweat and suffering for the sake of their mysteries and superstitions. But I detest their insatiable cupidity and the unworthy pleasure their kind show in mocking the ignorance of those they are careful to maintain in that same state of blindness.

They should content themselves with laughing at their own affluence, but at least let them not multiply their errors by abusing the blind piety of those who, with their simplicity, procure them so comfortable a life style. My brothers, you will no doubt render me the justice that is my due. The sensitivity that I have shown for your sufferings protects me against your suspicions. How many times have I not fulfilled the functions of my ministry without payment? And how many times has my tenderness been afflicted by my not being able to provide you with the succor that I would have wished to provide? Have I not always proven that I received more pleasure from giving than receiving? I have carefully avoided exhorting you to bigotry, and I spoke to you as rarely as possible of our pitiful dogmas. As a priest I had no choice but to fulfill my ministry, but how I suffered when I was forced to preach to you those pious falsehoods that I detested with all my heart. What contempt I felt for my ministry, and particularly for the superstitious mass and the ridiculous administration of the sacraments, especially when they had to be carried out with a solemnity that attracted your piety and excited your credulity? A thousand times I was on the point of publicly exploding. I wanted to open your eyes, but a fear stronger than my strength suddenly held me back, and forced me to remain silent until my death.

Excerpt from the Sentiments of Jean Meslier
addressed to his parishioners on a part of the abuses and errors in general and in particular, 15 March 1742

Chapter I
First proof, drawn from the motives that led men to establish religion.

Since there is no particular sect that doesn't claim to have been truly founded on God's authority and to be entirely exempt from all errors and impostures that can be found in the others, it is up to those who claim to establish the truth of their sect to show through clear and convincing proofs and testimonies that they were divinely instituted. Lacking this, it must be taken as certain that they were of merely human invention, full of errors and falsehoods. For it is not credible that an omnipotent, infinitely good God would have given laws and ordinances to men and that he wouldn't have wanted them to bear purer and more authentic marks of truth than those of the imposters that exist in such great numbers. Yet there is not a single Christ-lover, of whatever sect, who can clearly prove that his religion is truly of divine institution. As proof of this there is the fact that though for many centuries they have contested each other on this subject, going so far as to persecute with fire and blood in order to support their opinions, there has nevertheless been none from among them that has been able to convince the others through such evidence. This would certainly not be the case if there was on one side or the other clear and certain proof of divine institution. For, since no one of any sect or religion, enlightened and acting in good faith, claims to support and favor error and falsehood, and since on the contrary each side claims to support the truth—the true means of banishing all errors and of gathering all men together in peace with the same sentiments and in the same form of religion—these convincing proofs and evidence of truth should be produced, and in this way it would be shown that such-and-such a religion, and none of the others, is truly of divine institution. Then all will surrender to this truth, and no one will dare to combat this evidence, nor support the party of error and imposture without being at the same time confounded by contrary proofs. But since these proofs can be found in no religion, this leaves room for imposters to daringly support all sorts of falsehoods.

Here are yet other proofs that will no less clearly show the falsity of human religions, and especially the falsity of ours.

Chapter II
Second: Proof drawn from the errors of faith

Any religion that has an erroneous principle as the foundation of its mysteries, and that has an erroneous principle as the rule of its doctrine and morality, and that is also a harmful source of eternal troubles and divisions among men, cannot be a true religion, nor be of divine institution. Human religions, and principally the Catholic, have an erroneous principle as the foundation of their doctrine and morality. Thus I don't see how one can deny the first proposition of this argument. It is too clear and obvious to be put in doubt. I pass then to the second proposition, which is that the Christian religion takes what it calls faith as a rule of its doctrine and morality, that is, a blind, and yet firm and sure belief in a few laws or divine revelations and in a divinity. It must necessarily suppose thus, for it is that belief in some Divinity and divine revelations which give it all the credit and authority it has in the world, without which no one would take any notice of its prescriptions. This is why there is no religion that doesn't expressly recommend to its members to be firm in their faith. It flows from this that all Christ-lovers, take as maxims that faith is the beginning and the foundation of salvation, and that it is the root of all justice and sanctification, as was noted by the Council of Trent, Sess. 6 chap. 8.

But it is obvious that a blind belief in all that is proposed in the name and on the authority of God is an erroneous principle and a falsehood. As proof of this we have the fact that there exists no imposter in matters of religion who doesn't claim to cover himself with the name and authority of God, and who doesn't say that he is particularly inspired and sent by God. Not only is that faith and blind belief that they pose as foundation of their belief an erroneous principle, but it is also a harmful source of trouble and division among men for the maintenance of their religions. There are hardly any evil deeds they don't perpetrate against each other under this specious pretext.

It is not credible that an omnipotent God, infinitely good and wise, would want to use such methods or that He would take such a false path in order to make His will known to men, for this would manifestly mean wanting to lead them to error and to lay traps for them in order to have them embrace the party of falsehood. It is similarly not credible that a God who loves unity and peace, the good and the salvation of men, would ever have established as the foundation of His religion so fatal a source of eternal troubles and divisions among men. Thus, such religions cannot be true, nor have been instituted by God.

But I can see where our Christ-lovers will not fail to have recourse to their so called reasons for belief, and that they will say that though their faith and their belief are blind in one sense, they are nevertheless supported by such clear and convincing testimonies of truth that it would be not only imprudent, but rash and a folly to not surrender to them. They commonly reduce these so-called reasons to three or four headings.

They maintain the first through the so-called sanctity of their religion, which condemns vice and recommends the practice of virtue. According to them its doctrine is so pure, so simple, that it is obvious that it can only have come from the sanctity of an infinitely good and wise God.

The second reason for belief is drawn from the innocence and the sanctity of those who have embraced it with love and defended it to the death, suffering the cruelest torments rather than abandon it. It is not credible that such great personalities would have allowed themselves to be deceived in their beliefs, or that they would have renounced all of life's advantages and exposed themselves to such cruel persecutions in order to maintain errors and impostures.

They draw their third reason from the credibility of the oracles and prophecies that have for so long gone in their favor, and that they claim were fulfilled in such a way as to not be doubted.

Finally, their fourth reason for belief, which is really the principle one, is drawn from the grandeur and multitude of miracles performed in all times and places in favor of their religion.

But it is easy to refute all this vain reasoning and to make known the falsity of all these testimonies. For in the first place, the arguments our Christ-lovers draw from their so-called reasons for belief can serve to establish and confirm falsehood as well as truth. For we can in fact see that there does not exist a single religion, however false it might be, that does not claim to base itself on similar reasons for belief; there are none that don't claim to have a healthy and true doctrine and that don't, in their manner, condemn all vices and recommend the practice of all virtues. There are none that haven't had their learned and zealous defenders, who suffered harsh persecutions in supporting and defending their religion. Finally, there are none that don't claim to have prodigies and miracles performed in their favor.

The Mohammedans, the Indians, and the Pagans all make these claims in favor of their religions, as well as the Christians. If our Christ-lovers make much of their miracles and their prophecies, the same can be found in the religions of the pagans. Thus, the advantage that can be drawn from these so-called reasons for belief can be more or less found in all religions.

This being the case, as the histories and practices of all religions demonstrate, it obviously follows that all these so-called reasons for belief they put forward are equally found in all religions, and consequently cannot serve as certain proof and evidence of the truth of their religion, nor of the truth of any. The consequences are clear.

Secondly, to give an idea of the relation of miracles of paganism to those of Christianity, can it not be said, for example, that there is more reason to believe Philostratus concerning what he says in the eight books of the Life of Apollonius, than to believe all the Gospel writers together in what they say of the miracles of J.C., since we know, at least, that Philostratus was a man of intelligence, eloquent and well spoken, that he was the secretary of the Empress Julia, wife of the Emperor Severus, and that it was at the behest of this Empress that he wrote the life and marvelous acts of Apollonius? This is a sure sign that that Apollonius made himself famous through great and extraordinary acts, since an empress was so interested in having his life written. None of which can be said of J.C., nor of any of those who wrote his life, for they were ignorant, having come from the lowest ranks of the people, poor mercenaries, fisherman who didn't even have the intelligence to tell in their proper order the facts of which they spoke, and who often and wildly contradict each other.

As for he of whom they wrote the life and acts, if he had truly performed the miracles they attribute to him he would have made himself highly commendable by his good acts. Everyone would have admired him and statues would have been put up in his honor, as was done for the gods. But instead of this he was regarded as a man of no value, a fanatic, etc.

Josephus the historian, after speaking of the greatest miracles reported in favor of his nation and religion immediately lessens their believability and renders them suspect by saying that he leaves to everyone the freedom to believe whatever they want, a sure sign that he didn't have much faith in them. This also leaves room for the most judicious to look upon the stories that speak of these things as fabulous narratives. See Montaigne and the "Apology for Great Men." One should also see the account of the missionaries of the Isle of Santorini; there are three consecutive chapters on this matter.

All that is said on this subject allows us to clearly see that these so-called miracles can just as well be imagined to have occurred in favor of vice and falsehood as of justice and truth.

I prove this through the evidence of what the Christ-lovers themselves call the word of God, and by the testimony of he who they adore. For the books that they say contain the word of God, as well as Christ himself, who they adore as a God made man, expressly say there are false prophets, that is, imposters, who claim they were sent by God and who speak in his name, and who expressly say that they perform and will perform such great and prodigious miracles that it is possible that even the just will be seduced. See Matt. 24:5,11, 27 and elsewhere.

What is more, these so-called miracle workers want us to believe in theirs, and not in those performed by others in the opposite party, mutually destroying each other.

One day one of these so-called prophets, named Zedekiah, seeing himself contradicted by another named Micah, the latter slapped the former and said to him: 'Where now went the spirit of Jehovah from me to speak to thee?' By what path did the spirit of God pass from me to you?' See also 1Kings 18:40 and others.

But how can these so-called miracles testify to the truth when it is clear that they have not been performed? For one must know: 1- If those who are said to be the original authors of these narratives truly are; 2- Whether they were honest men, worthy of belief, wise and enlightened, and if they weren't prejudiced in favor of those about whom they speak positively; 3- If they thoroughly examined all the circumstances of the acts they report, if they knew them thoroughly and if they faithfully reported them; 4- If the ancient books or histories that report all these great miracles were not falsified and corrupted with the passage of time, as so many others have been.

If we were to consult Tacitus and many other celebrated historians on the subject of Moses and his nation, we would see that they are looked upon as a horde of thieves and bandits. Magic and astrology were then the only sciences *à la mode*, and since Moses was, it is said, learned in the wisdom of the Egyptians, it wasn't difficult for him to inspire veneration and attachment to his person in the children of Jacob, rustic and ignorant as they were, and to get them, in their misery, to embrace the discipline he wanted to impose on them. This is all quite different from what the Jews and our Christ-lovers would have us believe. By what rule can we know that we should believe these rather than any others? There is certainly no such likely reason.

There is just as little certitude, or even likelihood, concerning the miracles of the New Testament as there is of the Old to fulfill the preceding conditions.

It would serve no purpose to say that the histories that report the acts contained in the Gospels were regarded as holy and sacred and that they were always faithfully preserved without any alteration of the truths they contain. For it is perhaps for this very reason that they are most suspect and were even more corrupted by those who obtain advantages from them or who fear that they are not favorable to them, it being common among the authors who transcribe these kinds of histories to add, change, or modify whatever seems to best serve their designs.

Even our Christ-lovers can't deny this, since without speaking of other serious individuals who recognized additions, modifications and falsifications made at different times to what they called their Holy Scripture, their own St. Jerome, a famous learned man among them, says in several places in his prologues that they were corrupted and falsified. That they had already in his time been in the hands of a number of persons who added and subtracted whatever they wanted to in such a way that, he says, there were as many different versions as there were copies. See his prefaces to Paulin, his preface to Joshua, his epistle to the Galateans, his preface to Job, that on the Gospels to Pope Damasius, that on the psalms to Paul and to Eustachium, etc.

All the books of the Law of Moses and the prophets that could be found were burned at the time of Antiochus. The Talmud is regarded by the Jews as a book holy and sacred, and contains all the divine laws and notable sayings of the rabbis. Their exposition, both on divine and human law and a large quantity of other secrets and mysteries of the Hebrew language, is regarded by Christians as a book filled with reveries, fables, impostures and impieties. In 1559, by order of the Inquisitors of the Faith, they ordered burned in Rome twelve hundred of these Talmuds found in a library of the city of Cremona.

The Pharisees, who were a famous sect among the Jews, accepted only the five books of Moses and rejected all the Prophets. Among the Christians, Marcion and his followers rejected the Books of Moses and the Prophets and introduced other writings *à la mode*; Carpocrates and his followers did the same and rejected the entire Old Testament and maintained that Jesus Christ was nothing but a man like the others. The Marcionites and the Sovereigns attacked the entire Old Testament as evil, and also rejected most of the four Gospels and the Epistles of St. Paul.

The Ebionites only accepted the Gospel of St Matthew, rejecting the three others and the Epistles of St Paul. The Marcionites published a Gospel under the name of St. Matthias in order to confirm their doctrine. The Apostolics introduced other scriptures in order to support their errors, and to this end utilized certain acts that they attributed to St. Andrew and St. Thomas.

The Manicheans, Chron. p. 287, wrote a Gospel in their style and rejected the writings of the prophets and the Apostles. The Etzsaites spoke of a certain book that they said came from heaven, and they carved up the other scriptures following their fantasy. Origen himself, with all his great intelligence, nevertheless corrupted the Scriptures and forged allegories as he wished, in this way changing the meanings of the Prophets and the Apostles, and even corrupted some of the principal points of doctrine. His books are now mutilated and falsified; they are no longer anything but pieces gathered and stitched together by others who came later: and so we find there manifest errors and flaws.

The Allogians attributed the Gospel and Apocalypse of St John to the heretic Cerinthus, which is why they rejected them. The heretics of the last centuries rejected as apocryphal several books that the Roman Catholics regard as holy and sacred, like the books of Tobias, Judith, Esther, Baruch, the canticle of the three youths in the furnace, the story of Susanna and that of the idol of Baal, the Wisdom of Solomon, Ecclesiastes, the First and Second Books of Maccabees. To which uncertain and doubtful books one can add several others that have been attributed to other Apostles, like the Acts of St. Thomas, his travels, his Gospel and his Apocalypse; the Gospel of St. Bartholomew, that of St. Matthias, that of St. James, that of St. Peter, and that of the Apostles, as well as the Acts of St. Peter, his book of preachings and his Apocalypse, that of Judgment, that of the childhood of the Savior, and others of similar cloth, all of which are rejected as apocryphal by Roman Catholics, even by Pope Gelasius and by the Holy Fathers of the Roman Communion.

What confirms even more that there is no ground for certainty concerning the authority that is claimed for these books, is that those who maintain their divinity are forced to confess that they would have no grounds for certitude if their faith didn't assure them of this and didn't oblige them to believe. Since faith is nothing but an erroneous principle and imposture, how can faith, i.e., blind belief, render those books that are themselves the basis for that blind belief certain? What a pity and what madness.

But let us see if these books contain any of the characteristics of truth, such as erudition, wisdom, sanctity or any other of those perfections that are appropriate to a God, and if the miracles that are cited there are in agreement with what should be thought of the grandeur, the goodness, and the infinite wisdom of an omnipotent God.

First, it can be seen that there is no erudition, no sublime thought or any production beyond the ordinary strength of the human spirit. On the contrary, on one hand we see nothing but fabulous narratives, like that of the formation of woman from the rib of a man, or of the so-called earthly paradise, and of a snake who spoke and reasoned and who was even trickier than man; of an ass who spoke and who reproached its master for mistreatment; of a universal flood and an arc where animals of all kinds were contained; of the confusion of languages and the division of nations; not to mention a number of other vain tales on low and frivolous subjects that serious authors would not deign to report. All these narrations have no less the air of fables than those that were invented about the industriousness of Prometheus, Pandora's Box, the war of the Titans against the gods, and other such like that the poets invented to amuse the men of their time.

On the other hand one sees nothing but a mix of a number of laws and ordinances or superstitious practices touching on sacrifices, the purifications of the ancient law, and the vain discrimination between animals, of which it supposes some pure and others impure. These laws are no more worthy of respect than those of the most idolatrous of nations.

One can find there simple stories, true or false, of kings, or princes, or individuals who lived either well or badly, or who carried out a few good or evil acts; low and frivolous acts are reported there as well.

In order to do all this it's obvious that no great genius was required, nor any divine revelations. Thinking so doesn't do God any honor.

Finally, one can see in these books nothing but the discourses, the conduct, and the acts of these renowned Prophets who claimed to be particularly inspired by God. One can see how they acted and spoke, their dreams, their illusions, their reveries, and it would be easy to judge that they much more resembled visionaries and fanatics than they did men who were both wise and enlightened.

Nevertheless, there are in some of these books a few good teachings and some noble moral maxims, as in the proverbs attributed to Solomon, those in the Book of Wisdom and in Ecclesiastes. But this same Solomon, the wisest of their writers, is also the most unbelieving. He even doubts the immortality of the soul, and he concludes his work by saying there is no other good than that of enjoying in peace the fruits of our labor and living with what we love.

Besides, how far above these books that are said to be inspired by God are the authors who are called profane: Xenophon, Plato, Cicero, the Emperor Antonius, the Emperor Julian, Virgil, etc. I feel safe in saying that even the fables of Aesop are certainly more ingenious and instructive than all those crude and low parables that are told in the Gospels.

But what also makes obvious that these of books cannot have been divinely inspired is the fact that, aside from the lowness and crudity of style and the lack of order in the narration of particular facts—which are extremely circumstantial—one can see that the authors are not in agreement with each other, and that they contradict each other in several areas. They didn't even have enough intelligence or natural talent to correctly edit a history.

Here are a few examples of contradictions. The Gospel writer Matthew has J. Ch. descend from King David through his son Solomon until Joseph, the at least putative father of J. Ch. Luke has him descend from the same David by his son Nathan down to Joseph.

Speaking of Jesus, Matthew says that the word had been spread around Jerusalem that a new king had been born, and that the Magi had come seeking him so as to adore him. King Herod, fearing that the so-called new king would some day take the crown from him, had had all the babies born within the last two years in the area of Bethlehem killed, for it was there he was told this new king was going to be born. Joseph and the mother of Jesus, having been warned in a dream by an angel of this evil plan, had quickly fled to Egypt, where they remained until Herod's death, which occurred a few years later.

On the contrary, Luke says that Joseph and the mother of Jesus peacefully remained for six weeks in the place where their child Jesus was born, that in keeping with the law of the Jews he was circumcised there eight days after his birth. And when the time prescribed by that law for the purification of the mother had passed, she and Joseph her husband took him to Jerusalem to present him to God in His temple and also to offer a sacrifice, which was commanded by the law of God. After this they returned to Galilee to their city of Nazareth, where their child Jesus every day grew in grace and wisdom, and his mother and father went every year to Jerusalem on the solemn days of Passover. Luke makes no mention of their flight to Egypt, nor of Herod's cruelty towards the children of the province of Bethlehem.

As for Herod's cruelty, since the historians of those times don't speak of it at all, and neither does Josephus, the historian who wrote the life of Herod; and since the other Gospel writers make no mention of it, it's obvious that this voyage of the Magi led by a star, this massacre of little children, and this flight to Egypt are nothing but absurd lies. For it is not credible that Josephus, who condemned the vices of this king, would have passed silently over so black and detestable an act, if what this Gospel said were true.

On the subject of the duration of the public life of JC, according to what the first three Gospels say there could hardly have been three months from his baptism to his death, supposing that he was thirty when he was baptized, as Luke says, and that he was born on December 25. For from this baptism, which occurred in the 15th year of Tiberius' reign, and the year when Ananaias and Caiphas were the High Priests, until the first night of the next Passover, which was in the month of March, there were only about three months. According to what is said in the first three Gospels, he was crucified on the eve of the first day of the next Passover after his baptism, and the first time he came to Jerusalem with his disciples—for everything they say about his baptism, his travels, his miracles, his preaching, his death and his passion necessarily happened in the same year as his baptism. This is the case since the writers of the Gospels do not speak of a next year. It even seems, by the narration they give of his acts, that he did them all immediately after his baptism—one after another consecutively and within a short span of time—during which we can only see one interval of six days before his transfiguration, during which six days we don't see where he did a single thing.

One can see from this that he lived only about three months after his baptism, and if we subtract from this six weeks of forty days and forty nights that he passed in the desert immediately after his baptism, it follows that the duration of his public life, from his first preaching until his death, only lasted around six weeks. Following what John says, it would have lasted at least three years and three months, since it appears—according to the Gospel of that Apostle—that he went to Jerusalem three or four times during Passover, which only comes once a year.

Thus, if it is true that he went there three of four times after his baptism, as John testifies, it is false that he only lived three months after his baptism and that he was crucified the first time he went to Jerusalem.

If we say that the first three Gospels speak only of one year, but that they fail to distinctly mark off the others that passed after his baptism, or that John only means to speak of one Passover, though he seems to be speaking of several, and that it is only in anticipation that he several times repeats that the Passover of the Jews was near and that Jesus went to Jerusalem, and that consequently there is only an apparent contradiction among the Gospels on this subject, I would accept all this. But it is clear that these apparent contradictions arise from the fact they don't all agree on all the circumstances in the tale they are telling. Whatever the case, it is still possible to draw the conclusion that they were not inspired by God when they wrote their histories.

Another contradiction concerns the first thing he did immediately after his baptism, for the first three Gospels say that he was immediately transported by the Spirit to a desert, where he fasted forty days and forty nights, and he was several times tempted by the devil. According to John, two days after his baptism he left for Galilee, where he performed his first miracle by changing water to wine at the wedding in Cana where, three days after his arrival in Galilee, he could be found more than thirty leagues from where he had been.

As for the place where he first retreated after leaving the desert, Matthew says (ch. 4:13) that he went to Galilee, and that leaving the city of Nazareth he went to the city of Capernaum. And Luke (ch. 4:16 & 41) says that he at first went to Nazareth, and that he then went to Capernaum.

They contradict each other on the time and way the Apostles followed him. For the first three say that Jesus, passing along the banks of the Sea of Galilee, saw Simon and Andrew, his brother, and that further along he saw James and his brother John with their father Zebedee. On the contrary John says that it was Andrew, brother of Simon Peter, who was the first to join Jesus along with another disciple of John the Baptist, having seen him pass before them when they were with their master on the banks of the Jordan.

On the subject of the Last Supper, the first three Gospels say that Jesus Christ instituted the sacrament of his body and his blood in the form of bread and wine, as is said by our Roman Christ-lovers. But John makes no mention of this mysterious sacrament. John says (ch. 13:5) that after the Last Supper Jesus washed the feet of his Apostles, that he expressly ordered them to do the same for each other, and reports a long speech he made them at the same time. But the others Gospels make no mention of this washing of the feet, nor of a long speech that he then made. On the contrary, they testify that immediately after the Last Supper he left with his Apostles for the Mount of Olives, where he gave his soul over to sorrow, and that he finally fell into agony while the Apostles slept a short distance away.

They contradict themselves on the day of the Last Supper. On one hand they say he held it the evening of the eve of Passover, that is, the eve of the first day of unleavened bread, as it is said in Exodus 12:18. Levit. 25:5 Num. 28:16, and on the other hand they say he was crucified the day after the day of the Last Supper, at around noon, after the Jews had put him on trial for an entire night and a morning. According to what they say, the day after that Last Supper would not have been the eve of Passover. Thus, if he died the eve of Passover at around noon it wasn't the evening of the eve of that holiday that the Last Supper was held. There is thus a manifest error in this.

They also contradict themselves on what they report about the women who followed Jesus from Galilee. For the first three Gospels say that these women and all those he knew—among whom were Mary Magdalene, Mary the mother of James and Jesus, and the mother of Zebedee's children—looked from afar on what was happening when he was hung and attached to the cross. On the contrary, John says (19:25) that Jesus' mother and his mother's sister and Mary Magdalene were standing near the cross, along with the Apostle John. The contradiction is manifest, for if these women and this disciple were near him they thus weren't far away, as the others say.

They contradict themselves on the so-called appearances they report that Jesus made after his so-called resurrection. Matthew (ch. 28:16) only speaks of two appearances, one when he appeared to Mary Magdalene and to another woman also named Mary, and another when he appeared to his eleven disciples, who had gone to Galilee to the mountain he had shown them from which they could see him. Mark speaks of three appearances, the first when he appeared to Mary Magdalene, the second when he appeared to his two disciples who were going to Emmaus, and the third when he appeared to his eleven disciples, who he reproached for their lack of belief. Luke, like Matthew, only speaks of the two first appearances, and John the Evangelist speaks of four appearances, and adds to Mark's three that which he made to seven or eight of his disciples who were fishing on the sea at Tiberias.

They contradict themselves again on the location of the appearances, for Matthew says that they were in Galilee on a mountain, Mark says that they were when he was at the table, Luke says that he led them out of Jerusalem and brought them as far as Bethany, where he left them and rose to heaven, and John says that it was in the city of Jerusalem in a house where they had closed the doors, and another time by the sea in Tiberias.

Here then are quite a number of contradictions in the tale of these so-called appearances. They contradict themselves on the subject of his so-called Ascension to heaven, for Luke and Mark positively say that he rose to heaven in the presence of his eleven Apostles, but neither Matthew nor John makes any mention of this so-called Ascension. What is more, Matthew testifies quite clearly that he did not rise to heaven, since he positively says that Jesus Christ assured his Apostles that he would remain with them until the end of time: "Go then," he tells them in this so-called appearance, "teach all the nations and be assured that I will remain with you until the end of time."

Luke contradicts himself on this subject, for in his Gospel (ch. 24: 50) he says that it was in Bethany that he rose to heaven in the presence of his Apostles, and in his Acts of the Apostles, supposing that he was the author, he says that it was on the Mount of Olives. He again contradicts himself in another circumstance of that Ascension, for he says in his Gospel that it was the same day as the resurrection, or the first night following it, that he rose to heaven. But in the Acts of the Apostles he says that it was forty days after his resurrection, which certainly is not in agreement.

If all the Apostles had truly seen their master rise gloriously to heaven how could Matthew and John—who would have seen him like the others—have passed over in silence so glorious a mystery, and one so advantageous to their master, given that they reported so many other circumstances of his life and acts that are so much less considerable than this one? How is it that Matthew makes no express mention of this Ascension and doesn't clearly explain how he will forever remain among them, though he visibly left them to rise to heaven? It isn't easy to understand by what secret means he could remain with those he left.

I pass over in silence a number of other contradictions. What I have just said suffices to show that these books are not the product of divine inspiration, or even of human wisdom, and that consequently they don't deserve our having any faith in them.

Chapter III

But by what privilege do these Gospels and a few other similar books pass for holy and divine, while others that don't any less bear the title of Gospel, and which were once the first published under the names of a Apostles, do not? If it is said that the refuted Gospels were supposedly and falsely attributed to the Apostles the same can be said of the former group. If it can be supposed that some were falsified and corrupted, the same can be supposed for the others. There is no certain proof that can separate the ones from the others; whatever the Church decides, it is no longer credible.

As for the so-called miracles reported in the Old Testament, they were only performed in order to demonstrate an unjust and odious regard for peoples and individuals, and to deliberately overwhelm some with evils so as to favor others. The vocation and choice that God made of the Patriarchs Abraham, Isaac, and Jacob, to make of their posterity a people who he would sanctify and bless above all the other peoples of the earth, is the proof of this.

But, it will be said, God is the absolute master of his grace and beneficence; he can grant them to whoever he deems fit without anyone having the right to complain or accuse him of injustice. This reasoning is vain, for God—the author of nature, the father of all men—should love them all equally as his own works. Consequently, he should equally be their protector and benefactor, for he who gives being should give all that flows from this that is needed for their well-being. If this is not what our Christ-lovers mean, that their God expressly made creatures so as to render them miserable, then that it would certainly be an unworthy thought to have of an infinitely good being.

What is more, if all the so-called miracles of the Old and the New Testaments were true, it could be said that God showed more care in meeting the least needs of men than in their greatest and principal need; that he more severely punished slight faults in certain persons than he punished great crimes in others; and finally that he didn't show himself so beneficent in the most pressing of needs than in the least of them. All this is easy to show, as much by the miracles that he is said to have performed as by those he didn't perform and that he should more likely have performed than any other—if it were true he had done any. For example, to say that God had the kindness to send an angel to console and aid a simple servant when he left—and still leaves—to languish and die in misery an infinite number of innocents; that he would miraculously preserve for forty years the clothing and shoes of a miserable people, when he doesn't watch over the natural preservation of so many goods so useful and necessary for people's subsistence, and which every day are lost through different accidents. What! He sent to the first of the human race, Adam and Eve, a demon, a devil, a simple snake to seduce them and in this way to destroy all men? This simply isn't credible. What! He would have wanted, through a special grace of his providence, to prevent the king of pagan Geraris from falling into a minor error with a foreign woman, an error that would have had no ill consequences, yet he didn't want to prevent Adam and Eve from offending him and falling into the sin of disobedience, a sin which, according to our Christ-lovers, is fatal and caused humanity's destruction? This isn't credible.

Let's now come to the miracles of the New Testament. It is claimed that they consist of Jesus and his Apostles divinely curing all sorts of maladies and infirmities so that, when they wanted, they rendered eyesight to the blind, hearing to the deaf, speech to the dumb; that they made the lame walk, that they cured paralytics, that they chased demons from the bodies of the possessed, and they resurrected the dead.

Several of these miracles can be found in the Gospels, but many more can be seen in the books our Christ-lovers have written on the lives of their saints. We read in them that these so-called "happy ones" cured maladies and infirmities, chased demons almost whenever they met them, all of this solely using the name of Jesus or the sign of the cross. That so to speak they commanded the elements, that God so favored them that even after their deaths he granted them his divine power, and this unto the least of their garments, and even unto the shadow of their bodies and the shameful instruments of their deaths. It is said that the sock of Saint Honoré resuscitated a dead man on January 6, that the rods of Saint Peter, Saint James and Saint Bernard performed miracles. The same is said of Saint Francis' rope, the rod of Saint John of God, and the belt of Saint Melanie. It is said of Saint Gracilien that he was divinely instructed on what he should believe and teach and that through the quality of his preaching he made a mountain retreat that was preventing him from building a church. That there endlessly flowed from the sepulcher of Saint Andrew a liqueur that cured all kinds of maladies. That the soul of Saint Benedict was seen rising to heaven clothed in a precious cloak and surrounded by burning lamps. Saint Dominic said that God never denied him anything he asked of him. That Saint Francis commanded the sparrows and that they obeyed him, as well as swans and other birds, and they too obeyed him; and that often fish, rabbits and hares placed themselves in his hands or on his bosom. That Saint Paul and Saint Pantaleon, having had their heads cut off, milk instead of blood flowed from them. That the fortunate Peter of Luxembourg, in the first two years after his death, 1388 and 1389, performed 2400 miracles, among which there were 42 dead resuscitated, not counting more than 3,000 other miracles he performed afterwards, nor those he still performs every day. That the bodies of the fifty philosophers converted by Saint Catherine, having all been thrown into a great fire, were afterwards discovered whole, with not a single hair burned; that the body of Saint Catherine was raised by the angels and buried by them on Mount Sinai. That the day of the canonization of San Antonio of Padua all the bells of the city of Lisbon rang on their own without anyone knowing how that occurred; that this saint, being one day at the seaside, and having called on the fish in order to preach to them, they came to him en masse and, raising their heads from the water, attentively listened to him. We would never finish if we had to report all this nonsense. There is no subject so vain, so frivolous, and even so ridiculous that the authors of these lives of the saints don't take pleasure in piling up miracle on top of miracle, so able are they at forging beautiful lies. See also the sentiment of Naudé on this matter in his *Apologie des Grands-hommes,* vol 2, p. 13.

In fact, it is not without reason that these things are looked upon as vain lies, for it is easy to see that all these so-called miracles were only invented in imitation of the fables of pagan poets. Their conformity among themselves makes this quite visible.

Chapter IV
Conformity of ancient and new miracles.

If our Christ-lovers say that God truly gave power to his saints to perform all the miracles reported in their lives, so did the pagans say that the daughters of Anius, High Priest of Apollo, truly received from the God Bacchus the favor and the power to change all that they wanted into wheat, wine, oil, etc.

That Jupiter gave the Nymphs who watched over his education a ram's horn that provided him with milk during his childhood, and that had a special property in that it provided them with all they wanted in abundance.

If our Christ-lovers say that their saints had the power to resuscitate the dead, that they had divine revelations, the pagans said before them that Athalide, son of Mercury, had obtained from his father the gift of living, dying, and resuscitating whenever he wanted, and that he also knew of everything that happened in the world and in the after life. And that Aesculapius, son of Apollo, had resuscitated the dead, and that among others he resuscitated Hyppolite, son of Theseus at the request of Diane, and that Hercules resuscitated Alcestis, the wife of Admet, the King of Thessaly, in order to return her to her husband.

If out Christ-lovers say that their Christ was miraculously born of a virgin who had never known a man, the pagans before them already said that Remus and Romulus, the founders of Rome, were miraculously born of a Vestal Virgin named Ilia, or Sylvia, or Rea Sylvia; they had already said that Mars, Argus, Vulcan and others were born from the goddess Juno, without knowledge of a man, and had already said that Minerva, the goddess of science had been born from the brain of Jupiter, and that she came out fully armed from the force of a blow with which this god had smashed his head.

If our Christ-lovers say that their saints made fountains of water come out of rocks, pagans say the same thing, that Minerva made a fountain of oil spurt as a reward for a temple dedicated to her.

If our Christ-lovers brag of having miraculously received images from heaven, like that of Notre Dame de Lorette and of Liesse and several other presents from heaven, like the so-called holy ampoule of Rheims, like the white chasuble that Saint Ildefonse received from the Virgin Mary and other such things, the pagans bragged before them of having miraculously received from heaven their Palladium, or their simulacrum of Pallas which came, they said, to take her place in the temple that had been built in honor of that goddess.

If out Christ-lovers say that their Jesus Christ was seen by his Apostles rising gloriously to heaven, and that several souls of their co-called saints were seen being transferred to heaven by angels, the Roman pagans before them had already said that Romulus their founder was seen in his glory after his death, that Ganymede son of Tros, King of Troy, was transported by Jupiter to heaven to serve him; that the hair of Berenice, having been consecrated to the temple of Venus, was afterwards transported to heaven; they say the same thing of Cassiopeia and Andromeda, and even of Silenus' ass.

If our Christ-lovers say that the bodies of several of their saints were miraculously saved from corruption after their deaths, and that they were found through divine revelations after having been long lost, the pagans say the same thing about the body of Orestes, which they claim to have found with the aid of the Oracle, etc.

If our Christ-lovers say that the seven sleeping brothers miraculously slept for 177 years, that they were locked up in a cave, the pagans say that Epimenides the philosopher slept 57 years in a cave where he had fallen asleep.

If out Christ-lovers say that several of their saints miraculously still spoke after having their heads or tongues cut off, the pagans say that the head of Gabienus chanted a long poem after having been separated from his body.

If our Christ-lovers glory in the fact that their temples and churches are decorated with paintings and rich gifts that show the miraculous cures carried out through the intercession of their saints, then one can also see, or rather one once saw in the Temple of Aesculapius, a number of paintings of miraculous cures and healings he performed.

If our Christ-lovers say that several saints were miraculously preserved in burning flames without suffering any harm in their bodies or to their garments, the pagans said that the priestesses of the temple of Diana walked barefoot on burning coals without either burning or hurting their feet, and that the priests of the goddess Feronius and Hyrpicus also walked on burning coals during the fireworks in honor of Apollo.

If the angels built a chapel to Saint Clement at the bottom of the sea, Baucis and Philemon's small house was miraculously changed into a superb temple as a reward for their piety.

If several of their saints, like Saint James, Saint Maurice, etc., several times appeared before their armies, mounted and equipped to fight in their favor, Castor and Pollux several times appeared to battle for the Romans against their enemies.

If a ram was miraculously found to be offered in sacrifice in place of Isaac when his father Abraham wanted to sacrifice him, the goddess Vesta also sent a heifer to be sacrificed to her in place of Metella, the daughter of Metellus. The goddess Diana also sent a doe in place of Iphigenia when she was at the stake about to be sacrificed, and in this way Iphigenia was delivered.

If Saint Joseph fled to Egypt on the warning of an angel, Simonides the poet on several occasions avoided danger thanks to the miraculous warnings that were given him.

If Moses made water spring from a rock when he struck it with his rod, the horse Pegasus did the same by striking a rock with his hoof.

If Saint Vincent Ferrer resuscitated a dead man hacked to pieces whose corpse was already half-cooked, Pelops, son of Tantalus, King of Phrygia, having been cut in pieces by his father so he could be eaten by the gods, had his members gathered together, reassembled, and his life returned to him.

If several crucifixes and other images have miraculously spoken and given answers, the pagans say that their oracles divinely spoke and gave answers to those who consulted them, and that the heads of Orpheus and Polycrates gave oracles after their deaths.

If, as is said in the Gospels, God made known by a voice from heaven that Jesus Christ was his son, Vulcan made visible that Coeculus was truly his son by the appearance of a miraculous flame.

If God miraculously nourished a few of his saints, the pagan poets say that Triptoleme was miraculously nourished with divine milk by Ceres, who also gave him a chariot led by two dragons, and Phineas, son of Mars, though he came stillborn from his mother's belly, was nevertheless miraculously nourished with her milk.

If several saints miraculously calmed the cruelty and ferocity of the cruelest beasts, it is said that Orpheus attracted lions, bears, and tigers to himself through the sweetness of his song and the harmony of his instruments and calmed the ferocity of their nature; that he attracted stones and trees, and that even rivers stopped flowing so they could listen to him sing.

Finally, and to conclude—for many more stories can be reported—if our Christ-lovers say that the walls of Jericho fell at the sound of trumpets, the pagans say that the walls of Thebes were built by the sound of the musical instruments of Amphion; the stones, the poets say, put themselves in place thanks to the sweetness of the music, which is more miraculous and admirable than seeing walls tumble to earth.

All this certainly shows a conformity in miracles on one side and the other. Since it would be foolish to believe in the so-called miracles of paganism, it is no less so to believe in those of Christianity, since they all come from the same erroneous principle. It is for this reason that the Manicheans and the Arians, who existed in the early days of Christianity, had no use for so-called miracles performed through the invoking of saints, and mocked those who invoked them after their deaths and who honored their relics.

Let us now return to the principal end proposed by God in sending his son who was made man to earth. This was done, as it is said, to remove the sins from the world and to completely destroy the works of the so-called devil, etc. This is what our Christ-lovers maintain, as well as that Jesus Christ died for love of them, in keeping with the intentions of God his Father, which is clearly stated in all the so-called holy books.

What! An omnipotent God who wanted to become a mortal man for love of them and to spill his last drop of blood in order to save them all would then limit his power to curing only a few maladies and bodily infirmities in the few of the infirm who were presented to him, and who wouldn't have wanted to employ his divine goodness in curing all the infirmities of our souls, that is, curing all men of their vices and dissolutions, which are worse than the illnesses of the body? This isn't believable. What! So good a God would have wanted to preserve dead bodies from rot and corruption and would not also have wanted to protect from the contagion and vice of sin the souls of an infinite number of persons that he had come to redeem at the price of his blood, and that he should have sanctified with his grace? What a pitiful contradiction!

Chapter V
Third proof of the falsity of religion, drawn from so-called visions and Divine revelations

Now we come to so-called visions and divine revelations, upon which our Christ-lovers found and establish the truth and certainty of their religion.

In order to give a fair idea of this I don't think that one can do better than to say, in general, that they are such that if someone now dared to brag about having similar ones and tried to make much of himself he would be looked upon as a madman and a fanatic.

Here are the so-called visions and divine revelations:

God, say the so-called holy books, having appeared for the first time to Abraham, said to him: "Get there out of thy country (he was then in Chaldea), and from thy kindred and from thy father's house, unto a land that I will shew thee." This Abraham having gone there God, says the history (Gen. 12,1) appeared to him a second time and said to him: "Unto thy seed will I give this land." In recognition of this gracious promise Abraham built an altar to him.

After Isaac's death his son Jacob, going one day to Mesopotamia to find a wife, having walked all day and feeling tired from his walk, wanted to rest for the evening. Lying on the ground, his head resting on some rocks, he fell asleep. During his sleep he saw in a dream a ladder going from the earth to the farthest reaches of heaven, and he thought he saw angels ascending and descending this ladder. He saw God Himself on the highest rung, saying to him: "I am the Lord God of Abraham thy father, and the God of Isaac: the land whereon thou liest, to thee will I give it, and to thy seed; and thy seed shall be as the dust of the earth, and thou shalt spread abroad to the west, and to the east, and to the north, and to the south: and in thee and in thy seed shall all the families of the earth be blessed. And, behold, I am with thee, and will keep thee in all places whither thou goest, and will bring thee again into this land; for I will not leave thee, until I have done that which I have spoken to thee of." Jacob having awakened from this dream was seized with fear and said: "Surely the Lord is in this place; and I knew it not. How dreadful is this place! This is none other but the house of God, and this is the gate of Heaven." And having risen he prepared a stone, on which he spread oil in memory of what had just happened to him, and at the same time made a vow to God that if he returned safe and sound he would offer him a tithe of all he had.

Here is another vision. Guarding the flock of his father-in-law Laban, who had promised him that all the lambs of various colors that the sheep would produce would be his reward, he dreamed one night that he saw the males leap onto the females, and they produced lambs of various colors. In this beautiful dream God appeared to him and he said (Gen 31,12): "Lift up now thine eyes, and see, all the rams which leap upon the cattle are ringstraked, speckled, and grisled: for I have seen all that Laban doeth unto thee (...) now arise, get thee out from this land, and return unto the land of thy kindred." As he returned with all his family with all he had earned from his father-in-law, the story says that during the night he met an unknown man, who he fought all night until daybreak, and that man, not having been able to defeat him, asked him who he was. Jacob told him his name: "Thy name shall be called no more Jacob, but Israel: for as a prince hast thou power with God and with men, and hast prevailed." (Gen 32:25,28)

These were, in part, the first of these so-called divine visions and revelations. The others shouldn't be judged any differently than these. What appearance of divinity is there in these coarse dreams and vain illusions? If anyone came now to tell us such foolish tales and believed them to be veritable divine revelations; if, for example, some foreigners, some Germans, came to our France and, seeing all the beautiful provinces of the kingdom, were to say that God had appeared to them in their country and had told them to go to France, and that he would give them and their descendants all the beautiful lands, *seigneuries,* and provinces of this kingdom, which go from the Rhine and the Rhone to the Atlantic, that he will make an eternal alliance with them, that he will multiply their race, that he will render their posterity as numerous as the stars in the sky and the grains of sand in the sea, etc., who wouldn't laugh at such foolishness, and who wouldn't look upon these foreigners as madmen? There is no one who wouldn't look upon them as such and who wouldn't mock all these beautiful visions and divine revelations.

There is no reason to think or to judge otherwise about all that they have those great so-called holy patriarchs Abraham, Isaac, and Jacob say about the so-called divine revelations they said they saw.

As concerns the institution of bloody sacrifices, the holy books attribute it to God. Since it would be too tiresome to lay out the disgusting details of these of sacrifices, I send the reader to Exodus 25:1-27:1 and 21-28:3-29:1, ibid. v. 2,4,5,6,7,8,9,10,11.

But were men not mad and blind to think that they were doing honor to God by rending, killing, and burning His own creatures under the pretext of making sacrifices to Him? And even now, how can our Christ-lovers be so mad as to believe they are pleasing their God the Father by eternally offering in sacrifice His divine son in memory of his having been shamefully and miserably hung on a cross where he expired? This can certainly only be the result of a stubborn blindness of spirit.

As for the details of animal sacrifices, they only consist of colored garments, blood, guts, livers, jabots, kidneys, nails, skin, droppings, smoke, cakes, a few measures of oil and wine, all of it offered and infected by ceremonies as filthy and pitiful as the most extravagant magical operations.

What is even more horrible is that the law of this detestable Jewish people also commanded that they sacrifice men. The barbarians (for such is what they were) who wrote that atrocious law commanded (Lev. 27) that they kill without mercy anyone who had been pledged to the God of the Jews, who they called Adonai, and it was in accordance with this execrable precept that Jephtha sacrificed his daughter and that Saul sacrificed his son.

But here is yet another proof of the falsity of these revelations of which we have spoken: it was the failure to fulfill the great and magnificent promises that accompanied them, for it is a fact that these promises were never fulfilled.

The proof of this consists in three principal things; 1- Rendering their posterity more numerous than all the other peoples of the earth etc.; 2- Rendering the people of their race the happiest, the holiest and the must triumphant of all the peoples of the earth, etc.; 3- Rendering their alliance eternal and that they will forever possess the country he would give them. It is clear that these promises were never fulfilled.

First: it is certain that the Jewish people, or the people of Israel, which is the only one that we can regard as the descendants of the patriarchs Abraham, Isaac, and Jacob, and the only one for whom the promises should have been fulfilled, has never been so numerous so as to be comparable in number to all the other peoples of the earth, and is consequently far fewer than the grains of sand, etc.; for it can be seen that at the time when it was most numerous and flourishing it never occupied anything but the small sterile provinces of Palestine and its environs, which are almost nothing in comparison with the vast extent of the multitude of flourishing kingdoms that exist all over the earth.

Secondly: they were never fulfilled touching on the great blessings with which they were to have been favored for, though having carried off several small victories over poor peoples that they pillaged, this has not prevented them from being in most cases defeated and reduced to servitude, their kingdom as well as their nation destroyed by the Roman army. And even now we see that the remains of that unhappy nation is looked upon as the most vile and contemptible of the earth, having nowhere had either dominion or authority.

Thirdly and finally: these promises were not fulfilled with regard to that eternal alliance that God is supposed to have made with them, since we do not see—and we have never seen—any sign of that alliance. On the contrary, for several centuries they have been excluded from the possession of the small country that they claim to have been promised them by God for their eternal use. Thus, none of these so-called promises having had any effect, this is a certain mark of their falsity. Which again manifestly proves that those so-called holy and sacred books that contain them were not written through divine inspiration. It is thus in vain that our Christ-lovers claim they can use them as infallible evidence proving the truth of their religion.

Chapter VI

FIRST SECTION
On the Old Testament

Our Christ-lovers also put prophecies forward as a reason for belief and as a certain proof of the truth of their religion. These are, they claim, certain evidence of the truth of God's revelations and inspirations, God alone being able to predict future things so far in advance of their arrival, like those that were predicted by the prophets.

Let us now see what there is to these so-called prophecies, and if we should make as much of them as our Christ-lovers claim.

These men were nothing but visionaries and fanatics, who acted and spoke in keeping with the impulses and transports of their dominant passions, yet they imagined that it was through God's spirit that they acted and spoke. Or else they were imposters who pretended to be prophets and who, in order to more easily deceive the ignorant and the simple, bragged of acting and speaking through God's spirit.

I would like very much to know how an Ezekiel would be received who says (ch 3; 4) that God had him eat a parchment book, ordered him to have himself tied up like a madman, told him to lie down 390 days on his right side and 40 on the left, ordered him to eat shit on his bread and then, as a compromise, ox droppings. I ask how such a lunatic would be received among even the most imbecilic of our provincials?

What greater proof of the falsity of these so-called predictions than the violent reproaches that these prophets made against each other accusing each other of falsely speaking in God's name. Reproaches they made, they said, in God's behalf. See Ezekiel 13:1 Jer. 2:4.

They all say: guard yourselves against false prophets, just as the sellers of mitridate say to guard yourselves against counterfeit pills.

These unfortunates make God speak in a way that even a madman wouldn't dare speak. God says in ch. 23 of Ezekiel that the young Aholiba only loves those who have an ass' member and the sperm of a horse. How could these insane liars know the future? Not a single prediction in favor of their Jewish nation has been fulfilled.

The number of prophecies that predict the happiness and grandeur of Jerusalem is almost uncountable. It can be said that it is natural that a defeated and captive people would console itself for its real ills with imaginary hopes, just as there hasn't passed a single year since the destitution of King James that the Irish of his party haven't forged prophecies in his favor.

But if these promises made to the Jews were in fact true, then the Jewish nation for a long time would already have been, and would still be, the most numerous, the most powerful, the happiest, and the most triumphant of peoples.

SECOND SECTION
On the New Testament

We must now examine the so-called prophecies contained in the New Testament.

First. An angel appeared in dream to a certain Joseph, the at least putative father of Jesus son of Mary, and said to him: "Joseph son of David, do not fear to take to your house Mary your wife, for that which is in her is the work of the Holy Spirit (*How many similar stories are there, says Montaigne, of poor humans cuckolded by the gods*). She will give birth to a son who you will call Jesus, for it is he who will deliver his people from their sins."

That angel also said to Mary: "Have no fear, for you have found grace in the eyes of God. I declare that you will conceive in your womb and you will give birth to a son you will call Jesus. He shall be great and shall be called the son of the Most High. The lord God will give him the throne of David his father. He shall reign forever in the house of Jacob, and his reign will have no end." (Matt. 1:20 and Luke 1:3)

Jesus began to preach and to say: "Repent, for the kingdom of Heaven is nigh (Matt.4:17) Fear not and do not say what will we eat or what will we drink? Or how will we be clothed? For your heavenly father knows that all of these things are necessary. Seek first the kingdom of God and his justice and all these things shall be given to you in abundance." (Matt 6:30,31,32)

And now let any man who has not lost his senses examine if this Jesus was ever king, or if his disciples had everything in abundance.

This Jesus often promises that he will deliver the world from sin. Is there a more false prophecy? Is our century not eloquent proof of this?

It is said that Jesus came to save his people. What a way to save them! It is the greatest part that denominates a thing: for example, a dozen or two Spaniards or Frenchmen are not the French people or the Spanish people, and if an army of 120,000 men were taken prisoner of war by a stronger army of enemies, and if the head of that army ransomed only a few men, say ten or twelve soldiers or officers, by paying their ransom, we wouldn't then say that he delivered or saved his army. What then is a God who has Himself crucified and dies to save the world and leaves so many nations damned? What a pity and what a horror.

Jesus says that we only have to ask and we will receive, to seek and we shall find. He assures us that all we ask of God in his name shall be obtained and if we have faith that is as tiny as a mustard seed we could move mountains with only a word. If that promise were true nothing would appear impossible to our Christ-lovers, who have faith in their Christ. Nevertheless, the opposite occurs.

If Mohammed had made promises to his followers like those Jesus made to his, what would we say? We would cry out: "Liar! Imposter! You madmen who believe such an imposter!" Yet here are the Christ-lovers themselves in the same case, and they have been there for a long time without turning from their blindness. On the contrary, they are so ingenious in deceiving themselves that they claim that these promises have been fulfilled since the beginning of Christianity. It is the case, they say, that miracles occur in order to convince the unbelieving of the truth of their religion, but that their religion now being sufficiently established miracles are no longer necessary. Where is the certainty of this proposition?

In any event, he who made these promises didn't restrict them to a certain time or place, nor to certain persons in particular: he made them generally for all the world. "The faith of those who will believe," he says, "will be followed by these miracles: they will chase out devils in my name, they shall speak diverse languages, they shall touch snakes, etc."

As for the moving of mountains, he positively says that he who says to a mountain: "Move from there; I cast you into the sea," as long as he doesn't hesitate in his heart but rather believes, all that he orders shall be done. Are these not promises that are completely general, without restriction as to time, place, or person?

It is said that all the sects that are erroneous and false will come to a shameful end. But if Jesus Christ means only to say that he founded and established a society of followers who will not fall into vice or error, these words are absolutely false, since within Christianity there is no sect, society, or church that is not full of errors and vices, principally the sect or society of the Roman church, though it says it is the purest and holiest of all. A long time ago it fell into error; it was born there, or better yet, it was engendered and formed there. And now it even commits errors that are against the intentions, the sentiments, and the doctrine of its founder, since against his design it has abolished the laws of the Jews, which he approved of and which he himself said he had come *to fulfill and not to destroy,* and it has fallen into the errors and idolatry of paganism, as is seen by the idolatrous cult it renders to its God of clay, to his saints, to their images and relics.

I know that our Christ-lovers regard it as a vulgarity of the spirit to want to take literally the promises and prophecies as they were expressed. They abandon the literal and natural meaning of words in order to give them a meaning they call mystical and spiritual, and that they name allegorical and tropological. Saying, for example, that by the people of Israel and Judah—to whom these promises were made—one must understand not the Israelites of the flesh, but the Israelites of the spirit, that is the Christians, who are the Israel of God, the true Chosen People. That by the promise made to this enslaved people one should understand not a corporeal deliverance of a lone captive people, but the spiritual deliverance of all men from servitude to the devil, which is to be carried out by their divine savior. That by the abundance of riches and all the temporal happiness promised to this people should be understood the abundance of spiritual grace. And that finally, by the city of Jerusalem should be understood not the earthly Jerusalem, but the spiritual Jerusalem, which is the Christian church.

But it is easy to see that these spiritual and allegorical meanings, being nothing but foreign, imaginary meanings, subterfuges of the interpreters, they can not in the least serve to show the truth or the falsity of any proposition or promise at all. It is ridiculous to thus forge allegorical meanings since it is only in relation to the natural and true meaning that we can judge truth or falsehood. For example, a proposition, a promise that is found to be true in the proper and natural sense of the terms in which they were conceived does not become false in itself on the pretext that we want to give it a foreign meaning that it doesn't have. In the same way those found to be manifestly false in their proper and natural meaning do not become true in themselves on the pretext that one wants to give them a foreign meaning that they don't have.

It can be said that the prophecies of the Old Testament, added to the New, are things quite absurd and puerile. For example, Abraham had two wives, one of whom was only a servant according to the synagogue, and the other was a wife according to the Christian church. And based on the pretext that that Abraham had two sons, one of whom, from the servant, was said to prefigure the Old Testament, the other from his wife prefigured the New Testament. Who could help themselves from laughing at such a ridiculous doctrine? (*Spectatum admissi risum teneatis amici—de Arte Poetica Horat. 5 verse*)*

Is it not amusing that a piece of red cloth, exposed by a whore in order to serve as a signal to spies in the Old Testament, serves as the blood of Christ spilled in the New?

If in keeping with this manner of allegorically interpreting all that is said, done, and practiced in that ancient law of the Jews we were then to interpret all the speeches, actions, and adventures of the famous Don Quixote we would certainly find there just as many mysteries and meanings.

Nevertheless, it is on this ridiculous foundation that the entire Christian religion rests. This is why there is almost nothing in that ancient law that the Christ-loving scholars don't attempt to explain mystically.

The most false and ridiculous prophecy ever made was that of Jesus in Luke 22. It is predicted that there will be signs in the sun and the moon, and that the Son of Man will come in a cloud to judge men, and

---

* If you saw such a thing, could you refrain your laughter, friends?

he predicts this for the present generation. Did that occur? Did the Son of Man come in a cloud?

Chapter VII
Fifth. Proof drawn from doctrinal and moral errors

The Christian Apostolic and Roman religion teaches and obliges the belief that there is only one God, and that at the same time there are three divine persons, each of whom is truly God. Which is manifestly absurd, for if there are three who are truly God then there are truly three Gods. It is false to say that there is only one God, or if it is true to say it then it is false to say that there are truly three who are God, since it can not be said of the same thing that it is one and three.

It is also said that the first of these so-called divine persons, called the Father, engendered the second person, called the Son, and that these two persons together produced the third, who is called the Holy Spirit, and that nevertheless these three so-called divine persons do not depend upon each other and none of them is even any older than the other. This too is manifestly absurd, since a thing cannot receive its being from another without some kind of dependency upon the other, and that a thing must necessarily exist in order for it to give being to another. If, then, the second and third divine persons received their being from the first, they must necessarily depend for their being on that first person who gave them being or who engendered them. And, necessarily, that first, who gave being to the other two, must have existed before, for that which is not can give being to nothing. In any event, it is repugnant and absurd to say that a thing that was engendered or produced did not have a beginning. According to our Christ-lovers the second and third persons were engendered or produced; they thus had a beginning. And if they had a beginning, and the first person didn't, since he wasn't engendered or produced by any other, it necessarily follows that one was before the other.

Our Christ-lovers, who sense these absurdities, and who can't fend them off with any good reasons, have no other resource than to say that we have to piously close the eyes of human reason and humbly adore such great mysteries without wanting to understand them. But since what they call faith has been solidly refuted above, when they say that we must submit it is as if they said that we must blindly believe that which we don't believe.

Our Christ-lovers openly condemn the blindness of the ancient pagans who adored several gods. They laugh at the genealogy of their gods, or their births, their marriages and the generation of their children. But they don't notice that they say things much more ridiculous and absurd.

If the pagans believed that there were goddesses as well as gods, that these gods and goddesses wed and had children, they found all this nothing but natural, for they didn't yet imagine that the gods had neither bodies nor sentiments; they thought they possessed them in the same way men do. Why wouldn't there have been males and females? We can't see why there is any more reason to deny or recognize one any more than the other. And supposing that there were gods and goddesses, why wouldn't they have children in the ordinary way? If it were true that their gods existed there would be nothing ridiculous or absurd in this doctrine.

But in the doctrine of our Christ-lovers there is something even more ridiculous and absurd, for aside from their saying that one God makes three, and from three they make one, they say that this triple and unique God has neither body nor form nor face; that the first person of this triple and unique God, who they call the Father, engendered on his own a second person they call the Son and who is exactly like his Father, being, like Him, without body, form, or face. If this is the case, why is it that the first is called the Father, rather than the mother? And that the second is called the Son and not the daughter? For if the first is truly father instead of mother, and if the second is Son rather than daughter there must necessarily be something in the one and the other of these two persons that they be father rather than mother, and the other son rather than daughter. What could cause this if it's not that they are both male rather than female? But how can they be male rather than female since they have neither body not form nor face? This is unimaginable and self-refuting. Nevertheless, they still say that these two persons without body, form, or face—and consequently without any difference in sex—are nevertheless Father and Son, and they produced through their mutual love a third person they call the Holy Spirit, which person has, no more than the two others, neither body, form, or face!

Since our Christ-lovers limit God the Father's power to engendering but one son, why don't they want the second, as well as the third persons to have, like the first, the power of engendering a son like him? If that power of engendering a son is a perfection in the first person, it is thus a perfection and a power which is not in either the second or third persons. These two persons thus lacking a perfection and a power that are found in the first they can certainly not all be equals. If, on the contrary, they say that this power of engendering a son is not a perfection, then they shouldn't attribute it to the first any more than to the two others, since only perfections should be attributed to a being who is absolutely perfect.

In any case, they wouldn't dare say that the power of engendering a divine person is not a perfection, and if they say that that first person could have engendered several sons and daughters, but he only wanted to engender that one Son, and that, similarly, the two other persons didn't want to engender others, we can firstly ask them, how do they know that things are thus, for we don't see anywhere in their Holy Scriptures where these divine persons were positively declared. How then can our Christ-lovers know that this is the case? They only speak in keeping with their ideas and their hollow imagination.

Secondly, it can be said that if these so-called divine persons had the power to engender several children and they nevertheless didn't want to do so, it follows that this divine power would be without effect in them. It would be completely without effect in the third person, who would neither engender nor produce any, and it would be almost without effect in the two others since they want to so strictly limit it. Thus the power they would have to engender and produce a number of children would remain idle and useless in them, something it would be inappropriate to say of divine persons.

Our Christ-lovers censure and condemn pagans for attributing divinity to mortal men, and for adoring them like Gods after their deaths. They are correct in this, but those pagans only did what our Christ-lovers still do now, who attribute divinity to their Christ. They should condemn themselves as well, since they commit the same error as the pagans and they adore a man who was mortal, and so mortal that he shamefully died on a cross.

It would be of no use for our Christ-lovers to say that there is a great difference between their Jesus Christ and the gods of the pagans on the pretext that their Christ is, as they say, true God and true man all together, since the divinity is veritably incarnated in him. By means of this the divine nature, finding itself joined and united hypostatically, as they say, with human nature these two natures together made of Jesus Christ a true God and a true man; something that was never, despite what they say, done with the gods of the pagans.

But it is easy to show the feebleness of this answer, for on the one hand would it not have been just as easy for the pagans as for the Christians to say that the Divinity incarnated itself in the men they adored as gods? On the other hand, if the Divinity had wanted to incarnate itself and unite hypostatically with human nature in their Jesus Christ how do they know that same Divinity would not have wanted also to become incarnate and unite itself hypostatically with human nature in the person of its great men and admirable women who, by their virtue, by their good qualities, or by their good acts excelled over the common run of men and who thus were adored as gods and goddesses? And if our Christ-lovers don't want to believe that the Divinity was ever incarnated in these great individuals, why do they want to persuade us that it was incarnated in their Jesus? Where is the proof? In their faith and their belief, which the pagans had in exactly the same way as them. Which shows that they are both in error.

But what is more ridiculous in Christianity than in paganism is that the pagans ordinarily only attributed divinity to its great men, authors of the arts and sciences and who excelled in those virtues useful to their country. But who do our Christ-lovers attribute divinity to? To a man with nothing, vile and contemptible, who had neither talent, nor science, nor skill; born of poor parents and who, from the time he wanted to make an appearance in the world and have himself spoken of, was never taken for anything but a madman and a seducer and who was despised, mocked, persecuted, whipped, and finally hung like most of those who wanted to play the same role when they lacked courage and ability.

In his time there were several other similar imposters who said they were the true messiah promised by the law, among others a certain Judah the Galileean, a Theudas, a Bar-Kochba and others, who on a vain pretext abused the people and attempted to have them rise up in order to attract them, but all perished.

Let us pass now to his speeches and some of his acts, which are the most remarkable and the most singular of their kind. "Repent," he said to the people, "for the Kingdom of Heaven is nigh. Believe the good news." And he went all around Galilee, preaching the so-called approach of the kingdom of heaven. Since no one has yet seen any appearance of the coming of this Kingdom, it is eloquent proof that it was only imaginary.

But let us now see in his other preaching the elegy for and the description of this beautiful Kingdom:

This is how he spoke to the people: "The Kingdom of Heaven is likened unto a man which sowed good seed in his field. But while men slept, his enemy came and sowed tares among the wheat, and went his way (...) (It) is like unto treasure hid in a field; the which when a man hath found, he hideth, and for joy thereof goeth and selleth all that he hath, and buyeth that field. (It) is like unto a merchant man, seeking goodly pearls, who, when he had found one pearl of great price, went and sold all that he had, and bought it. (It) is like unto a net, that was cast into the sea, and gathered of every kind, which, when it was full, they drew to shore, and sat down, and gathered the good into vessels, but cast the bad away. The kingdom of heaven is like to a grain of mustard seed, which a man took, and sowed in his field, which indeed is the least of all seeds: but when it is grown, it is the greatest among herbs." Is this how it is in speeches worthy of a God?

We would still judge him the same way if we were to closely examine his actions. For example: 1—Running around an entire province preaching the imminent arrival of a so-called kingdom. 2—Having been transported by the devil to a high mountain, from which he thought to see all the kingdoms of the world. This is only fitting for a visionary, for it is certain that there is not a mountain in the world from which you could even see one entire kingdom, except for the tiny Kingdom of Yvetot, which is in France. It was thus only in imagination that he saw all these kingdoms and was transported to that mountain, as well as onto the pinnacle of the temple. 3—When he cures the deaf mute, which is spoken of in Saint Mark, it is said that he selected him out in particular, that he put his fingers in his ears and, having spit, he pulled on his tongue. And then, casting his eyes to the heavens, he gave out a large breath and said to him: Ephphatha. Read whatever you like that is reported about him, and judge for yourself if there is anything in the world as ridiculous.

Having put before your eyes a part of the foolishness attributed to God by the Christ-lovers, let us continue by saying a few words about their mysteries. They adore a God in three persons, or three persons in one God, and they grant themselves the power of making Gods of clay and flour, and even of making as many as they want. For in keeping with their principles they only have to say four words over such and such a number of glasses of wine, or over these tiny images of dough, and they then make as many Gods as they like, even into the millions. What madness! With all the so-called power of their Christ they couldn't make the tiniest fly, yet they think they can make Gods in the thousands. One must be struck with a strange blindness to put up with such pitiful things, and this on so vain a foundation as the ambiguous words of a fanatic.

Don't these blind scholars see that it means opening wide the door to all kinds of idolatries to have images of dough thus adored on the pretext that priests have the power to consecrate them and to change them into Gods? Couldn't, and can't, all the priests of idols brag of having the same character?

Do they not also see that the same reasons that demonstrate the vanity of gods or idols of wood, stone, etc., that the pagans adore in the same way demonstrate the vanity of Gods and idols of clay and flour that our Christ-lovers adore? Why do they mock the falsity of the gods of the pagans? Is it not because they are the handiworks of men, images mute and unfeeling? And what then are the Gods that we keep enclosed in boxes for fear of mice?

What then will be the vain resources of the Christ-lovers? Their morality? Essentially it is the same as in all religions, but cruel dogmas have been born of it and have taught persecution and disorder. Their miracles? But what people don't have their own, and what wise men don't hold these fables in contempt? Their prophecies? Have we not demonstrated their falsity? Their morality? Is it not often unspeakable? The establishment of their religion? But did fanaticism not begin, intrigue not raise, and force not visibly support that edifice? Their doctrine? But isn't it the height of absurdity?

I believe, my dear friends, to have provided you with sufficient protection against so many follies. Your reason will provide you with even more than my discourse, and may it please God that we not have reason to complain that we have been deceived. But since the time of Constantine human blood has flowed for the establishment of these impostures. The Roman Church, the Greek, the Protestant, so many vain disputes, so many ambitious hypocrites have ravaged Europe, Africa, and Asia. Add together, my friends, with the men these quarrels have slaughtered, those multitudes of monks and nuns who have been rendered sterile by their state. See how many creatures have been lost and you will see that the Christian religion has made half of humanity perish.

I will finish by begging God, so outraged by that sect, to deign to recall us to natural religion, of which Christianity is the declared enemy. To that simple religion that God placed in the hearts of all men, which teaches us that we only do unto others what we want to have done unto us. Then the universe will be composed of good citizens, of just fathers, of submissive children, of tender friends. God gave us this religion in giving us reason. May fanaticism no longer pervert it! I die more filled with these wishes than with hopes.

This is the exact summary of the in-folio testament of Jean Meslier. We can judge how weighty is the testimony of a dying priest who asks God's forgiveness.

On the Great Good and Advantages for Men if They All Lived Peaceably, Enjoying in Common the Goods and Conveniences of Life[*]

If men equally possessed and enjoyed in common the goods, wealth, and conveniences of life, if they were all unanimously occupied in some honest and useful exercise, or some honest and useful labor of the body or spirit, and if they wisely managed the goods of the land and the fruits of their labor and industry, they would all have sufficient place to live happy and content, for the earth almost always produces sufficient and even abundantly enough to nourish them and sustain them, if they would always make good use of these goods, and it's quite rare that the earth fails to produce the necessities of life; and thus all would have enough to live peacefully, no one would lack what is necessary to him, no one would suffer in order to have for himself or his children what they need to live or clothe themselves; no one would suffer for himself or his children not knowing where he would be lodged or sleep, for all would find all of this surely, abundantly, easily and comfortably in a well regulated community; and thus no one would have any interest in resorting to fraud or shrewdness and falsehood in order to surprise his neighbor. No one would have any interest in lawsuits to defend his goods. No one would have any interest in envying his neighbor, nor to be envious of each other, because all will be more or less in a state of equality. No one would have any interest in stealing what others might have, no one would have any interest in killing or murdering anyone in order to have his purse or his money or his goods, for this would do him no good as an individual; no one would have any interest in so to speak killing himself with work and fatigue, as is now done by countless numbers of poor people, who are more or less forced to kill themselves with work, to kill themselves with tasks and fatigues in order to barely have what they need to live as well as to meet the expenses and taxes that are rigorously demanded of them. No one, I say, would have any interest in killing himself in this way with tasks and fatigue, because each for his part would assist in supporting the sufferings of labor, and no one would remain uselessly idle while others occupy themselves usefully at labor.

---

[*] From *Mémoire contre la religion*, in *Oeuvres Complètes*. Anthropos, Paris, 1970.

You are surprised, my dear friends? You are surprised, poor peoples that you have so much evil and so much suffering in life? It's that all alone you bear the weight of the day and the heat, like the workers spoken of in a parable in your Gospels. It's that you and your like are charged with all the burdens of the state, you are charged not only with all the burdens of your kings, your princes who are your tyrants, but you are also charged with the entire burden of the nobility, with the entire burden of the clergy; you are charged with the entire burden of monkery and all those of the justice system, you are charged with all the lackeys and all the stable boys of the great and the servants and maids of the others, you are charged with all the warriors, with all those who claim taxes not due, of all the watchmen over salt and tobacco; and finally, of all the do-nothings and the useless of the world; for it is only on the fruit of your difficult labors that all these people live; you furnish by your labors all that is necessary for this, but even more all that could serve their entertainments and pleasures. What, for example, would the greatest princes and the greatest potentates of the earth be if the people didn't support them? It is only from the people (who they hardy treat kindly) that they draw all their grandeur, all their wealth, and all their power; in a word they would be nothing but weak and small men like you if you didn't support their grandeur; they would have no more wealth than you if you didn't give them theirs. And finally they would have no more power or authority than you if you didn't submit to their laws and will. If all these men I am speaking of shared with you the difficulties of labor, and if they left for you as they do for themselves a fitting portion of those goods you earn and you so abundantly bring forth by the sweat of your brows, you would on the one hand be less charged and much less tired; on the other you would also have much more rest and sweetness in life than you now have. But no, all the suffering is yours and your like, and all the good is for the others, though they deserve it less, and this is why the poor people have so much evil and so many sufferings in life.

We see, says M. de la Bruyère in his "Characters," *certain ferocious animals, male and female, spread about the countryside, black and livid and burned by the sun, attached to the land that they dig through and up with an invincible stubbornness; they have a voice that is almost articulated, and when they stand on their feet they show a human face, and in fact they are men. At night they retreat into their lairs where they live on black bread, water, and roots; they spare other men the suffering of planting, laboring and harvesting in order to live, and so deserve,* he says, *to not lack this bread they planted and that they have brought forth in so much suffering.* Yes, to be sure they deserve not to lack for it, and even more they deserve to eat it first, and to have the better part, as well as to have the better part of the good wine that they also bring forth in so much suffering and fatigue. But, O, inhuman and detestable cruelty, the rich and the great of the earth steal the better part of the fruits of their hard labors, and leave them nothing but the straw of the good grain, and the dregs of the good wine they bring forth with so much suffering and labor. The author I quoted doesn't say this, but he makes it clearly enough understood. If as I said all goods were wisely governed and dispensed, no one would have any interest in fearing either famine or poverty for himself and his own, for all goods and riches would be equally for all, which would certainly be the good and the greatest happiness that could arrive for men.

In the same way, if men do not stop their vain and harmful distinctions between families, and if they were to truly look upon each other as brothers and sisters, as they should in keeping with the principles of their religion, no one of them would prevail or brag of being of better or nobler birth than their companions, and consequently they would have no reason to detest each other or to insultingly reproach each other for their birth or family; but each would find himself worthy of esteem in keeping with his own personal merit and not according to the imaginary merit of a pretended better or more noble birth; which would also be a great good for men.

In the same way, if men, and particularly our Christ-lovers, didn't make marriages indissoluble as they do, and if on the contrary they always left conjugal unions and friendship free among them, without forcing the ones or the others, that is without forcing men or women to remain their entire lives inseparably bound against their inclinations, we would certainly not see so many bad marriages or so many unhappy couples as there are among them, and there would not be as much discord and dissension as there is between husbands and wives; they would have no interest in resorting every day to reproaches or insults or ill treatment as they so often do against each other, they would have no interest in so often being angry with each other; they would have no interest in speaking ill of each other, they would have no interest in beating each other or of tearing each other apart with such fury, as they often do to each other, because they could freely quit each other peacefully as soon as they ceased to love or be happy together, and they could each freely seek their happiness elsewhere. In a word, there would no longer be unhappy husbands or unhappy wives, as there are now so many who are unhappy throughout their lives under the fatal yoke of an indissoluble marriage. On the contrary, they would both always have, agreeably and peaceably, their pleasures and contentment with whomever is fitting for them, for from that point it would always be good fellowship which would be the principal and main reason for their conjugal union, which would be a great good for both. Also as for the children who would issue from this, because they wouldn't be like so many poor children who remain orphaned of father or mother and often of both together, and who for this reason are as if abandoned by all, and who we often seem unhappy under the law of brutal stepfathers or evil stepmothers who force them to starve and mistreat them with blows, or under the guidance of tutors or guardians who neglect them and who even eat up and dissipate their goods; they would also not be like so many poor children who we see unhappy under the guidance of their fathers and mothers and who suffer from their most tender years all the miseries of poverty: the cold in the winter, the heat in the summer, hunger, thirst, lack of clothing; who are always in filth and ordure, without an education, without instruction and who can't even grow or flourish because they lack the sustenance necessary for life.

But they would all be equally well raised, all equally well nourished and given all they need because they would all be raised, nourished and maintained in common from the public and common goods. In the same way as well they would be equally instructed in good morals and honesty, as well as in the sciences and arts to the extent it would be necessary and fitting for each of them to be so in relation to public utility and the need there might be of their services, in such a way that, all being instructed in the same principles of morality and in the same rules of good conduct and honesty, it would be easy to make them all wise and honest, to have them all work together for the same good, and to make them all capable of usefully serving their fatherland. Which would certainly be advantageous for the public good and human society. Things are not the same when men are raised and educated in different principles of morality and they have taken on different rules and different ways of living, for from that point this diversity of education, instruction and ways of living only inspires contrariety and a diversity of humors, opinions, and sentiments that ensures that they can't peacefully accommodate each other nor, consequently, unanimously work together for the same good, which causes continual troubles and divisions between them. But when they are all brought up and educated from youth in the same moral principles, and they have learned to follow the same rules of life and conduct, from that point all sharing the same sentiments and having the same views they all work more easily together for the same good, which is the common good of all.

It would this be better for men to always permit freedom of marriage and conjugal unions. It would be better for them to have all their children equally well raised, fed, maintained and educated in good morals as well as the sciences and the arts. It would be better for them to look on each other and love each other as brothers and sisters. It would be better for them to not make family distinctions among themselves and to not believe themselves from a better family or of better birth than each other. It would be better for all of them to occupy themselves with some good labor or some honest and useful exercise, and for each to bear his part of the harshness of labor and the inconveniences of life, without unjustly leaving to one group all the suffering and the entire weight of the burden, while others do nothing but take their pleasure and contentment. Finally, it would be better for them to possess everything in common and to peaceably enjoy in common the goods and the conveniences of life, and all of this under the guidance and the leadership of the wisest; they would certainly all be incomparably happier and more content than they are, for we would no longer see any destitute, or any unfortunates or even any poor on earth, so many of whom we see every day.

M. Pascal in his "Reflections" testifies clearly to having the same sentiments when he remarks that the usurpation of all the land and all the ills that have followed from it only come from the fact that each individual has wanted to appropriate those things they should have left in common. *This dog is mine, these poor children said, and that is my place in the sun. This,* that author says, *is the beginning and the image of the usurpation of all the land.* Plato, divine Plato, wanting to construct a republic whose citizens could live agreeably with each other rightly banished from it the words of mine and yours. Know well that as long as there will be something to share there will always be found discontent, from which is born troubles, divisions, wars and law suits.

Error, Illusion, and Imposture (1729)[*]

All Religions are nothing but error, illusion and imposture.

Know then, my dear friends, that all that is spread about and practiced in the world in the way of cults and adoration of gods is naught but error, abuse, and imposture. All laws and ordinances published in the name of and by authority of God, or gods, are really nothing but human inventions, like all those beautiful festivals at holidays and sacrifices and divine offices, and all the other superstitious practices of religion and devotion that are done in their honor. All these things, I say, are naught but human inventions which were ... invented by clever and tricky politicians and then cultivated and multiplied by seducers and imposters, blindly accepted by the ignorant, and finally maintained and authorized by the laws of princes and the great of the earth, who used these human inventions in order to more easily bridle the common run of men and to do with them what they willed. But in the end, these inventions are nothing but bridles for calves, as Montaigne said, for the only serve to bridle the spirit of the ignorant and the simple. The wise do not bridle themselves, and don't allow themselves to be bridled, for in fact it is only the ignorant and the simple who accept this and allow themselves to be led. And what I am here saying in general on the vanity and falsity of religions I am not only saying about those pagan and foreign religions that you already look upon as false, but I am also saying it about your Christian religion, because in fact it is no less vain, no less false than any other, and I can even say that, in a sense, it is perhaps even more vain and more false than any other, for there is perhaps no other as ridiculous or absurd in its principal points as this one, nor any that is so contrary to nature itself and reason. This is what I am telling you, my dear friends, so that you not allow yourselves to be any longer deceived by the beautiful promises it makes to you of the so-called eternal rewards of a paradise that is only imaginary, and so that you put your spirits and hearts at rest regarding all the vain fears it instills in you about the so-called eternal punishments of a hell that does not exist. For all that is told you of the beauty and magnificence of the one and the terror and frights of the

---

[*] Written: by Jean Meslier, 1729. From *Mémoire des Pensées et Sentiments in Oeuvres de Jean Meslier*, prefaces et notes par Jean Deprun, Roland Desne, Albert Soboul. Paris, Editions Anthropos, 1970.

other are nothing but fables: after death there is neither good nor evil to fear. Wisely profit then from your time by living well and by soberly, peacefully, and joyously enjoying life's goods and the fruits of your labor, for this is your part and the best thing you can do. For death, in putting an end to life, also puts an end to all knowledge and all sentiments of good and evil. ...

Paul-Henry Thiry, Baron d'Holbach (1723-1789)

The representative figures of the Enlightenment, Voltaire, Diderot, and D'Alembert, have come down to us as eaters of priests, ferocious enemies of the established order. Yet their relations with the royals of the era, Catherine the Great and Frederick of Prussia, were cozy to say the least. And despite their reputations as enemies of religion (Voltaire's famous *"ecrasez l'infame"*, for example) we find in the Encyclopedia, that most extensive expression of the Enlightenment world view, that atheism is caused by "ignorance and stupidity," by "debauch" and the "corruption of morals;" that atheists want nothing so much as "to be talked about and that it is their vanity that pushes them to seek a reputation for being "impious." What the leading lights of the Enlightenment sought was less the destruction of religious belief than the shaking of the Catholic Church and the freeing of God from the church's shackles.

If the likes of Voltaire, Diderot, and Rousseau during the Enlightenment were less the atheists than they were thought to be, it is perhaps not surprising that the one true atheist in the group is someone who has been virtually eclipsed: Baron d'Holbach. He died only five months before the revolution for which his writings did so much to prepare.

The Baron served as one of the first great examples of the cosmopolitanism and the internationalism of the French revolutionary tradition. He was a German who discovered France and the French language as an adolescent (the Swiss Rousseau was at least a native French speaker). D'Holbach's itinerary exemplifies the cosmopolitanism of the intellectuals of the period: born German, educated in Holland at the University of Leyden, maintained an intellectual salon in Paris, translated from English, wrote countless books on the natural sciences, religion, and philosophy in French, and contributed 400 articles to Diderot and d'Alembert's Encyclopedia.

Starting in 1761, he was the tireless author of anti-religious works that stemmed from the strain of atheism begun by Jean Meslier:

"Christianity Revealed, or an Examination of the Principles and Effects of the Christian Religion" (1761), "The Sacred Contagion" (1768), "Hell Destroyed, or a Reasoned Examination of the Eternity of Punishments" (1769). A work commonly attributed to Meslier, "The Good Sense of the Curé Meslier," was in fact a work of the Baron's. In his last years he wrote important works on ethics, philosophy, and politics.

His writings, like those of Meslier before him and of Sylvain Maréchal after him, are a careful and well-reasoned demolition of the religious edifice, tearing down the "God-lovers'" redoubt stone by stone, holding the contradictions of the Bible, its inconsistencies and improbabilities, before the eyes of all who cared to see, and positing a materialist philosophy in opposition to what he called the "fables" that ruled humanity. His examination of religion was always clear-eyed, bringing religion down to earth. In "On Religious Cruelty" he said that "men always give the Gods they adore the passions they themselves have," a statement that echoes Xenophanes, who maintained that if oxen, horses, and lions could draw, the gods they drew would resemble oxen, horses, and lions. His critique grounded religion in the concrete realities of society, binding materialism and atheism together in a way that takes us back to the materialists of Greek antiquity. For d'Holbach, atheism gladly assumes the role of the demolisher of the old world, as it does throughout this French tradition.

On Religious Cruelty (1769)[*]

In this essay I am going to examine the different kinds of religious cruelty. Under this name I include those religious opinions that proceed from this cruelty or give birth to it, those acts of barbarism imposed by religion itself, and those its zealots take as an obligation occasioned by its service and love.

The belief in God being the foundation of every religion, it is in general the idea we have of the Supreme Being that imprints a character on the worship we render him. If men imagine for themselves a tyrannical, capricious or wicked God their religion will breathe slavery, inconsistency, and cruelty. But if they sincerely look upon the divinity as a being infinitely wise and good we would be justified in concluding that their religion will be full of reason and benevolence and will lead to conducting oneself in an honest way of. Those who adore a single God doubtless say that this being is endowed with infinite wisdom and goodness. But if they attribute cruel acts to him, if they think that we can please him with vain and puerile practices or through barbaric actions, if they think that God himself has ordered such things, then the idea they truly have of the Divinity will be directly opposed to what they say, and will constitute the essence of their religion.

Without even being aware of it, many people believe in a cruel God, and they are consequently cruel when it comes to religion. In this realm they impose on themselves and on others. But let them question themselves in good faith and let them, deep in their hearts, ask themselves how they imagine the Supreme Being will treat the largest part of the men he has created, namely the infidels, in the world to come. Let them ask themselves how they themselves, if they had the power, would treat in this world the people who disagree with them on religious matters or dogmas. These questions, carefully and thoughtfully examined and candidly answered, will make men's opinions concerning the Divinity visible and cast their religion in a light very different from that with which it was originally envisaged.

Though most men agree that due to their consequences there are no opinions more important than those that have God and religion as objects, there is nevertheless no other that we so commonly take at face

---

[*] From *De la cruauté réligieuse*. 1769, [n.p.] London.

value. The symbolism and the catechism are learned by rote, much like vaudevilles and songs, and we don't reason any more about the one than about the other.

A great number of articles of faith are warmly embraced, stubbornly supported, and courageously defended, not because they are found to be reasonable, but because we have been accustomed to respect them from an early age, or because they are in accordance either with our temperament or our interests. We are disposed to think that the opinions we were penetrated with in our childhood and which habit has, in a certain sense, caused to grow along with us, are the result of our own reasoning, though we have never examined them. There are some that are so obviously true that it is of little import to know whether we discovered them ourselves, or if they were simply acquired. But as for those about which there can be the least doubt it is essential that we only admit them after careful reflection. This alone gives us the right to look upon them as truly ours.

...

Men always give the Gods they adore the passions they themselves have.

We know nothing either clear or satisfying about the creation of man[1].

We thus do not know the original opinion he had of his creator and what, at the beginning, was the object of his adoration.

If our first fathers admitted the excellence of a Being eternal, infinite, omnipotent, of an infinite goodness, the creator of the universe, it is obvious that almost their entire posterity soon lost both this knowledge and any reasonable sentiment regarding the divinity[2]. According to the most ancient testimonies we have of our history, the men of the earliest ages adored the strangest of gods: there is nothing more ridiculous than their different opinions concerning that multitude of divinities. They are so absurd that if we didn't have incontestable proofs of them it would be impossible for us to believe that a man, gifted with any kind of intelligence, could so deprave himself as to fall into such a pit of unreason. These notions were both absurd and changeable, and this must necessarily have been the case. In fact, if the truth is by its very nature circumscribed and always the same, error has neither fixed form nor limits.

But though straying from the truth by different routes, men have in general thought similarly when it comes to their gods: they have attributed to them the dispositions and passions that they themselves feel, and often a corporeal resemblance[3]. For what has been more common among most nations and religions than representing gods with a human likeness?

Among the Christians themselves, and especially among the monks of Egypt, there was once a sect that professed anthropomorphism. It based this sentiment on the fact that it is said that man was created in the *image of God*. The opinion of these monks was taken to such a degree of madness that they would have assassinated Theophilus, their bishop, who had written against the idea, if he hadn't had the quick wittedness to calm them by saying: *when I see you I see the face of God*[4]. Tertullien and Epiphanus, those two great antagonists of heretics, were accused of this error. In fact, what is more common among those called Christians than to see the omnipotent, the incomprehensible, the invisible creator of the universe represented as a feeble mortal[5]?

It is obvious that most men take themselves as the model for the idea they have of gods and even of one God. In this they only aggrandize their own dimensions. A God for them is nothing but a colossal man or, if you will, man is a pigmy God. It is likely that if other animals, whether reptiles or insects, were capable of imagining gods, they would make them resemble themselves; these would be elephant or ant gods; lamb or lion gods.

This general propensity of men, to give their divinities those dispositions and passions that dominate them, explains quite well the cruelty they have always attributed to their gods. At the same time, it is an extremely strong proof of the natural cruelty of the human heart.

Through their own experience and that of others men feel how strongly power is connected to tyranny and cruelty. For this they have examples drawn from the conduct of masters with their servants, husbands with their wives, fathers with their children, teachers with their pupils, absolute monarchs with their slaves. And just as they've attributed an unlimited power to their gods they put no limit to their tyranny and cruelty[6].

It is obvious from countless examples that the greatest part of humanity, at all times, in all nations, in all religions, has regarded cruelty as an attribute of the gods. Pagans generally supposed that they were punished with the greatest calamities, like famines or plagues, usually for the omission of some vain and ridiculous ceremony, or for having held in contempt some absurd tale from their divines or priests. If they believed their gods capable of being irritated by subjects so frivolous, they also thought they could appease them through expiations of the same type. For this a few songs, dances, or games in their honor were often employed[7]. The Romans in particular, when afflicted with some contagion, would attempt to expiate their sins and appease the gods by naming a dictator whose functions were limited to attaching a nail to Jupiter's temple. He would abdicate his magistracy after that noble ceremony.

There is nothing to be surprised about that pagans, who often deified their like and particularly their most odious princes, should attribute cruelty to the gods who were the makers of their vices as well as their virtues. But it is as absurd as it is astonishing that those who adore an infinitely good God should insult him in the same way.

Nevertheless, it is well known that the Jews, Christians and Mohammedans, who all claim to believe in the same God, represent him as even more cruel than the pagan gods. The opinion taught by the Jews, adopted and spread by Christian sages, is of a God merciful and beneficent, full of patience, rich in goodness, full of tender compassion, ready to pardon iniquities, transgressions and sins, but who nevertheless wants to cruelly punish the guilty, take vengeance for the iniquities of the children on the children, and on the children of the children until the third and fourth generations[8].

The Old Testament provides us with many other examples of the Jews' belief that God punished the innocent for the crimes of the guilty. A unique but remarkable example of this will suffice. We read in the book of Chronicles, chapter 21, that King David ordered a census of the people of Israel. It is likely that this was motivated by vanity. Nevertheless, this wasn't so horrible a crime, nor was it comparable in atrocity to many others committed by *this man according to God's heart*. Nevertheless, God was so irritated that he struck Israel with the plague and made 70,000 men perish. If a census was a crime it was that of David and not that of the people. He himself felt this so strongly that here is what David's prayer was: *Is it not I who ordered the census? It is thus I who sinned, but what did this flock do?* It is obvious that the people could no more prevent a census being taken than could a flock of sheep, and that it was no more guilty. Nevertheless, after God had destroyed for this reason as many as 70,000 men, as we said, *he repented of the evil he had done and said to the exterminating angel: that is enough, stay your hand now.* This gives an idea of the cruelty with which the pagans and Jews imagined that their gods punished them in this world. Nevertheless, the worst temporal punishments are nothing but mild afflictions in comparison with the eternal torments reserved to sinners in the other world by the God of goodness, if we are to believe those who admit the dogma of the future life. In fact, according to most Christians eternal misfortune will be the share not only of atrocious and stubborn scoundrels, but also of sinners who, all things being weighed, couldn't prevent themselves from falling into certain errors, the necessary result of their fragility. The same sentences are distributed for the omission, even absolutely involuntary, of certain ceremonies that assuredly cannot purify either the heart or the conscience. This is the case for children who die without having been baptized.

All infidels and unbelievers are still threatened with eternal damnation. Thus the belief in the true God having been, during many centuries, exclusively granted to an obscure, contemptible, wicked people (as they are depicted by their own historians and prophets), given that this people inhabited a small country that had but little commerce with its neighbors, it follows that since they lacked knowledge of the true God the rest of humanity had to be eternally unhappy. We are forced to believe that the Aristideses, the Phocions, the Timoleons, the Epaminodas, the Socrateses, and the Platos, in a word, that the most excellent pagans were included in that cruel sentence. Since Christ's arrival we must damn both those who didn't believe in him, though they never heard of him, and those who recognize him as God but haven't accepted the same type of cult or doctrine taught by some particular sect. This is what the Roman Catholics dare to maintain, and this is what a great number of Protestants presume. And this, if you believe the Mohammedans, is the way that God will treat those men who didn't recognized their prophet and who didn't regard the Koran and its doctrine as having emanated from heaven.

"Truly," says this so-called celestial book," we will cast into the fires of hell those who do not recognize the signs of our faith. When they are well grilled we will give them new skins in exchange, so they can suffer even worse torments, for God is powerful and wise." And elsewhere: "Boiling water will fall on their heads; their entrails and their skin will be torn and they will be continually beaten with iron clubs. Each time they attempt to leave hell in order to avoid torments they will be dragged back there and their executioners will tell them: savor the torment of fire."

In a word, many Christians have believed and taught that God condemned the greatest part of humanity, millions and millions of His own creatures, to suffer in a place where all the faculties of he body and the soul will be tormented continuously and without pause.

"It is there, oh sinner, that you will live in an eternal prison of external shadows, where the only order shall be confusion and horror. Where nothing will be heard but screams and blasphemies, no other sound but the gnashing of teeth, where there will be no other society but that of the devil and his angels who, tormented themselves, will have no other relief than that of making you feel their fury. *St Mathew chap 13 verse 42 and chapter 25 verse 36, etc.* It is there that punishment will be without pity, misery without grace, pain without consolation, wickedness without measure, torment without rest. *Apocalypse chapter 14 verses 10 & 11.* God's anger will penetrate the body and the soul, as the flame does with a block of sulfur or of pitch. *Daniel chapter 7 verse 10.* In this flame you shall be forever burned without ever being consumed, forever dying without expiring, forever groaning in the anguish of death without ever being delivered from it or even having the power to hope for the end of your suffering, in such a way that after having endured them as many thousands of years as there are blades of grass on the earth, sand in the ocean, hairs on the head of all the children of Adam born or to be born, you will be no closer to the end of your torments than you were the day you were cast there. Far from finishing, they will do naught at every instant but begin, for it will be some relief to envisage a possible end to your misfortune after so many thousands of years; but each time that your spirit shall recall that word 'never,' and it will recall this every instant, your heart shall be torn with rage and by a horrible despair, that horrible idea shall sharpen your unbearable pains that already exceed any power to explain or imagine. This shall be a new hell in the midst of the very hell."

With what surprise must such a shocking, such a terrible tale is read. The ideas it postulates of the manner in which God treats his creatures seem to have been proposed to transform him into a demon.

I can't leave behind the subject of God thus condemning men to eternal and unheard of torments without posing a question to those who are unfortunate enough to admit so blasphemous and diabolical a doctrine. I especially pose it to those who, without believing it, are cowardly or perverse enough to teach it and propagate it.

I would thus ask of them: what could be the legitimate and advantageous end of all this punishment? Is it not, in the first place, to correct the guilty, which is certainly very much to be desired? In second place is it not to turn men away from the committing of the crimes for which they see others punished? Finally, is it not to exile or to isolate from society those members which it fears? Such are the unvarying notions that men should formulate about the goals of punishments. And so, eternal punishments fulfill none of these legitimate views. The guilty cannot be corrected and it would even be useless to do so since, corrected or not, they will still be tormented. His example cannot help others turn away from crime; his conduct as well as his destiny are irrevocably determined. Finally, it cannot be imagined that among the damned any could be dangerous to society.

Is it possible for men to fall into so manifest a contradiction as to represent God as a being of infinite goodness, or even of the most ordinary equity, and at the same time to believe or teach that he punishes his creatures in such a way? Should they not rather represent him as a barbaric demon, as in infinitely unjust and cruel being? Through an act of pure will he created man in order to then condemn the work of his hands to eternal misery! What is the cause of this rigor? He is punished for things that did not at all depend on him. Is there a man ferocious enough to want, in cold blood, for whatever reason, to condemn to eternal torments his own children, or even a declared enemy? Is there anyone so pitiless as to not spare torments without measure to any being at all? Will a good man not want, on the contrary, to spread happiness as far as he can? Will not his only desire be to procure happiness for all created beings? Though these unworthy and absurd ideas about the divinity originally emanated from a barbaric disposition that many people bear within them, and which is inspired in others by other means, they are taught these opinions and they are more or less profoundly impressed on their souls according to the degree to which they are temperamentally disposed to cruelty. But we should be attentive to the fact that far from serving religion, by inculcating the doctrine of eternal punishment reasons are furnished for the atheism that annihilates all religion. And, on the other hand, we throw into despair a great number of honest, simple, and timorous souls without restraining the intrepid and hardened wicked ones, whose excesses, as experience proves, cannot be repressed by distant fears.

Notes by d'Holbach

1. The stories of all pagan authors concerning the origin of man are indubitably fables. And the stories in the book of Genesis attributed to Moses are regarded by many learned men as a pure allegory. In fact, they more

nearly resemble allegory than history. At the very least it is quite true that the story is obscure and not very satisfying.

2. According to what we are taught, as well as commonly received opinion, all men descend from one man and one woman, but this opinion seems unsustainable for several reasons, especially due to the impossibility of black and white men coming from the same parents. But whether there were at the beginning one or several couples of created men changes nothing in the matter in question.

3. The Lacedemonians, the most bellicose people on earth, always represented their gods, and even their goddesses, in warrior garb. In his account of the Cape of Good Hope Mr. Pierre Kolbe tells us that some Hottentots, the filthiest men that exist, who cover their bodies with soot mixed with grease, and who only clothe themselves in animal skins, say that in his color, his face, and his clothing God resembles the most handsome among them.

4. See the French translation by Cousin, chap II page 472.

5. Paintings of God the Father as an old man are very common in Roman Catholic countries. The author of this essay saw in Lyon a God the Father sporting a fashionable three-cornered hat, apparently to represent the Trinity.

6. In antiquity and in pagan countries most servants were slaves and treated with an extreme barbarism. Doctor Jortin in his excellent "Discours sur la religion chrétienne" observes that Christianity proscribed a great number of atrocious usages, especially those relating to the treatment of servants. We would owe a great debt to Christianity if it had abolished all those barbarisms about which the doctor speaks, and especially this one. In Europe, where servants are not slaves, where they serve willingly and are under the protection of the law, it is not in the power of masters to treat them as cruelly as they'd like. Nevertheless it must be admitted that in our colonies in America many Christians treat their slaves with a cruelty unknown to the pagans themselves. The worthy and scholarly author who I just cited gives in a footnote an example of the manner in which Seneca, who was a pagan, pleads the cause of servants. His defense speech is so humane that I can't but transcribe it here. 'They are slaves, but they are also men. They are slaves, but they are your like. They are slaves, but they are unfortunate friends. They are slaves, but

they are your brothers, if you think that fortune might treat you like them, etc.' Beginning of Ep. 47 of Seneca.

We must nevertheless concede that there are very few servants faithful enough, attached enough, caring enough to be looked upon as unfortunate friends. It is no less certain that their masters should always remember that they are of the same species as them and consequently treat them with indulgence and humanity.

7. The reader will have doubtless see that in these expiations, as well as in many other religious practices, the pagans were very closely imitated by a great number of Christians.

8. Christians have carried this opinion much farther than the third and fourth generation. They have extended divine vengeance from the first man to the last: by Adam's sin all of his posterity finds itself punished.

Essay on the art of crawling, for the use of courtiers (1775)[*]

The courtier is, without contradiction, the most curious product of the human race. He's an amphibian animal in which are commonly assembled all contrasts. A Danish philosopher compares the courtier to the statue composed of different materials that Nebuchadnezzar saw in a dream. He says: "The head of a courtier is of glass, his hair of gold, his hands of resin, his body of plaster, his heart is half steel half mud, his feet are of straw, and his blood of water and quicksilver."

It must be admitted that so strange an animal is difficult to define. Not only can he not be known by others, he can barely know himself. Nevertheless, it appears that, all things considered, he can be categorized in the class of men, with this difference: ordinary men have only one soul, while the courtier seems to have several. In fact, a courtier is sometimes insolent and sometimes groveling; sometimes sordidly avaricious and sometimes insatiably avid; sometimes extremely prodigal, sometimes audacious; sometimes of a shameful cowardice, sometimes of the most impertinent arrogance and sometimes of the most careful politesse. In a word, he is a Proteus, or rather a god from India, who is represented with seven faces.

Whatever the case, it is for these rare beings that nations seem to exist. Providence has destined them for their least pleasures: the sovereign himself is only their business agent When he does his duty he has no other task than that of fulfilling their needs and their fantasies, only too happy to work for these necessary men who the state cannot do without. It is in their interest that a monarch imposes taxes, makes war or peace, imagines a thousand ingenious inventions to torment and gouge the people. In exchange for this, the grateful courtiers pay the monarch with gratitude, assiduity, flattery, and meanness; and the talent of trading thanks for these important merchandise is that which is perhaps most useful to the court.

Philosophers, who are commonly ill-humored, in truth look upon the métier of courtier as low, as infamous, as that of a poisoner. The ungrate-

---

[*] From *Correspondance littéraire, philosophique et critique addressée a un souverain d'Allemagne pendant une partie des années 1775-1776, et pendant les années 1782 a 1790 inclusivement.* Tome V. Paris, F. Buuisson, libraire, 1813.

ful people don't feel the entire extent of the gratitude they owe to these generous ones who, in order to maintain their sovereign in a good mood, devote themselves to boredom, sacrifice themselves to his caprices, continually sacrifice to him their honor, their probity, their *amour propre*, their shame and their remorse. Don't those imbeciles know the cost of these sacrifices? Don't they think what it must cost to be a good courtier? Whatever force of spirit one might have, however armored the conscience by the habit of holding virtue in contempt and crushing probity under foot, ordinary men always find it difficult to stifle in their hearts the cry of reason. There is only the courtier who manages to reduce that importunate voice to silence. He alone is capable of so noble an effort.

If we examine things from this point of view, we can see that of all the arts, that of crawling is the most difficult. This sublime art is perhaps the most marvelous conquest of the human spirit. Nature placed in the hearts of all men an *amour propre*, a pride that is, of all dispositions, the most difficult to vanquish. The soul revolts against everything that tends to depress it; it vigorously reacts whenever it's wounded in that sensitive spot. And if at a young age we haven't developed the habit of fighting, repressing or crushing this powerful spring, it becomes impossible to master it. This is what the courtier works at during his childhood, a study much more useful that all those that are so emphatically vaunted, and, in those who have acquired the faculty of subjugating nature, announces a strength with which few being find themselves gifted. It is through these heroic efforts, these combats, these victories that a skillful courtier distinguishes himself and reaches the point of insensitivity that leads him to credit, honors, and those grandeurs that are the object of the envy of his peers and of public admiration.

Let them exalt after this the sacrifices religion imposes on those who want to gain heaven. Let them talk of the strength of soul of those haughty philosophers who claim to hold in contempt all that men esteem. Believers and sages could not defeat *amour propre*; pride seems to be compatible with devotion and philosophy. It is only reserved to the courtier to triumph over himself and to carry off a complete victory over the sentiments of his heart. A perfect courtier is without contradiction the most amazing of all men. Don't talk to us about the abnegation of the pious; true abnegation is that of a courtier for his master: see how he obliterates himself in his presence. He becomes a pure machine, or rather he is nothing: he awaits his being from him; he seeks to find in his traits those he should have himself. He is like wax ready to receive all the impressions made on it.

There are a few mortals who have a narrow spirit, a lack of suppleness in the spine, a lack of flexibility in the neck: this unfortunate organization prevents them from perfecting themselves in the art of crawling and renders them incapable of advancing at court. Serpents and reptiles reach the heights of mountains and rocks, while the most fiery of steeds can never climb there. The court is not made for these haughty, inflexible personages who don't know how to give themselves over to the caprices, to surrender to the fantasies or even, when need be, to approve or favor those crimes grandeur deems necessary for the well being of the state.

A good courtier should never have an opinion; he should only have that of his master or minister, and his sagacity should always make sure he knows this, which presupposes a consummate experience and profound knowledge of the human heart. A good courtier should never be in the right: it isn't permitted him to have more wit than his master or the distributor of his graces. He must know that the sovereign and the men in place can never be wrong.

The properly raised courtier must have a stomach strong enough to digest all the affronts he receives from his master. From his youngest age he must learn to command his physiognomy for fear that it betray the movements, the secrets of his heart, or that it reveal an involuntary spite that an insult might cause. In order to live at court one must have complete control over the muscles of one's face in order to experience disgust without flinching. A pouter, a man either moody or touchy cannot succeed.

In fact, all those who hold power commonly don't accept that we feel the stings that they have the goodness to inflict or that we take it into our heads to complain. Before his master the courtier must imitate the young Spartan who was whipped for having stolen a fox. Though during the operation the animal, hidden in his coat, gnawed away at his belly, the pain didn't draw from him the least cry. What art, what self-control aren't supposed by that profound dissimulation that forms the main character of the true courtier. Under the cover of friendship he knows how to lull his enemies, show an open, affectionate face to those he most detests, embrace with tenderness the enemy he'd like to suffocate. Finally, the most impudent lies mustn't produce any alteration in his face.

The great art of the courtier, the essential object of his study, is to make himself aware of the passions and vices of his master in order to be able to seize him at his weak point. He is then assured of having the key to his heart. Does he love women? He must procure them. Is he pious? He must become so or become hypocritically so. Is he suspicious? He must implant suspicions about all those who surround him. Is he lazy? He must never speak to him of affairs. In a word, he must serve him in keeping with his style, and especially must continually flatter him. If he's a fool one risks nothing in flattering him, even if he is far from deserving it. But if by chance he has intelligence or good sense—which one must rarely fear—then a bit of care must be taken.

The courtier must learn to be affable, affectionate, and polite towards all those who can help or harm him. He can only be haughty towards those he has no need of. He must know by heart the price of all those he meets; he must deeply bow to the *femme de chambre* of a lady in favor, familiarly chat with the *Suisse* or the butler of a minister, caress the dog of the *premier commis*. Finally, it is not allowed to him to be distracted for a single minute; the life of the courtier is a continual study.

Like Harlequin, the true courtier must be everyone's friend while not having the weakness of attaching himself to anyone. Obliged to triumph over friendship and sincerity, it is only to the man in place that his attachment is owed, and that attachment must cease as soon as power does. It is indispensable to immediately detest whoever has displeased the master or the favorite of the moment.

Judge from all this if the life of a perfect courtier is anything but a long train of painful labors. Is it possible for nations to correctly pay a body of men so devoted to the service of a prince? The entire treasury barely suffices to pay heroes who sacrifice themselves completely to public happiness. Is it not just that men who damn themselves with such good grace for the good of their fellow citizens be at least well paid in this world?

What respect, what veneration should we not have for these privileged beings—whose rank, whose birth naturally render them so proud—when we see the generous sacrifice they ceaselessly make of their pride, their hauteur, their *amour propre*. Do they not every day push this sublime abandonment of themselves to the point of filling the same functions for the prince that the least of valets fills with his own master? There is nothing low in all they do for him. What am I saying? They take glory from the lowest jobs attached to his sacred person. Night and day they aspire to the joy of being useful to him. They keep him in sight, make ministers indulgent of his pleasures, take upon themselves his foolishness or hasten to applaud it. In a word, a good courtier is so absorbed in the idea of his duty that he often takes pride in doing things an honest lackey would never do. The spirit of the gospels is humility. The Son of Man told us that he who exalts himself shall be humiliated. The opposite is no less certain, and people of the court follow the precept to the letter. Do not then be more surprised if providence rewards them without measure for their flexibility, and if their abjection procures for them the honors, wealth, and respect of well-governed nations.

Jean-Paul Marat
(1743-1793)

Jean-Paul Marat is the prototype, the forerunner of the professional revolutionary, and he bears many similarities to the most exemplary of modern revolutionaries, Che Guevara. The similarities are striking: Marat, the Friend of the People of the French Revolution was, like Che, a foreigner in his revolutionary homeland, the former Swiss, the latter Argentinean. Both were physicians, though Marat, unlike Che, was a practitioner with a number of medical texts to his credit. The activities of both men were inhibited, though not halted, by physical ailments: Marat had a severe eczematic condition that made him a (literal) sitting target in his bathtub for his assassin, while Guevara had asthma that slowed him down in the mountains where he met his death. Most importantly, both men died in action, Marat pen in hand writing the names of suspects given him by his assassin, the Argentinian captured in battle and murdered.

The similarities of their respective fates extend as far as their roles as icons of their respective eras. Immediately after Marat's assassination, the Convention commissioned Jacques-Louis David, Jacobin and later immortalizer of the pomp(osity) of Napoleon's coronation, to paint a final image of the murdered Marat, a painting stunning in its directness, simplicity, and nudity, and which was hung in the halls of the Convention to serve as a model to those deliberating there. In the case of Che, it is not the final picture of the murdered guerrilla with his untamed hair, ragged beard, and dead, vacant eyes that became iconic. Rather it was the young man of just a few years earlier, gazing heroically into the future (with Jean-Paul Sartre out of frame nearby) that was to be—and remains —the inspiration for countless thousands of followers, decades after his death. In a real sense, the line of Marat-esque revolutionaries expired in Bolivia in 1967 with the murder of Che.

Marat was not a man of the sword, though he never hesitated in calling for the guillotine's blade for those who opposed the revolutionary line. Revolutionary purity was all that mattered to him.

He was the principal, if not the sole, author of the pages of his various newspapers, and the number of pages he filled is uncountable, an almost unimaginable feat in a man of action. Unlike many later revolutionaries, who flattered the people and made them feel that the fault for their losses and failings lay elsewhere, Marat's voice was more often than not hectoring, flagellating the people for their weaknesses and their flaws. He called the French "vain," castigating them for believing in the goodness of a constitution that he considered defective: he wasn't chary of reminding them of their blindness, their inability to recognize how wrong were the things they considered right. Furthermore, failure to listen to him could only bring ruin. "What haven't I done to make the scales fall from your eyes? Today there remains no means of putting off your ruin, and your faithful Friend has no other obligation to you than that of deploring your sad destiny; than that of shedding, over your too great disasters, tears of blood," he wrote in 1791. "Ignore me at your peril" would seem to have been Marat's watchword.

In Marat's writings, it is the Friend of the People who sees all, who knows all, who alone has discovered the traps laid before the people. Without his guidance they cannot but go astray. Marat was a one-man Leninist vanguard party, but he was also, like the later anarchists of late nineteenth century France, the lone man who arrogated to himself the right to decide who merited punishment. He contained the greatness and the flaws of the entire revolutionary ideal.

Prospectus for *L'Ami du Peuple* (1789)

Now that the French have, arms in hand, re-conquered liberty; that a crushed despotism no longer dares raise its hand, that the disturbers of the state have been forced to flee, that the enemies of the Fatherland are obliged to put on a mask, that disconcerted ambition fears to show itself; that the barriers of prejudice are everywhere overturned by the voice of reason, that the rights of man and the citizen are going to be consecrated, and that France awaits its happiness from a free constitution, nothing can oppose the Nation's wishes but the play of prejudices and passions in the assembly of its representatives.

It depends on wise men to prepare the triumph of the great truths that will bring about the reign of justice and freedom and solidify the foundations of public happiness. Thus, the greatest present to offer the nation in the current conjuncture, or rather, the only thing that it needs, would be a periodical in which one can attentively follow the work of the National Assembly; where one can analyze with impartiality each article; where correct principles will ceaselessly be recalled; where the rights of man and the citizen will be established; where the successful organization of a wise government will be outlined; where the abuses to be corrected will be pointed out; where the agents of power will be watched over; where their maneuvers, their machinations, and their attacks will be repelled; where the defense of the oppressed will be espoused; where the means to dry up the sources of the state's misfortunes will be developed; and where unity, abundance and peace will be brought about by solidifying freedom. Such is the plan of this journal, which the public will see scrupulously fulfilled in accordance with its point of view, the extent of its knowledge, and the well-deserved success of the political works of its author, though the public is already certain of this, thanks to the issues that have previously come out.

In order to better serve the Fatherland M. Marat has, for a long time, shown no concern for his reputation. But his name is too well known today for it to be necessary to observe that his pen has only been guided by his love for truth, humanity and justice. We can even add that his touch is so original that those writers who tried to continue his journal during his retirement were never able to reach the second issue.

M. Marat has not simply served the Fatherland with his pen, he has also served it with his person from the first instant of the revolution. It is he who caused the project to fail that was formed by the enemies of the state to surprise Paris on the night of July 14 by transporting there, under the mask of friendship, several regiments of German cavalry, numerous detachments of which had already been received and led in triumph. It is he who determined that the Parisians would march on Versailles on October 5 and prevent France from again being plunged into the abyss. It is he who, renewing before our eyes the functions of the Roman censors, had the courage to present himself to the Paris municipality in order to denounce to it its corrupted members and force it to purge itself.

The zeal of this intrepid citizen, whose name is inscribed among those of the liberators of the Fatherland, has no limits. And who would not be amazed by the indomitable courage with which he has defended the public cause for the last six months; the audacity with which he attacks all who are guilty of abuse and pursues without rest the representatives of the nation who abuse their powers, as well as the agents of authority who embezzle, and the judges who prevaricate; the generosity with which he defends the oppressed? His paper, having become the bogeyman of the evil, has made for him legions of redoubtable enemies. A price was put on his head by the leaches of the state. Cowardly assassins have tried to bring an end to his days; heedless judges have cast a fiery decree against him. Taken from his home by his friends he was, for two months, in a kind of exile. Finally, he was arrested in his retreat by a large body of soldiers. By his virtue, his courage, his steadfastness, he has triumphed over all. He was returned with honors of war by the enemies he had trampled. He forced them to repair the wrongs they'd done him. Today his paper circulates freely, and all good citizens proffer wishes that nothing will alter its course.

This paper, the only one truly consecrated to the salvation of the Fatherland, is more necessary than ever.

It appears regularly every day. Subscriptions in the provinces can be taken at all bookstores and postmasters, and in Paris at the author's offices at 39, rue de l'Ancienne Comédie Française, where the price of a subscription should be sent postage paid, as well as all letters to the Friend of the People.

The price of a subscription is 12 livres the trimester, postage paid.

Illusion of the Blind Multitude on the Supposed Excellence of the Constitution (1791)[*]

The public's infatuation with the constitution is the fashionable folly of the moment. There's no reason to be surprised by this; it's a thing absolutely new among us, and for this alone it can't fail to seduce light and frivolous men, equally incapable of seizing its defects and of calculating its ill effects. How could it fail to infatuate the French, of all people in the world the least reflective?

To this fury for novelty should be added the pitfalls of vanity. When it enters the head of a people who have broken their chains, nothing in the world is more apt to flatter self-love than the idea of an indefinite freedom supported by the supreme power, and one can conceive just how far the enthusiasm of limited but honest citizens for the new order of things might be carried. And it's not that the scoundrels at the head of affairs haven't taken pains to inspire this infatuation. What strings haven't they played on with this end in sight?

In the first place, a mass of bought-off pens have represented the constitution as the most sublime work ever given birth to by the human spirit; as an eternal monument to wisdom and virtue, as the infallible guarantor of the nation's happiness. These pompous elegies have been circulated throughout the empire, while no occasion has been missed to flatter the self-love of the people by presenting to it a false image of its strength and its freedom, at the very moment when new chains are being forged for it. Credulous Parisians! Remember the inscriptions that decorated the altar of the Fatherland the day of the military federation. It said to the people: You are the sovereign. You are also the legislator. The law is still against you. And the blind multitude, puffed up with vanity, didn't see that this whole foolish apparatus had no other goal than that of metamorphosing the soldiers of the Fatherland into henchmen of the executive power, and to chain them to the maintaining of the evil decrees that returned authority to the hands of the prince.

In the midst of the cries of enthusiasm that filled the air the voice of the Friend of the People vainly spoke out to reveal the trap and recall you to wisdom. What he said to you then—and what he said a hundred

---

[*] From *L'Ami du Peuple*, No 334, January 8, 1791.

times—I repeat to you today: the constitution is a failure, a complete failure and so completely failed that it forms the most dreadful of governments, for in the last analysis it is nothing but an administration of royal commissioners still connected to the *noblesse de la robe* and followed by armed henchmen, i.e., a true military and noble despotism.

The Flight of the Royal Family (1791)*

The farewell to the Fatherland by the Friend of the People if the Parisians reject his final advice.

Citizens, the flight of the royal family was prepared from afar by the traitors of the National Assembly and above all by the Committees of Investigation and of Reports. In order to pass intelligence between the counter-revolutionary commandants of Alsace and Lorraine and the fugitive Capets and the Austrians, it was necessary to crush the patriotic party. These infamous committees have perpetually imposed upon you the authors of the troubles in Haguenau, Colmar and Wissembourg, etc. In order to fool you there is no variety of trickery that Broglio, Reignier, Noailles, Voidel and other scoundrels haven't committed. So it is the National Assembly that prepared the success of the invasion of its provinces, or rather who opened the frontiers of the Kingdom to its enemies. At the same time, in order to come to terms with the enemies of the revolution—the headquarters of the departments—the Parisian general, by his machinations, did all he could to paralyze the national forces and put them in the hands of the King.

Citizens, friends of the Fatherland, you are reaching the moment of your ruin. I won't waste time raining down upon you vain reproaches for the misfortune you have brought down on your own heads by your blind confidence and your fatal sense of security. Let us only think about your salvation.

There is only one means left to pull you back from the precipice to which your unworthy chiefs have led you to, and that's to immediately name a military tribune, a supreme dictator, to put down the principal known traitors. You will find yourself lost without any resources if you lend an ear to your present chiefs, who will never cease cajoling you and lulling you to sleep, until the day the enemy arrives before your walls. Let the Tribune be named today. Let your choice fall upon the citizen who has, until this day, shown the most enlightenment, zeal and fidelity. Swear to him an inviolable devotion and obey him religiously in all he commands you in order to shed yourselves of your mortal enemies.

---

* From *L'Ami du Peuple*, No. 497, June 22, 1791.

The moment has arrived to make the heads of the ministers and their subalterns fall, those of Mottié, of all the scoundrels at headquarters and all the anti-patriotic battalion commanders, of Bailly, of all the counter-revolutionary municipal officers, of all traitors in the National Assembly. Begin by assuring yourselves of their persons, if there's still time[1]. Seize the moment to destroy the organization of the National Guard that destroyed freedom. In these moments of crisis and alarm, you have been abandoned by all of your officers. What need have you of these cowards who hide themselves in the moment of danger, and who only show themselves in times of calm in order to insult and mistreat patriotic soldiers and to betray the Fatherland? You should immediately send messengers out to the departments asking for reinforcements, call the Bretons to your assistance, take over the arsenal, disarm the *alguazils* on horseback, the guards at the gates, the hunters at barriers. Be ready to avenge your rights, to defend your freedom, and to destroy your implacable enemies.

A tribune, a military tribune, or you are lost without resources! I have done everything in human power up to the present to save you. If you neglect this salutary advice, the only one left to me to give you, then I have nothing more to say to you, and I take my leave of you forever. In a few days Louis XVI, taking again the despot's throne, in an insolent manifesto will treat you as rebels if you don't head off the yoke. He will advance on your walls at the head of all the fugitives, of all the discontented, and Austrian legions will block your way! One hundred cannon mouths will threaten to bring down your city with fiery cannon balls if you put up the least resistance, while Mottié, at the head of the German hussars, and perhaps the *alguazils* of the Parisian army, will disarm you. All among you who are fervent patriots will be arrested; the people's writers will be dragged into the dungeons, and the Friend of the People, whose last breath will be for the Fatherland, and whose faithful voice still calls you to freedom, will have a burning oven for his tomb. A few more days of indecision and there will be no more time to come out of your lethargy. Death will surprise you in the arms of sleep.

Note by Marat

1. I wager you a thousand that Mottié, all the informers of headquarters, and all the anti-patriotic battalion commanders have fled with the king.

Freedom is Lost (1791)[*]

One had to witness the session of last Monday to see just how poor the Assembly is in enlightened and upright members, in friends of freedom and the public good; just how vile and corrupted, how gangrened; how much it is the enemy of the revolution, how much it is prostituted to the will of the prince.

The ministerial party is all-powerful there: nothing equals their audacity. And among the handful of patriots who could have opposed their maneuvers, their machinations, their sacrilegious attacks on the sovereignty of the nation and the rights of citizens, there cannot be found even one man with insight, one man of character, not one man who devotes himself to the Fatherland. So not one decree, however lacking in energy, has been passed against public functionaries who have deserted their posts, embezzled, prevaricated, against the machinating ministerial agents. There is not a single decree that is even the least bit favorable to the people that isn't revoked after a reading of the previous day's proceedings. This was the fate met by he who ordered the sending of the antipatriotic and traitorous address of the department of Paris to the other departments, after the most indecent scenes in which the henchmen of despotism exposed their shameful maxims with unexampled effrontery.

And there is no device[1] sufficiently destructive of freedom, vexing enough, disastrous enough that they don't have the art to have enacted, always with objections, often without opposition.

What defenders of the Fatherland do you have to oppose this formidable conspiracy of the representatives of the nation, of the prince, of the ministers, of public functionaries, of chiefs of the army and the National Guard, and the officer corps and henchmen of despotism? A mass of club members, of talkers and vain petitioners who hide at the moment of crisis, leaving their fellow citizens to be slaughtered, and who afterwards present themselves with bravado at the bar of the senate to display their stupidities and gravely assure the conscripted fathers that soon LIBERTY WILL ROLL ALL THE TYRANTS OF THE UNIVERSE IN THE DUST. People: these are the heroes who should be taking up your defense and seeing to your triumph. As if a few ridiculous phrases were enough to crush the countless enemies of freedom. O foolish nation!

---

[*] From *l'Ami du Peuple*, No. 625, December 14, 1791.

Why haven't you renounced your vain babbling and followed the advice of your friend, armed yourself with rope, with daggers, and ended the days of those of your defeated enemies who would have the audacity to rise up again.

Yes, freedom is lost among us, and lost without a chance of return. But while waiting for the tyrant to be re-established in his power, cast a glimpse on the excesses of despotism that the fall of our current tyrants will soon bring about.

It is certain that the tyrant will burn to re-establish the nobility, but he won't re-establish either the high clergy or the robe, two redoubtable barriers that limited his authority. As long as the public treasury, for which he has the keys, is filled from the sale of national goods, and as long as the confidence in paper money is not destroyed, Louis Capet will have in his pay a numberless army of henchmen formed of all the embezzlers, informers, and cutthroats ready to sell themselves, as well as all the intriguers jealous to share his power. It is they who will, for a certain time, support his tyrannical rule. But as soon as his resources are used up—and the time for this is not distant—a shameful bankruptcy will lose him all the creditors of the state, who will join the mass of the oppressed. Soon the onerous taxes that will weigh down citizens in order to satisfy the bought-off satellites will repel the artisans, the merchants and the cultivators, who will augment the party of the oppressed and denuded citizens with a mass of the discontented.

All the ambitious, who the cupidity of the court can no longer satisfy, and the public functionaries it can no longer corrupt, will throw themselves into this party. The successive uprisings will be followed by a general uprising, and the satellites and the privileged henchmen of the prince will fall beneath the blows of the discontented, while he himself will be thrown from the throne and proscribed along with his unworthy family. The kingdom will be torn apart by different factions. From the fire of civil dissension several federated republics will be born; the most audacious and skillful citizens will usurp the empire, will subject the multitude to a new yoke, and the government will have changed form without having re-established freedom.

O my Fatherland! What a terrible fate the future reserves for you! A fatal decree of pitiless destiny will always tie over your eyes the blindfold of illusion and error in order to prevent you from profiting from your resources and to deliver you, defenselessly, into the hands of your cruel enemies! What haven't I done to make the scales fall from your eyes? Today there remains no means of putting off your ruin, and your faithful Friend has no other obligation to you than that of deploring your sad destiny, than that of shedding tears of blood over your too great disasters.

Note by Marat

1. Such as those that authorize the king to crush the inhabitants of the colonies, who are friends of liberty; to have perish on the scaffold the patriots from Avignon; to provoke a rupture with the German princes and the Spaniards; to protect the monopolies in grain and currency. And such is that which solicits Duport—alias Dutertre—to put the high national court under the surveillance of the minister under the pretext of reminding him of his obligations, and by orders of the prince to have correspond with him the procurator of the nation charged with the pursuit of crimes. A decree that will very probably pass.

The Hébertists Back Marat (1792)[*]

Forced into exile for a few months, upon his return Marat placed the following notice from the Cordelier Club, presided over by the leader of the working class—the sans culottes—Jacques Hébert, at the head of the first two weeks' worth of issues of L'Ami du Peuple.

> Cordelier Club
> Society of the Friends of the Rights of Man and the Citizen
> From the proceedings of the meeting of April 7, 1792, the 4th year of freedom:
> The Society of the Friends of the Rights of Man and the Citizen testified to the Friend of the People, the severe and courageous Marat, its wish that he once again take up his journal.
> Ever devoted to the Fatherland, this writer has decided to take up his pen again, sharpened by crime and tyranny's new maneuvers. More than ever, Marat will pierce crime through the heart, support the friends of freedom, encourage and enlighten the people, astonish slaves, and make the evil blanch.
> How painful it was for the Friend of the People to flee to a foreign land when, proscribed, his death sworn to by the court and Lafayette, he left thousands of victims defenseless, struck by the same blow as him! But what could he have done in those times of horror when most of the popular writers were cowards or had sold out? Would it have served the cause of humanity to continue his journal when the most peaceful citizen couldn't pronounce the name of the Friend of the People without being dragged to a prison cell?
> Now that the Catilines only infest this city at intervals, today when others are perhaps forming but when there is still time to ward off the storm, Marat is going to take up his pen again! Among a recently freed people patriotic writers should not allow the ambitious to wear a mask. They should whole-heartedly rain infamy down upon the traitors; they should pitilessly denounce those shameless representatives who prostitute themselves to the executive power or who insult the majesty of the people by not recognizing their rights.

---

* From *L'Ami du Peuple*, No 631 April 16, 1792.

The Cordelier Club hastens to make the intentions of the Friend of the People known to the patriotic societies so they can second him and assist him in strengthening the constitution and the indestructible foundations of the Declaration of the Rights of Man and the Citizen.

All citizens are thus advised that it is truly Marat who has taken up the pen again.

The Cordelier Club has named to carry this decree to the societies: MM Vincent, Dubois, Salbert, Baron, Berger, and Machaut.

Signed: Hébert, President
Naud, Secretary

Louis Capet at the Bar of the Convention (1792)[*]

Tuesday the 11th of this month, at 3:00 in the evening, Louis Capet appeared at the bar of the National Convention in order to submit to an interrogation and recognize the evidence.

It was quite a new and sublime spectacle for the philanthropic thinker; that of a despot, no longer surrounded by splendor, pomp and the formidable apparatus of his power, stripped of all the imposing signs of past grandeur, and brought like a criminal before a popular tribunal to receive the penalty for his crimes. Has the reign of servile prejudices finally passed? Yes it has, and with no chance of return, not even for those classes of society most degraded by despotism and among who thought could least make the dignity of the human person bloom, for the tribunes saw the ex-monarch appear without giving the least sign of approbation or reprobation; I would even say with the most perfect indifference, if they could have been indifferent to the judging of the tyrant.

What must have passed through the mind of the former despot of the French, brought like a criminal before an assembly of these men, upon whom he once disdained to cast his gaze; of these men he called his subjects; of these men he only remembered in order strip them of everything; of these men he made wait in his antechambers when they came to ask of him some grace; of these men who insolent valets, covered in the colors of servitude, rudely pushed away, insulted with effrontery, and oppressed with impunity. Judging by his air and his bearing one would think him insensible to the change in his fortunes. What? The loss of a sparkling throne and all the pleasures of a voluptuous court are thus nothing in his eyes? One could believe this given the way he used them when they were in his possession. How many times, ceding to a natural taste, did he quit the joys that are the object of desire of ambitious hearts to attend to the labors of the most common arts as if instinct, despite pride, had brought him to the place nature defined for him.

It is owed to truth to say that he presented and comported himself at the bar with decency, however humiliating his position was. He heard himself called Louis Capet 100 times without flinching—he who had only heard resound in his ears the name of "majesty"—and he never showed

---

[*] From *Journal de la république française*, No 73. December 12, 1792.

the least impatience the entire time he was kept standing, he before whom no man had the privilege of sitting.

How great he would have been in my eyes if in his humiliation he had been innocent and full of feelings, and if this apathetic calm had come from the resignation of a sage to the laws of necessity.

His responses to the questioning proved that he is less stupid than is thought, if it weren't more than probable that they were suggested to him[1]; he passes for having an excellent memory. With the exception of a few answers they were all evasive, i.e., impudent lies.

What then is the idea that should be formed of Louis Capet? That of a man without a soul, a man never worthy of the throne; of a despot whose courtiers always had him maintain a conduct that changes according to the circumstances; of a tyrant who they pushed into all crimes. His conduct has always been a tissue of inconsistencies and horrors: sometime haughty, insolent, low, base, begging; he always showed himself hard, barbarous, ferocious, false, cheating, traitorous; he always dipped his hands without regret in the blood of the people, and if he isn't himself the author of the plots hatched against public freedom, he consented to them and is no less criminal in the eyes of justice.

Notes by Marat

1. How suggested? I don't know, but the extreme dilatoriness in the triage of the papers and in reporting to the commissions of 24 and 12 seemed to me to be concerted in order to allow the members of these committees the means to prepare the historical act and charges; while the delays in their presentation had as their goal not allowing the assembly the time to examine and correct it.

The Execution of the Tyrant (1793)[*]

The head of the tyrant has just fallen under the sword of the law; the same blow has overturned the foundations of monarchy among us. I finally believe in the republic.

In order to wrest him from his execution, the despot's henchmen sought to inspire fear in us of the affects of his death. How vain these fears were. The precautions taken to maintain tranquility were imposing, without a doubt; they were dictated by prudence, but they nevertheless proved to be superfluous: one could have confidence in public indignation from the Temple to the scaffold; not one voice cried out for grace during the execution, not one voice was raised in favor of the man who once decided the destiny of France. A profound silence reigned all around him, and when his head was shown to the people, from all around there arose the cries of *Vive la nation! Vive la république!*

The rest of the day was perfectly calm; for the first time since the [Festival of the] Federation[†] the people seemed animated by a serene joy: one would have thought they had just participated in a religious celebration, delivered from the weight of oppression that had weighed on them for so long; and, penetrated by the sentiment of fraternity, all hearts gave themselves over to the hope for a happier future.

This sweet satisfaction was only troubled by the sorrow caused by the horrible attack on the person of a representative of the nation[1] for having voted for the death of the tyrant.

The execution of Louis XVI is one of those memorable events that mark an epoch in the history of nations. It will have a prodigious influence on the fate of the despots of Europe, and on those peoples who have not yet broken their chains.

In pronouncing the death penalty on the tyrant of the French, the National Convention no doubt showed itself to be great, but it was the wish of the nation, and the manner in which the people watched the punishment of its former master, that raised them far beyond their repre-

---

[*] From *Journal de la république française*, No 105. January 23, 1793.
[†] Celebration of the first anniversary of the Revolution on July 14, 1790.

sentatives for, have no doubt, the same sentiments that animated the citizens of Paris and the *federés** animate the citizens of all departments.

The execution of Louis XVI, far from troubling the peace of the state, will only serve to strengthen it, not only by containing the internal enemies through terror, but also the external enemies. It will also give the nation new strength to repel the ferocious hordes of foreign henchmen who would dare bear arms against it. For there is no way of going back, and this is the position in which we find ourselves today: we must win or perish, a palpable truth that Cambon rendered in a sublime image when he said at the tribune the day before yesterday: "We have finally docked on the isle of freedom, and we have burned the vessel that brought us there."

Note by Marat

1. The assassin is that Paris who last year insulted patriots in cafes, and who had some affair with Boyer in which he came out badly. Last Sunday he was with five thugs at the home of a food supplier at the palace of d'Egalité where Pelletier† usually took his meals. Exiting from a neighboring room at the moment Pelletier was paying his bill he asked him if he had voted in favor of death [for the king]. Upon hearing the affirmative he plunged his saber in his belly, a wound from which the virtuous deputy died during the night.

---

* Supporters of the Revolution, who wanted France to be a federation.
† Louis-Michel Lepelletier, 1760-1793.

The Enragés and Jacques Hébert

Inchoate rage was the dominant feature of the far left of the French Revolution, and was also to be a contributing cause of its failure. The Jacobins have long been viewed by the Marxist (predominately Communist) left in France as the truest voices and defenders of the Revolution, particularly thanks to the work of one of the greatest of twentieth century historians of the Revolution, Albert Soboul. For those farther to the left, the Enragés and the Hébertists, the uncouth, the unmannered, the "bare-armed," the "sans culottes," stood as the true voice of the people; a people who fought, died, won, and had its victory stolen from them so that the rich could profit. The attitude, the means of attack of the Enragés, is expressed by the definition of their name: the word means "enraged," but it is also the word used to describe a rabid dog.

For the Revolution was not only the Terror, the war against leagued royals, fiery oratory at the Convention, the execution of the King and his family, it was also—and after its initial days had become for the working class primarily—inflation, scarcity, and the struggle for survival.

The Enragés, among them Jacques Roux, a priest and the son of a magistrate, and Anacharsis Cloots, son of the Prussian nobility who had moved to Paris to participate in the Revolution, denounced those who had become wealthy thanks to the Revolution and cried out against the stranglehold the rich had on the poor, against speculation in currency and land. In order to forestall the Enragé threat from their left, the Jacobins would periodically adopt measures against hoarding and impose maximum prices on subsistence goods, measures that were sufficient to disarm these potential rivals for a brief while and hold the popular classes in their own base of support.

The Manifesto of the Enragés demanded that "the goods necessary for all must be delivered at a price all can afford" and called for the Jacobin deputies to climb the stairs of the buildings of "the revolutionary city" to "witness the sobs of an immense multitude without bread or clothing." And it condemned the Jacobins, the deputies of the Mountain who were ready "to declare war on the external tyrants but were so cowardly as to not crush the internal ones."

The Enragés, Jacques Hébert, and later Gracchus Babeuf, also gave voice to the fears of Jacobin dictatorship, of the stifling of the press, which was a redoubtable arm against the royalists, but also a potent weapon against the left. In fact, when reading left-wing texts from the period of the Jacobin ascendancy, you can see that the writing has a tone remarkably close to what you would expect from its opponents on the right. But the hatred of the Enragés was for a party, a government of men who came from an alien class, and who they felt were silencing the voice and failing to meet the needs of the people.

When the Jacobins finally appropriated the heart of the Enragé program, the above-mentioned maximum and mollified the potentially rebellious masses, they were free to crush the movement. In the aftermath of Marat's assassination, the Jacobin leader Robespierre was able to take advantage of an old quarrel between Roux and the Friend of the People to discredit Roux. Arrested and almost certain to be executed, he committed suicide.

Hébert and his followers assumed the left-wing mantle and continued to press Robespierre, pushing for de-Christianization in 1793 and then, in 1794, leading the people in riots against rising prices and scarcity. An anti-Jacobin uprising was in the planning stages when in March 1794 the Jacobins—whose police apparatus was outstanding—moved first and arrested Hébert, putting an end to both the left and the most left-wing phase of the revolution. A purge of Hébertists from the popular clubs left the revolution completely disarmed when, on the 9th Thermidor of the year II of the Republican calendar (July 27, 1794), Robespierre and the Jacobins were deposed. The people had been demobilized, and the path was clear for the Directory to begin undoing whatever progress had been made during the Jacobin years.

Jacques Hébert (1757-1794)

Fuck the Pope (1790)[*]

The great anger of Père Duchesne against the bishop of Rome, who has just excommunicated all the French and who, with the Cardinals, the Bishops and all the fucking priests, cooked up the plot to slaughter the National Assembly, the Jacobin Club and all good citizens. The nomination of a Patriarch to govern the clergy of France.

Who does he take us for, that bastard of an indulgence seller? Does he think that with his toilet paper—his bulls—his cannons without primers, and all the thunder and idiocies that he used to put to sleep or scare our fathers, fuck, does he still believe he leads the French of today? We're no longer in the time of King Dagobert, and today we're no longer such dupes as to buy the pardons that priests trafficked in in past centuries, or to be upset by an interdiction that the bishop of Rome will cast upon the Kingdom. The hell with them; we won't let ourselves be fooled by those sons-of-bitches of priests. Their confessions, their purgatory, their absolutions, their indulgences are nothing but feed for the foolish. The so-called keys of St. Peter, that the Pope's criers once opened the doors to the great salon of the eternal father, now seem to us to be nothing but skeleton keys that the Latin pontiff wants to use to pry open our houses and our coffers so as to take what we own.

How does this bastard still have the audacity to use such methods today? It's said that he has responded to all the mitred Ravaillacs who fired him up against the French nation and he issued a brief of excommunication against us. O lord, what is going to become of us? In order to make a greater impression on people's spirits, it's during the fortnight of Easter that the lightning bolts are going to be thrown at us; all the croziered—and soon-to-be-clubbed—priests must, during this holy time, make a last effort to overthrow the constitution. At the head of the devoted, escorted by knights of the dagger, in groups the fuckers are going to lay siege to the house of every deputy to the National Assembly, and those of all the members of the Society of the Friends of the Constitution

---

[*] From *Le Père Duchesne*, No 44, 1790.

and kill them during the night, and then fall upon the guards of the Tuileries and take away the King.

These are the peaceful projects of these sons-of-bitches of priests, and they dare flatter themselves that the French will back them in this abominable enterprise; they think that upon hearing their voices brother will arm himself against brother, son against father, and finally, that for the second time, we'll give them the abominable joy of a new St. Bartholomew's Day Massacre.

They've lied, these rascals, and we'll know how to handle them. I can reply for the Parisians, fuck, and our pals from the faubourg Saint Antoine are all disposed to fix them. I pity the bastard who will dare assume his pulpit to pronounce the excommunication they threaten us with. He can be sure it'll be only one small leap from there to the lamppost. And if the sons-of-bitch priests think they'll do better in the Departments; if they flatter themselves that the same brigands who they armed with daggers in Nîmes, Montauban, and Vannes will back up their efforts, then, fuck, 20,000 of us are ready to recall them to order.

And so, fuck, all their projects, all their plots will fail miserably, and these bastards of sons-of-bitches would do well to make of necessity a virtue and take the side of the constitution. This is the only choice left to them, and it is in vain that they place their hopes in Capet the Redhead. Despite him, despite the Germans, despite his army of Savoyards, despite his bandits from Spain, we'll accomplish our task, fuck, and we will maintain the constitution.

So let the old rascal put away his baubles; let him remain peaceably in his Vatican. Let him feast with all the red donkeys of his fucking college, let him sip the good wines of France and Spain every day with the gluttonous de Bernis, or let him amuse himself with tender young thing, but fuck, let him not trouble his old age by messing in politics.

The bishops we'll name, fuck, will be worth as much as those of la Guimard[1], and those who will have benefices granted by the people will deserve their confidence more than all those valets of the court, those schemers, those payers of debts due who won bishoprics and abbeys and who lived off the patrimony of the poor as once was done. But to ward off the blows that those damn low-lives want to deal us, I make the motion to cut off the living of those conspirators, and to take from them the pensions that the nation still accords them, and that we name a patriarch for France, and that the most virtuous of prelates be chosen for that eminent post, and fuck the court of Rome, its cardinals, its bishops, its abbots, its indulgences, its pardons and the Pope himself.

Note by Hébert

1. The traffic that dancer carried out in benefices while the bishop of Orleans was among her pursuers is well known. A doctor who, as a price for the precision and dexterity with which he rubbed that beauty down during her frequent indispositions asked her to accord him a post. Become a priest, Guimard answered him, I don't know how to read—what difference is it. ... But don't you know that between my legs I have a page of benefices. He became a priest had a priory worth 20,000 livres.

The Reawakening of Père Duchesne (1790)[*]

To fuck up the aristocrats and all the enemies of the constitution. His great excursion to the plain of Grenelle under the tents of the brave buggers who are camped there; his farewell before his departure.

Yes, fuck, I'm reawakening to pulverize all the enemies of the nation; I've been quiet for too long. Annoyed to see a bunch of worthless fucks take my name and mouth a thousand stupidities under this borrowed mask, I was afraid that in the end I'd be confused with them, and I had taken the decision not to write a line until these slimy buggers shut their mouths. One of them, I heard, a postal clerk, calls himself the Truest of the True Père Duchesne , and he has managed to convince many idiots that he really is. But since he allowed a tip of his ears to stick out of his mask, the good citizens didn't fall for it. And because of his smooth style the clerk was recognized, and not the frank and loyal furnace merchant. Fuck, Père Duchesne doesn't darken paper for little misses, and he has never been so clumsy as to take an aristocratic sign as his emblem. We've never seen a Cross of Malta on his pages. But the marks of his trade, two furnaces, these are his arms, and he'll never be such a good for nothing as to blush for this.

I learned that another lunatic stuck his nose in this mess having called for murder and carnage everywhere. I hope that in such ravings no one recognized Père Duchesne. All those who've read my paper over the last two years know that I have always recommended respect for the law; that no good action has been carried out without my praising it and testifying to my joy in it. But I've also not spared the worthless bastards and disturbers of public peace. We all know how many times I've been beside myself with rage! How many times I cursed upon discovering new plots against freedom! In the end, all that is known of me are my joys and my fury.

But we've talked enough about me; let's get back to the matter at hand. I say, fuck, that I am again going to declare war on all aristocrats, on all the buggers who conspire against the nation, on all the scoundrels who, under a lambskin, hide the ferocity of tigers. Those false patriots who seek to overturn everything; those ambitious ones who want to run the country in order to enrich themselves had better watch out. I'm fol-

---

[*] From *Le Père Duchesne*, No 65, 1790.

lowing the trail of all these worthless bastards and all the rogues, and I'll be such a good sentinel that not a single one will escape.

This is how those who have themselves published should act; it's not through long involved reasoning that men should be judged, but by their acts. So when I find someone in the wrong I don't waste a beat and, fuck, I tell him exactly what I think.

It has never been more difficult to learn the truth. You don't know who to believe, all you find are fucking scoundrels everywhere who try to fool you and take you down the wrong path. Some want to force you to admire, to find worthy those that you know to be worthless bastards; other make it a crime to love and respect the most honest men, the most zealous defenders of freedom. This one is a traitor, one person tells you; but I say he's a good bugger, answers the other. This is how the fools manage to mix things up. So I repeat, no one should be judged on hearsay: people should only be judged based on what they do, but at the same time, you must be on your guard about everyone. Never allow yourself to be led to be for or against without knowing why. I never want to erect idols for fear of having to later smash them, but I also can't help myself from praising those who go straight ahead and who never falter. Obey the law, this is the first obligation of a citizen. This is the touchstone which I use to distinguish true patriots from false; when a law is good, it's a crime to violate it; if it's bad we're still required to blindly follow it. That which is worth nothing can't last a long time; that which is good can never die. The more revolting a tree is, the quicker it is destroyed. If there had never been a de Brienne* or de Callone† there would never have been a revolution. It was those buggers who, because they oppressed us, made us feel the price of freedom and forced us to make a constitution. There are still today many worthless bastards who resemble them, and who think they will have us through their cabals, but like the other ones, they'll end up burned. Yes, the more effort is taken to enslave us the freer we'll be. The revolution has been completed, because this has been accomplished in public opinion. There is not one single Frenchman who wouldn't prefer to die rather than return to the *ancien régime*.

---

* Etienne Charles de Lomenie de Brienne (1736-1818) Former Archbishop of Paris who repudiated Catholicism, later arrested and died in prison.

† Charles Alexandre de Calonne (1727-1802) Pre-Revolutionary Controller General of Finance.

Yes, fuck, we'll triumph over all the enemies within and without; sooner or later all the traitors will be sacrificed; it's impossible to force things on a people of 24 million armed for their defense, and where the whole country is covered with pikes, bayonets and cannons.

What a pleasure it was to see in their camp those young buggers who are going to fly to the defense of the frontiers; they wait as if it were a holiday the day when they can finally reach that worthless bastard de Bouillé‡; let that old shit de Condé come here at the head of his black army and he'll be properly received. Oh how well I was received by these young citizens! I had barely stepped foot in camp before this one took me by the arm, that one by the hand, the other one hugged my neck and "c'mon along Père Duchesne! Come into our tent drink to the health of the nation."

It's there, great gods, that by cursing the aristocrats I earned friends where it counts. After having joyously passed the day like that I left our young warriors and made my farewell. Oh fuck, my friends, if I wasn't such an old bugger, I said while leaving them, I would follow you, I'd want to march at your head. Don't worry, Père Duchesne, there are enough of us to fuck up the enemy without; you should fucking just watch over the one within.

---

‡ Francois Claude Amour, Marquis de Bouillé (1739-1800) Cousin of Lafayette and a violent opponent of the Revolution.

Deputy to the Second Legislature (1790)*

His great joy at being able to denounce all the worthless bastards, to make known the real sectarians, and to block the conspiracies intended to return us to slavery

Finally, fuck, its going to be convoked, that legislature that is our only hope. We all sobbed hoping for the decree that would call for elections. And now the campaign's started up again, praise god. Now I'm at peace and I swear by all that's holy that everything is going to go just right. There's no more reason to twist and turn: even if some commit some real stupidities, others will know how to repair them.

And they want to make me a member of that assembly. What, you? said to me the fat ass Mathieu of the rue Vivienne? Yes, me, fuck, why not? Aren't I as worthy as a bugger like you, as a blood-sucker of the people like you? It's true that I don't know how to be a speculator; the money that I get out of my furnaces and my scribbling, as I get it I stuff it in a piggy bank, and when I need some to go out I break it and promptly take what I need. But since Mère Duchesne is a good homemaker, when I make a hole she sticks in a piece, and she does this so well that after having amassed one *sol* after another by her economies I found myself rich without knowing it. As soon as the decree on the priests was passed, as happy as I on that glad occasion, she went to get me her little sack. Here, my dear, she said, here's something to build a nest for a working-man's son. Buy one of the 800 farms from that renegade from the Third Estate. Oh, wife of god, I cried out, there's no one like you in the world, thy will be done.

So the next day, fuck, I took up the wagon and set out for Peronne. Upon arriving I learn that the remains of our aristocrat were going to be sold the next day to the highest bidder. I presented myself at the auction and I'm the winner of a big, fat farm. I quickly went to tell Mère Duchesne of the success of my voyage. For joy, fuck, that evening my friend Jeambart was invited, and we drank to friendship.

Well, I said to him between the pear and the cheese, take a look at what I've become. Yesterday I was nothing but a poor bugger of an active citizen, nothing else, and now, thanks to Mère Duchesne who, unbeknownst to me, saved a few sols, here I am a big shot, I'm one of

---

* From *Le Père Duchesne*, No 66, 1790.

the elite of the country. Nevertheless, I don't feel that I'm worth any more, and I'm no more intelligent or honest. Fuck, how funny it would be if for the next legislature Père Duchesne would be chosen.

And so, fuck, this beautiful dream has been realized; our electors, when they were handed the ballot box, were about to elect me; and now there they are assembled and they're going to work for real, they want to name me. Fuck, I'll be like a beautiful woman and I'll let them have their way. Anyway, in that position I see that I'll do every bit as much good as some, and much less evil than others.

Oh fuck, what joy for Père Duchesne to take up this honorable position! I won't speak in beautiful rounded sentences at the tribune, but fuck, when I'll appear there it'll be to fill the worthless bastards full of holes. I'll denounce all the abuses, I'll chase all the rogues and traitors all the way to hell. If someone comes to tempt me with the civil list they'll see just how heavy my arm is. If I have any credit with the assembly I won't use it to put the assembly to sleep, to make them croak, or lead them to make some kind of ignorant mistake. If the ministers prevaricate, watch out for a bomb fuck; they'll be turned over to the tribunals, not to the low lives of judges like those at Châtelet, who'll whitewash them and send them back white as milk, but god damn it, if there's still one Guignard[*], one Champion, one Necher[†], one de la Tour-du-Pin[‡], the guillotine will take care of them. Never, fuck, will we be stupid enough to address compliments to buggers worthy of the wheel; if there's someone scoundrel enough to carry out a massacre like that in Nancy we won't waste time, fuck, and I won't allow crowns to be sent to someone for whom there aren't enough tortures in the world.

If I meet among us some hypocrite who, under the mask of probity hides a soul of mud, a gangrened heart, one of those wretches who are always for sale to the highest bidder, I'll do every fucking thing I can to make it known, despite his apparently beautiful patriotic motions. Deep down still perfidious, he'll be seen for what he really is; he could make the cock sing all he wants (if the cock is still alive), he can call for peace, unity, I'll make it known that he's nothing but a fucking humbug, an

---

[*] Francois-Emmanuel Guignard de Saint-Priest (1735-1821) Much detested as Minister of the Interior in 1790.

[†] *sic*; read Jacques Necker, (1732-1804) Pre-Revolutionary Minister of Finance.

[‡] Jean-Frédéric de Paulin de la Tour du Pin, Minister of War.

assassin who cajoles his victim in order to better slaughter him. No, fuck, not as long as there remains a single breath in Père Duchesne will he suffer such a bugger to impose himself upon the second legislature, that he spread discord there, that he disunite the best citizens in order to hand them over to their tyrants.

Before taking up my functions I would like first to make a motion that instead of 18 livres per diem and small change for letters, we be paid only six livres. This is enough to live reasonably well. You don't become a representative of the people in order to pile up money but, fuck, to grab glory, and the nation isn't made to pay for our fantasies and debauches, to maintain our mistresses, or repair our losses at dice games. A worthy deputy should only be concerned with the happiness of the people, with defending freedom; he must watch day and night over the well-being of the Fatherland, face all perils, make every sacrifice. He must have no other passion but that of the love of his fellow citizens and the hatred of tyrants. In a word, he has to be what Péthion* and Robespierre have never ceased being. Such will be Père Duchesne, fuck!

---

* Jerome Pétion (1756-1794) Girondin deputy to the Convention and member of the Committee of Public Safety. Proscribed for his moderate views, he committed suicide.

The Great Anger of Père Duchesne (1791)[*]

Against the fucking slanderers of the ladies of Les Halles and the flower sellers of the Palais Royal on the subject of the beautiful speech they made to the King

You can't do anything without a bunch of fucking asses finding a reason to complain. Fuck, the most patriotic women constantly do whatever they can to serve the revolution and a thousand venomous tongues set out to poison their efforts. What is so wrong about going to look for the King so as to tell him that his aunts are crazy to want to undertake a ridiculous trip, a trip that alarms all good citizens because they don't trust the people around them? Fuck! If I had in my hands one of these buggers who speak ill of noble national acts it would be my pleasure to give them a fucking hard time. As for me, when I meet these brave women who, when it comes to virtue, are as good as the Maid of Orleans I run up to them, I take them in my arms and I'll be fucked if we don't share bacchic libations in honor of the fatherland. What's so bad about this? You should have seen the other day, when they defended the Tuileries, how I gave them my hand and complimented them on the beautiful speech they made to the King. Père Duchesne, they said to me, here is a copy of our speech, and since you're a good patriot we ask you to publish it in your marvelous writings. We know you well enough to know that you're a man who'll punch out all the fucking asses who hearts won't be moved when they read it. So it's in order to keep the promise that I made to these brave women that I am going to give it to you exactly as Thousand-Tongue Marie pronounced it.

"Sire, we love you like a good father and we have come here to show you our sorrow at the way your family is abandoning you on all sides. We already came to see you to ask of you the return of the princes. We had hoped that they wouldn't put up for so long with the pain of being far from you. We beg of you again, sire, to recall to them the sentiment that their blood must have given them, to recall them to your side. We will celebrate this as soon as they appear alongside your dear person, and our love for you will also touch them. Let Your Good Majesty not suffer that your aunts, who have always been so dear to you, abandon us again. If they wound your heart and if they obtain from your respect for the Declaration of the Rights of Man a decision (under the name of permission)

---

[*] From *Le Père Duchesne*, [n.p.] [n.d. 1791?].

calling for their absence, they can leave peacefully and no one will forget that you allowed this. But if they are pursued by remorse for having left you, let them remember that we tried to save them from this. And then sire we, your people, we will take the place of your family: you will always find us so, we who will never abandon you, who will always be faithful to you."

This, fuck it, is what is called real eloquence, which comes from deep down in the heart; that which is cooked up in the Academy is not worth as much as this one. Only that of M. Bailly* comes close to this, and even so I don't like his theatrical gestures; he looks like he's crying when he speaks to us when in reality he's laughing at our good faith. At a performance, fuck it, all he has to do is show up and our arms fall; his face has the same effect on us as sunrays. We close our eyes and we don't dare say anything else; we listen to him in silence and with our mouths hanging open we look like fly traps.

I don't know if the speech of the ladies of the Halles and the flower girls of the Palais Royal has an effect. But, fucked if I don't hear anyone talking about anything else; thousands of aristocrats haven't stopped yammering that these women are mixing themselves in stuff that doesn't concern them, that they'd do better to sell their fish rather than soiling the palace of the Kings with their presence. Oh these fucking asses! Isn't anyone of whatever position a citizen? And doesn't he or she have the right to speak to his king, especially when he says he's the father of his subjects? And fuck, you do all you can to ruin commerce and you want them to stay in their place, yawning the day away? But as for you buggers, when you were in your time of splendor at the court, whenever there arrived an interesting moment for the kingdom—either the marriage of a prince or a great victory—it didn't bother you when they came to compliment you and they provided you with amusement, even more because they were simple and new to you. Their witticisms, their frank and daring repartee filled your worn out hearts with joy, but today, when they go to speak to our good King, whose fate interests you but little, since you have let him drop, this no longer pleases you. I am mad about this, and my dear women of Les Halles, of the Saint Martin market and of the Place Maubert are no less good patriots for all that.

---

* Jean Sylvain Bailly (1736-1793) Astronomer and President of the Third Estate. Guillotined in 1793.

So put your ill humor aside, don't pout any longer, return to your homes to live among us and you will see them come to greet you, ask you how you are doing, and compliment you that you haven't allowed the fact that you are aristocrats suffocate you. They are good people, have no rancor, and the great majority of the people allow themselves to be led by their influence. Believe me, fuck, the revolution is made in my head, and that about says it all. You can form plans all you want to come back the way you were, you'll end up like those little lead toys who, when you put them down on their heads, fall on their asses. Fuck! Think well on the advice of Père Duchesne, return home like good citizens as if nothing has happened and don't slander the women of Les Halles and the flower sellers of the Palais Royal.

On the Confiscation of Chateaux (1793)*

The great joy of Père Duchesne on the subject of the famous decree that confiscates the chateaux, palaces and all the belongings of the drunken good-for-nothing bastards and upon seeing that the scum who had their palms greased so they'd ask for the prisons to be opened have failed. His good advice that we throw into the hold all the loudmouths and journalists from Coblentz, and that we send them with the rest of the devil's cargo that's leaving for the Mississippi.

In this world everyone has his supporter. Each one has his coterie, and each coterie wants to come out ahead of the others. This, fuck, is the cause of all the disputes, of all the quarrels of three quarters of all men. Instead of following the route that reason has traced for them, they seem to seek out stones they can break their necks on, and all the cliffs they can fall over. They forge a thousand chimeras, they build castles in Spain; they all want to be happy, yet they turn their backs on happiness. They detest slavery, and all they do is forge chains. Always the dupes of charlatans and knaves, they hold in contempt those who offer them good advice, and they yawn when they are spoken to of reason. They seek the truth, yet they cover their eyes when its flame lights their way, they're deaf to its voice.

I pardon these defects, all these vices in poor buggers stupefied by slavery, but, fuck, I'm beside myself when I see republicans dispute amongst themselves about nothing. I'm furious when I think of all the misfortunes their divisions are capable of causing, and I want to strangle with my own hands all the worthless bastards who fool them and lead them astray. There are scoundrels who only seek out wounds and bumps; there are monsters who only breathe murder and carnage in order to fatten themselves like crows on the corpses of the sans-culottes.

These birds of prey had disappeared for a while, fuck, and as long as terror was the order of the day, they remained hidden in their holes. The people began to breathe, there were goods in abundance, *assignats* were at par, and the patriots, with reason, looked upon the holy guillotine as the philosopher's stone. But, fuck, since the renegades from the Sans-Culotterie proposed the opening of the prisons and the setting free of all the brigands, the knaves and conspirators once again are champing at the bit and they have dared to raise their heads more than ever. Good for

---

* From *Le Père Duchesne*, No. 350, 1793.

nothing bastards, who we don't know from Adam, have fallen like clouds on the sections and popular societies, wearing red bonnets and wide pants. They have blown hot and cold and found a way to confuse things and to set citizens on each other like cats and dogs. The best patriots have been attacked, dragged through the mud by the vilest of good for nothing bastards; naked buggers who have never strayed since the taking of the Bastille have been thrown into dungeons. No one knows who to listen to, or what branch to grab on to. The knaves who build their fortune on public ruin have profited from this disorder so they can fish in troubled waters. Fuck, while the patriots were obliged to defend themselves, no one thought about the other ones, and they had a moment of respite.

Great gods, they won't take it with them to hell, and their joy will be cut short before much time has passed. Already, fuck, all the true republicans are reawakening. They won't be fooled by appearances much longer. It's in vain that an attempt is made to treat with consideration both the goat and the cabbage, and that people seek to save the scoundrels who have conspired against liberty. Justice will be done, despite the bores who want to have us go backwards. Now we know who is hurting us. Order, security, abundance, the salvation of the Republic depend upon our courage and energy. This last sign of life that the aristocrats just gave us will only hasten their punishment. The people know their true enemies despite the masks with which they over themselves. They have them in their sights and, fuck, at the first signal they're going to be exterminated. Not a one will escape the punishment he has deserved. The Sans-culottes won't allow themselves to be had by schemers. They were burned last year by having remained with their arms folded while the infamous Dumouriez[*] cooked up his schemes with the *Brissotins*[†]. The buggers who today want to resuscitate federalism, the worthless bastards who accuse the Sans-Culotte generals and who use all means to put at the head of our armies certain rascals who we all know; these schemers, all this game for the guillotine will fail miserably and, like the *Brissotins*, will finish by doing the big tip-over into the guillotine.

---

[*] Charles Francois Dumouriez (1739-1823) Victor at the important revolutionary victory at Valmy in 1792. He opposed the execution of Louis XVI and later defected to the royalists.

[†] Followers of moderate rightist Jacques Brissot.

What's more, I'm at peace, fuck. The Convention, in the midst of all these storms and surrounded by all kinds of intrigues is still on the right path. While writing I have learned that it has just rendered a decree that's going to have all the enemies of the people chewing their nails and put the conspirators on notice. Bravo, fuck, bravo, the scoundrels who drink till they're drunk will never soil the land of freedom. The hell with all the notions of Coblentz and all the *phillipotins,* the hell with the clemency tribunal: the great judgment of the people on all suspects will be executed. It's been decreed, fuck, that at the signing of peace they'll all be embarked for the Mississippi, and their chateaux, their palaces, all they own is to be confiscated for the profit of the republic. How many good-for-nothings have had their provisions cut off. All those scribblers that they buy off, all those brigands whose palms they grease in order to starve us will hang up their fangs. In this way, fuck, this salutary decree will return peace to the interior and will procure new resources for the Republic for combating its enemies and to reward its brave defenders. It's fucking maddening that we didn't immediately deliver ourselves of such a plague because, fuck, as long as that bugger of a canaille breaths among us we must expect to always be on the alert. The parents, the friends of these rogues will still fight, they'll intrigue in all possible ways to prevent this devil's cargo from arriving in the Indies. But we won't fall asleep, fuck, and whoever will dare take up their defense will, like them, be thrown deep into the hold.

Courage, brave *Montagnards**, continue to deserve the benedictions of the people by every day rendering such decrees. Strike while the iron is hot and never put off till tomorrow what you can do today. Just a few more days and all the crowned brigands will be at your feet. While with one hand you hold the lightning to crush the despots and their vile slaves, offer the other to the unfortunate, ensure work for all citizens, give assistance to the elderly and the infirm and, to crown your labors, promptly organize public instruction. This will be your masterpiece for, fuck, without instruction there is no freedom, fuck.

---

* Mountain-dwellers, i.e., the primarily Jacobin left, so-called because their seats were at the top left of the semi-circle of the Convention.

Anacharsis Cloots
(1755-1794)

Speech on Behalf of the Committee of Foreigners (1790)[*]

The imposing fasces of all the flags of the French Empire that are to be deployed on July 14 on the Champs de Mars, in the same place that Julian crushed all prejudices, where Charlemagne surrounded himself with all virtues, this civic solemnity will be not only the festival of the French but, even more, the festival of the human race. The trumpet that sounded the resurrection of a great people has reverberated in the four corners of the globe, and the songs of joy of 25,000,000 free men have awakened peoples buried under a long period of slavery. The wisdom of your decrees, messieurs, the unity of the children of France, this ravishing tableau causes despots bitter worries, and just hopes in enslaved nations.

To us, too, has come a great thought, and we dare say it will complement the great national day! A number of foreigners from all the countries of the earth ask to be allowed to line up in the middle of the Champ de Mars, and the liberty bonnet they'll raise with joy will be the guarantee of the imminent deliverance of their unhappy fellow citizens. At Roman triumphs they were all too happy to drag the vanquished behind their chariots. You, honorable messieurs, in the most honorable of contrasts, you will see in your cortege free men whose fatherlands are in chains, and whose fatherlands will be free one day under the influence of your unshakeable courage and philosophical laws. Our vows and our homage will be the bonds attaching us to your triumphal chariots.

Never was there a more sacred ambassadorship. Our letters of appointment aren't written on parchment; our mission is engraved in ineffaceable characters in the hearts of all men. And thanks to the authors of the DECLARATION OF RIGHTS these characters will no longer be unintelligible to tyrants.

---

[*] From the original broadsheet, 1790.

Messieurs, you have genuinely recognized that sovereignty resides in the people. Everywhere the people are under the yoke of dictators who, despite your principles, call themselves sovereigns. Dictatorship is usurped, but sovereignty is inviolable, and the ambassadors of tyrants cannot honor your august festival as can most of us whose mission was tacitly acknowledged by our compatriots, by the oppressed sovereigns.

What a lesson for despots! What consolation for unfortunate peoples when we will teach them that the first nation of Europe, in gathering together its banners, gave us a sign of the happiness of France and the two worlds!

We will await, messieurs, in a respectful silence, the result of your deliberations on our petition, dictated to us by the enthusiasm of universal liberty.

Response of the President to the deputations of the different foreign countries:

> Messieurs:
>
> You have today proved to the entire universe that the progress made in philosophy and in the knowledge of the Rights of Man by one nation equally belong to other nations. It has been shown that there are eras that influence the happiness and the unhappiness of all parts of the globe, and France dares today to flatter itself that the example it has just given will be followed by those peoples who, knowing how to appreciate liberty, will teach monarchs that their true grandeur consists in commanding free men and executing laws, and that they can only be happy by causing the happiness of those who chose them to govern.
>
> Yes, messieurs, France will honor itself in admitting you to the civic festival whose preparation the National Assembly has just ordered. But as the price for this beneficence, it believes it has the right to demand of you a striking testimony of your recognition. After the august ceremony, return to the places of your birth. Tell your monarchs, tell your administrators, whatever name they bear, that if they are jealous of passing their memory on to the most distant posterity, tell them that they have only to follow the example of Louis XVI, the Restorer of French Liberty.
>
> The National Assembly invites you to participate in its session.

Religion is the Greatest Obstacle (1793) *
Speech pronounced at the Tribune of the national Convention 27 Brumaire, year II [November 17, 1793].

Will you allow me, Citizen Colleagues, to put you in a position to repair an outrage to reason committed by the Legislative Assembly which, on the Christian observations of the Bishop of Calvados of guillotined memory put off the reception of one of my philosophical productions, the fruit of fifteen hours of work daily for four straight years? This work, unique in its methods and tactics and interesting in its details and development, with one blow undermined all revealed religions, both ancient and modern. It is entitled: "The Certainty of the Proofs of Mohammedanism," for I throw a Moslem at the legs of other sectarians, who fall one after the other. My book takes the place of a vast library.

The philosophical explosion striking our revolutionary gaze is the result of fifty years of labor and persecution. It is by attacking with courageous tenacity all false revelations that we have arrived at the revelation of good sense. The conversion of a great people proves that philosophers have not planted in barren soil and that the proselytism of error is less rapid than that of eternal principles. It is today that the benedictions of truth make us forget the maledictions of falsehood. I am glad to have been persecuted by an Archbishop of Paris when I see the entire clergy of France abjure a doctrine against which I threw volumes ten years before the taking of the Bastille. Under the reign of kings and priests I was never forgiven my favorite motto: *Veritas atque Libertas.*†

I owe to my continual voyages and my independent cosmopolitanism the fact that I have escaped the vengeance of sacred and profane tyrants. I was in Rome when they wanted to incarcerate me in Paris, and I was in London when they wanted to burn me in Lisbon. It was by shuttling from one end of Europe to the other that I was able to escape the hired assassins and informants of all the masters and their valets. The revolution has finally arrived, and I am in my natural element, for *it is liberty and not the place that makes the citizen,* as Brutus so aptly said, and as our *rappor-*

---

* From Jean Meslier, *Oeuvres Complètes*. Paris, editions Anthropos, 1970.
† Truth and freedom.

teur on the law against foreigners has so clearly forgotten.* I too was ungrateful enough to forget the cradle of my birth in thinking only of the cradle of the Universal Republic—if spreading enlightenment in the capitol of the world means forgetting your native land. Whatever the case, my emigration came to an end when the emigration of the villains began. Regenerated Paris was the post of the "Orator of the Human Race,"† and I haven't left it since 1790.

It was then that I redoubled my zeal against the so-called sovereigns of heaven and earth. I loudly preached that there is no other God but nature, no other sovereign than the human race: the people-God. This people is self-sufficient in meeting its own needs. It will forever stand: nature doesn't kneel. Judge the majesty of the free human race by that of the French people, which is but a fraction of it. Judge the infallibility of all by the sagacity of a portion, which on its own is making the slave world tremble. The more the mass of free men grows, the less will great personages be feared. The suspect will disappear with tyrants. Universal leveling stands in opposition to any rebellion at all. The Surveillance Committee of the Universal Republic will have less work than the committee of the least Paris section. It will be thus for all ministerial offices. My republic is the antidote for bureaucracy: there will be few offices, few taxes, and no executioners. General confidence will replace a necessary mistrust. Reason will unite all men in one representative fasces, with no other connection than epistolary correspondence. This will be the true republic of letters.

Citizens, religion is the greatest obstacle to my utopia. But beyond a doubt, this obstacle is not invincible, for we see Christians and Jews dispute for the honors of the most solemn abjuration. It will be the same everywhere that the *Montagnarde* constitution‡ is accepted, everywhere that men have five senses. A constitution that leaves nothing to priests but their mummeries, forcing them to restore to us our morality and our money, this constitution, by showing imposture in its horrifying nudity, will accomplish without cease the marvels that now pass before our eyes.

---

* Saint-Just, who had presented and had adopted a law ordering that foreigners born subjects of governments the republic was at war with would be detained until peace was declared.
† Nickname Cloots had given himself in 1790.
* Jacobin constitution of 1793.

And this is even more the case because the requisition of men and things is leading all spirits towards the theatre of the war of liberation.

I will not refute the illogic of those who see counter-revolutionary intrigues in this and who imagine that we are leading the people to a precipice. Rest assured, good people, that the people do not allow themselves to be led; they have burned their ties and know more than all the learned men in the world. As for the disguised aristocrats who repeat their old slanders against the central commune, adding that the departments aren't mature, I send them to the Nièvre, the Somme, to Rochefort, to Ris, etc.,† unless they would prefer a stay in the Vendée, whose holy furies have accelerated the healing of our victorious republicans. Note, Citizens, that most of those who now play at the role of tremblers were the first to condemn the prudence of the Jacobins, who last fall opposed the premature motion of a member of the Finance Committee.‡ And these same Jacobins, always ready to catch the ball on the bounce, rise today to crush the religious hydra-head for good and all. A salutary terror is dissipating all fantastic terrors. An ancient said: "We only possess vigor the first day following a bad reign." Let us profit from this first day, which we will prolong until the day after the deliverance of the world.

It is thus recognized that the adversaries of religion have deserved well of the human race. It is in keeping with this that I request a statue in the Temple of Reason for the first ecclesiastical abjurer. It will suffice to give his name to obtain a favorable decree from the National Convention: it is the intrepid, the generous, the exemplary Jean Meslier, curate of Etrépigny in the Champagne, whose Testament brought desolation to the Sorbonne and among all Christ-lovers. The memory of this honest man, condemned under the *ancien régime*, should be rehabilitated under nature's regime.

Citizen Colleagues, you will honorably receive my two proposals, for the Archbishops of Paris and the Bishops of the Calvados are no longer on the order of the day.

---

† Regions where the dechristianization movement were especially strong.

‡ Cambon, who had proposed in November 1792 the removing from the 1793 budget of the expenses of the Catholic religion.

Jacques Roux (d. 1794)

Manifesto of the Enragés (1793)[*]

Address presented at the National Convention in the name of the Sections of Gravillers, Bonne-Nouvelle and the Cordelier Club by Jacques Roux

> People, I brave death to support your rights; prove to me your recognition by respecting persons and property—Jacques Roux

Delegates of the French people!

One hundred times this hall has rung with the crimes of egoists and knaves; you have always promised to strike the bloodsuckers of the people. The constitutional act is going to be presented to the sovereign for sanction: have you proscribed speculation there? No. Have you called for the death penalty against monopolists? No. Have you determined what freedom of commerce consists of? No. Have you forbidden the sale of minted money? No. Well then, we say to you that you haven't done everything for the happiness of the people.

Freedom is nothing but a vain phantom when one class of men can starve another with impunity. Equality is nothing but a vain phantom when the rich, through monopoly, exercise the right of life or death over their like. The republic is nothing but a vain phantom when the counter-revolution can operate every day through the price of commodities, which three quarters of all citizens cannot afford without shedding tears.

Nevertheless, it's only by stopping the brigandage of trade, which must be distinguished from commerce, it's only by putting comestibles within the reach of the sans-culottes that you will attach them to the revolution, and that you will rally them around the constitutional laws.

And is it because unfaithful representatives, the statesmen, have called down on our unfortunate fatherland the plague of foreign war that the rich should declare a more terrible one internally? Is it because 300,000 Frenchmen, traitorously sacrificed, perished by the homicidal

---

[*] From Jacques Roux, *Scripta et Acta. Textes presentés par Walter Markov.* Akademie-Verlag, Berlin, 1969.

steel of the slaves of kings that those who remained in their homes should be reduced to devouring stones? Is it necessary that the widows of those who died for the cause of freedom pay, at the price of gold, for the cotton they need to wipe away their tears, for the milk and the honey that serves as food for their children?

Representatives of the people, when you had among you the accomplices of Dumouriez, the representatives of the Vendée*, the royalists who wanted to save the tyrant; those execrable men who organized the civil war, those inquisitorial senators who considered patriotism and virtue as a crimes, the Gravilliers Section suspended its judgment ... it saw that it wasn't within the power of the Mountain to do the good that was in its heart, it rose up ...

But today, when the sanctuary of the laws is no longer soiled by the presence of Gorsas†, Brissot‡, Barbaroux§ and other chiefs of the appellants¶; today when these traitors, in order to escape from the scaffold, have gone to hide their nullity and infamy in those departments they've whipped up against the Republic; today when the National Convention has been returned to its dignity and vigor, and when in order to do good it only has to want to do so, we call on you, in the name of the salvation of the republic, to strike speculation and monopoly with a constitutional anathema, and to decree the general principle that commerce doesn't consist in ruining, rendering hopeless, or starving citizens.

For the last four years the rich alone have profited from the advantages of the Revolution. The merchant aristocracy, more terrible than the noble and sacerdotal aristocracy, has made a cruel game of invading individual fortunes and the treasury of the republic; we still don't know what will be the term of their exactions, for the price of merchandise rises in a frightful manner, from morning to evening. Citizen Representatives, it is time that the combat unto death that the egoist carries out against the

---

* Region that rebelled against the Revolution.

† Antoine-Joseph Gorsas (1752-1793) A Jacobin who later became a Girondin. Was executed after attacking Marat.

‡ Jacques Pierre Brissot (1754-1793) Girondist leader. Executed.

§ Charles Jean-Marie Barbaroux (1767-1794) Jacobin who later turned on them. Executed.

¶ Those who called for an appeal to the people before the execution of Louis XVI.

hardest working class of society come to an end. Pronounce against speculators and monopolists: either they'll obey your decrees or they won't. In the first hypothesis you will have saved the fatherland; in the second case you will still have saved the fatherland, for we will have been able to identify and strike the bloodsuckers of the people.

And can the property of knaves be more sacred than the life of a man? Armed force is at the disposal of administrative bodies; how can they not be able to requisition those goods necessary to life? The legislator has the right to declare war, i.e., to have men massacred; how could he then not have the right to prevent the grinding down and starvation of those who guard their homes?

The freedom of commerce is the right to use and to make use of, and not the right to tyrannize and prevent use. Those goods necessary to all should be delivered at a price accessible to all. Pronounce then ... The sans-culottes with their pikes will execute your decrees.

You didn't hesitate to strike with death those who would dare propose a king, and you did well; you have just outlawed those counter-revolutionaries who, in Marseilles, reddened the scaffold with the blood of patriots, and you did well. You would have deserved well of the fatherland if you would have put a price on the head of the fugitive Capets and the deputies who deserted their posts; if you would have expelled from our armies the nobles and those of the court who held their places; if you would have taken hostage the wives and children of émigrés and conspirators; if you would have held the pensions of the *ci-devant* privileged to pay the costs of the war; if you would have confiscated for the profit of volunteers and widows the treasures acquired since the Revolution by bankers and monopolists; if you would have chased from the Convention the deputies who voted for the appeal to the people [for the execution of the King]; if you would have turned over to revolutionary tribunals the administrators who provoked federalism; if you would have struck with the sword of justice the ministers and the members of the executive council who allowed a counter-revolutionary nucleus to form in the Vendée; finally, if you had arrested those who signed anti-civic petitions, etc., etc. ... And monopolists and speculators, aren't they every bit as guilty, if not more? Like the others, aren't they veritable national assassins?

So don't fear having the thunder of your justice burst over these vampires; don't fear making the people too happy. To be sure, it never calculated when it was a question of doing everything for you. It proved to you, notably on the days of May 31 and June 2, that it wanted total liberty. In exchange, give them bread and a decree; prevent the good people from being "put to the question ordinary and extraordinary" by the excessive price of comestibles.

Up to the present moment the big merchants who are by principle criminals and by habit accomplices of kings, have abused the freedom of commerce to oppress the people; they have falsely interpreted that article of the Declaration of the Rights of Man that establishes that it is permitted to do all that is not forbidden by the law. Well then, decree constitutionally that speculation, the sale of minted money, and monopolies are harmful to society. The people, who know their true friends, the people who have suffered for such a long time, will see that you are sorrowed by their lot and that you seriously want to cure their ills. When it will have a clear and precise law in the constitutional act against speculation and monopolies it will see that the cause of the poor is closer to your hearts than that of the rich; it will see that there don't sit among you bankers, arms merchants and monopolists; finally, it will see that you don't want the counter-revolution.

It is true that you have decreed a forced loan of one milliard on the rich; but if you don't uproot the tree of speculation, if you don't put a national brake on the avidity of monopolists, then the following day capitalists and merchants will raise this sum from the sans-culottes through monopoly and fraud. It would thus not be the egoist, but the sans-culotte that you will have struck. Before your decree the grocery store owner and the banker ceaselessly pressured citizens; what vengeance will they not exact today, now that you make them pay; what new tribute will they not raise on the blood and tears of the unfortunate?

It will be objected in vain that the worker receives a salary in keeping with the increase in the price of goods. In truth there are some whose industry is better paid; but there are also many whose labor is less well paid since the revolution. Besides, all citizens are not workers, and all workers are not occupied, and among those who are there are those with eight or ten children incapable of earning a living, and in general women don't earn more than 20 *sous* a day.

Deputies of the Mountain, if you would climb from the third to the ninth floor of the houses of this revolutionary city you would be touched by the tears and the sobs of an immense multitude, without bread or clothing, reduced to a state of distress and misfortune by speculation and monopoly because laws have been cruel to the poor, because they were only made by and for the rich.

Oh rage, oh shame of the 18th century! Who could believe that the representatives of the French people, who declared war on the enemies without were so cowardly as to not crush those within? Under the reign of Sartines* and Flesselles† the government wouldn't have tolerated that goods of prime necessity be paid for at three time their value. What am I saying? They even fixed the price of arms and viands for the soldier. And the National Convention, invested with the force of 25 million men, will allow the merchant and the rich egoist to continually bear it a mortal blow by arbitrarily taxing the things most useful to life? Louis Capet, in order to carry out the counter-revolution, had no need to provoke the wrath of foreign powers. The enemies of the fatherland had no need to flood with a rain of fire the departments of the West: speculation and monopolies suffice to overturn the edifice of republican laws.

But, it will be said, it's the war that is the cause of the dearness of goods. Then why, representatives of the people, did you provoke it? Why, under the cruel Louis XVI, did the French have to repel the league of tyrants, and why didn't speculation spread over this empire the standard of revolt, of famine and devastation? And under this pretext it is permitted to the merchant to sell candles at six francs the pound, soap at six francs the pound, oil six francs the pound. Under pretext of war the sans-culotte will thus pay for shoes at 50 *livres* the pair, a shirt at 50 *livres*, a poor quality hat 50 *livres*. ... So it can be said that the predictions of Cazalès* and Maury† have been fulfilled: in this case you will have conspired with them against the freedom of the fatherland. What am I saying? You will have surpassed them in treason. And so the Prussians and the Spaniards can say: we are free to enchain the French, for they

---

* Antoine de Sartines (1729-1804) Lieutenant general of the Police of Paris. Chief administrator of the city under Louis XV.

† Jacques de Flesselles (1721-1789) Provost of Paris. Killed during the taking of the Bastille.

* Jacques Antoine Marie de Cazalès (1758-1805) Pre-Revolutionary cavalry officer. Emigrated in 1792.

† Jean-Sifrein Maury (1746-1817) Archbishop of Paris and representative to the Estates General.

lack the courage to enchain the monsters that devour them; and so we can say that in spreading around millions, in associating bankers and big merchants with the party of the counter-revolutionaries, the republic will destroy itself.

But it's paper, it can be said, that is the cause of the dearness of things. Ah, the sans-culotte doesn't see that there's much in circulation; in any event, its prodigious issuance is proof of its value and the price attached to it. If the *assignat* has a real value, if it rests on the loyalty of the French nation, the quantity of national effects takes nothing from their value. Just because there is much money in circulation, is that a reason to forget that we are men, to commit brigandage in taverns of commerce, to make oneself master of the fortunes and lives of citizens, to employ all means of oppression suggested by avarice and party spirit, to excite the people to revolt and force it, by famine and the torture of unfulfilled needs, to devour its own entrails?

But the *assignats* lose much in commerce. Why then do the internal and foreign bankers, businessmen and counter-revolutionaries, fill their coffers with them? Why do they have the cruelty to diminish the salaries of certain workers and why don't they offer an indemnity to others? Why don't they offer a discount when they acquire national lands? England, whose debt perhaps exceeds by twenty times the value of its territory and who flourishes only on the paper of its bank, does it proportionally pay for its goods as dearly as we do? Ah, Minister Pith [*sic*, read Pitt] is too skillful to allow the subjects of George to be crushed in this way. And you, citizen representatives, you the deputies of the Mountain, you who boast of being among the numbers of the sans-culottes, from the height of your immortal rock you refuse to exterminate the constantly reborn hydra of speculation!

But, it is added, we get many articles from overseas, and they only want money in payment. This is false: commerce is almost always carried out through exchange of merchandise for merchandise, and paper for paper. In many cases effects are preferred over money. The metallic monies that circulate in Europe would not suffice to cover the one hundred-thousandth part of the bills in circulation. So it is clear as day that speculators and bankers discredit *assignats* only in order to sell their money more dearly, to find the occasion to monopolize with impunity and to traffic at the counter in the blood of patriots they burn to spill.

But it isn't known how things will turn out. It's certain that the friends of equality will not always suffer that we have them slaughtered beyond the borders, and that within them they be besieged by famine. It's certain that they will not always be the dupes of that public plague, of charlatans who eat away at us like worms: the monopolists whose storehouses are nothing but dens of swindlers.

But when the death penalty is pronounced against whoever will attempt to re-establish the royalty; when the countless legions of citizen soldiers form a vault of steel with their weapons; when they spit out saltpeter and fire from all sides on a horde of barbarians, can the baker and the monopolist say that they don't know how things will turn out? In any event, if they don't know it, we've come to tell them: *The people want freedom and equality, the republic or death*; and this is precisely what drives you to despair, vile henchmen of tyranny!

Not having succeeded in corrupting the heart of the people, in subjugating it through terror and calumny, you employ the last resources of slaves in order to stifle the love of liberty. You take control of manufacturing and seaports, of all branches of commerce, of all the products of the land in order to make the friends of the fatherland die of hunger, thirst and lack of clothing, and to push them to throw themselves into the arms of despotism.

But the knaves will not reduce to slavery a people that lives only by steel and liberty, privations and sacrifices. It is reserved to partisans of the monarchy to prefer ancient chains and treasures to the republic and immortality.

And so representatives of the people, to demonstrate heedlessness much longer would be an act of cowardice, a crime of *lese-nation*. You mustn't fear incurring the hatred of the rich, that is, the evil. You mustn't fear sacrificing political principles to the salvation of the people, which is the supreme law.

Agree with us then that it is through pusillanimity that you authorize the discrediting of paper; that you prepare bankruptcy by tolerating abuses and crimes that despotism would have blushed before in the last days of its barbarous power.

We know that no doubt there are evils that are inseparable from a great revolution; that there are sacrifices that must be borne to make liberty triumph, and that we cannot pay too dearly for the pleasure of being republicans. But we also know that the people have been betrayed by two legislatures; that the vices of the constitution of 1791 were the source of public calamities, and that it's time that the sans-culottes who smashed the scepter of kings see the end to insurrections and all types of tyranny.

If you don't quickly remedy this how will those who have no estate, those who have only two, three, four, five, six hundred *livres* in annuities—and this not well paid, either in land rents or personal accounts—how will they subsist if you don't stop the course of speculation and monopolies, and this by a constitutional decree that is not subject to the variations of legislatures. It's possible that we won't see peace for twenty years. The costs of the war will cause a new issuance of paper. Do you thus want to perpetuate our ills during this whole time by a tacit authorization of speculation and monopolies? This would be the means for expelling all foreign patriots and preventing the slave peoples from coming to France to breathe the pure air of liberty.

Is it not enough then that your predecessors, for the most part of infamous memory, left us the monarchy, speculation and war without your leaving us unclothed, starving and in despair? Must it be that the royalists and the moderates, under the pretext of the freedom of commerce, continue to devour manufactories and landed property, that they grab the fruits of the fields, the forests and the vine, of the very skin of animals; and that they still drink under the protection of the law from cups gilded with the blood and tears of citizens?

Deputies of the Mountain: No! No! You will not leave your work in a state of imperfection. You will found the bases for public prosperity; you will not consecrate the general and repressive principles of speculation and monopoly; you will not give to your successors the terrible example of the barbarism of powerful men over the weak, of the rich over the poor. You will not end your career in infamy.

With this full confidence, receive here the new oath we swear to defend unto the grave liberty, equality, and the unity and indivisibility of the republic and the oppressed sans-culottes of the departments.

Let them come, let them quickly come to Paris to solidify the ties of fraternity! Then we will show them those immortal pikes that overthrew the Bastille; those pikes that brought down in putrefaction the Commission of Twelve* and the faction of statesmen; those pikes that will render

---

* Commission charged with pursuing counter-revolutionary activity.

justice to the intriguers and the traitors behind whatever mask they wear, and of whatever country they inhabit. It's then that we will lead them to the young oak where the Marseillais and the sans-culottes of the departments abjured their error and vowed to overturn the throne. Finally, it's then that we will accompany them to the sanctuary of the laws where, with a republican hand, we will show them the side that wanted to save the tyrant, and the Mountain that pronounced his death.

Long live the truth, long live the National Convention, long live the French Republic!

[In the printed version of the speech Roux continues:]

After this exposé of this evidence I will ask of the National Convention, which I respect, of my cruelest enemies, who I do not fear, of all the sans-culottes, who I'll defend unto the grave; I'll ask them if I deserved the insults and the calumnies which journalists have poured over my head. There is nevertheless a reproach that they are right to make with impunity; that's that I am a priest ... yes, unfortunately, my father gave me no other estate.

But if all priests, like me, had taken the civic oath without being forced; if like me they had employed their time in striking down pride and fanaticism; if like me they had exposed the crimes of the court at the moment when counter-revolution was going to break out; if like me, they had led Louis Capet to the scaffold; if all, like me, had made the commitment to soon wed a virtuous woman; if all, like me, had set out in pursuit of the traitors of the three legislatures; if all, like me, had signed the petition of the Champ-de-Mars and the one against the faction of statesmen; if all, like me, had declared that they did not hold with the Pope who, at this time, is a counter-revolutionary and an assassin; if all, like me, had voted for the universal republic; finally, if all, like me, made religion consist of the happiness of our fellows; if they didn't know any other cult than that of the fatherland, any other flame than that of liberty, then we would attack priests less relentlessly. In any event, Cazalès and Barnave weren't priests, and they betrayed the cause of the people; Brissot[*] and Barabaroux weren't priests and they wanted to save the tyrant;

---

[*] Jacques Pierre Brissot (1754-1793) leader of the moderate Girondists. Died guillotined.

Manuel wasn't a priest and he received *assignats** from the court; and many others who play at being patriots aren't priests, and they starve the republic ... but they can't put it in irons.

Journalists have too often covered me with insults for me not to resist, patriotically, to oppression.

I will thus oppose to all those who call me a fanatic, blood-thirsty, a counter-revolutionary, a formidable arm: the address I presented last May 31 at the National Convention under the banner of the Gravilliers Section, and which had the honor of being inserted in the bulletin.

Note: When I attack monopolists and speculators I am far from including in this infamous class a great number of grocers and merchants who have rendered themselves praiseworthy by their *civisme* and humanity.

---

* Paper money issued by the Revolutionary government that functioned as bonds.

On the Decree Relating to the Arrest of Suspects (1793)[*]

> To arrest Romans on simple suspicions
> Is to act like tyrants, we who punish them
> - Voltaire

The great art of the legislator consists, not in proposing many laws, but in rendering their execution easy; not in reigning over men by terror, but in rendering himself master through wisdom and the mildness of government; not in establishing inquisitorial commissions in order to find the greatest number of guilty, but in principally striking the chief conspirators and being indulgent towards weak and repentant citizens who have gone astray.

Whether a people is in a state of revolution or not, its principles are those of eternal reason, of eternal justice. As Robespierre observed: *Tyranny cannot save the state and freedom.* When laws are made retroactive, when we needlessly multiply violent measures, we announce ourselves to be ignorant or cruel. Fear only engenders slaves; humanity alone carries out the conquest of liberty, and only crime should be punished on earth.

Let us now examine the law relating to the arrest of suspects. To start with, the countless treasons that have broken out everywhere have determined the National Convention (which more than ever is the rallying point of true republicans) to decree severe measures. Thus it has justly struck with the death penalty those who would attempt to re-establish royalty, who conspire against the unity and indivisibility of the republic, and against the sovereignty of the French people.

But the vague interpretation that can be given to that law (which is wise in itself) is such that if it were rigorously followed a prodigious number of Frenchmen would be at risk of incarceration.

I won't speak of those who were refused certificates of *civisme,* who were suspended from their functions, or who weren't able to justify that which their civic obligations demanded. The presumption against these people is too strong for society not to have the right to arrest them. He who doesn't pay public charges is certainly an enemy of the government and doesn't deserve to be protected by the law he breaks.

---

[*] From *Le Publiciste de la République Française par l'ombre de Marat,* no. 279.

I will allow myself only a few reflections on the decree, of which this is the tone:

Are considered suspect those who, by their conduct, their relations, their statements or their writings announce themselves to be partisans of tyranny or federalism and enemies of liberty, etc., etc., and who have not constantly manifested their attachment to the Republic.

I maintain that that law is not executable because of the great number of victims that would have to be struck. Consequently, it is faulty.

It's a fact that the great majority of persons from whom the Revolution took their privileges, their fortune, and their status were not able to calmly look upon the new order of things: man in general doesn't pardon an insult. How could he be calm when everything is taken from him except life, and when we work to render it unbearable to him by persecutions and tortures? So I say that at the term of this decree it would be necessary to incarcerate all the families of *ci-devant* nobles, all the noblesse of the robe, the financiers, and all the agents of the obliterated castes. It would be necessary to arrest all the judges, all the lawyers, the procurators, the court officers, the scribes and all the clerks attached to the old tribunals. It would be necessary to arrest all the tax agents, the tobacco agents, the officers of the *gabelle** and customs, the police informers and all the impure leftovers of the public bloodsuckers. It would be necessary to snatch the engravers, the etchers, the enamel makers, the embroiderers, the painters and all the artists who spread about the signs of feudalism and slavery. It would be necessary to snatch all the charlatans; the doctors, the pedants of the colleges who made their students kneel before the statue of a tyrant; the priests who still sell to the dying that god in whom they no longer believe themselves. It would be necessary to snatch all those who read with pleasure "*Le Journal de la cour et de la ville,*" the pages of "*L'Ami du Roi,*" of the "*Actes des Apôtres,*" who subscribed to the "*Chronique,*" "*Le Moniteur,*" "*Le Patriote Français*" and the "*Gazette Universel,*" it would be necessary to snatch the printers, sellers and distributors of the diatribes against the left of the Constituent Assembly, the Legislative Assembly, and against the holy Mountain that saved the fatherland. It would be necessary to snatch all those who raised to the heavens the traitors Lameth, Barnave, Mirabeau, Lafayette, Custine, Gorsas, Brissot, etc., etc. It would be necessary to snatch all those who wrote

---

* Much hated salt tax.

on their hats, who cried out in public places *Pétion or death*; who raised Philippe d'Orléans and Manuel to that legislature, who supported the motions of the intriguers, who proposed to the popular societies the generals who surrendered our forts and the general assemblies of the sections; the judges who spared conspirators and the magistrates who squandered the treasury of the Republic. It would be necessary to snatch the signatories of insidious or perfidious petitions, club members who have worked with the Jacobins, those who were stained with the principles of *feuillantisme,* federalism, and royalism and who didn't believe in the virtue of the idols of the day. It would be necessary to snatch the cooks, the domestics, the chambermaids, the coachmen, the suppliers, the *parfumeurs* who had relations with the émigrés, with the *ci-devant* barons, counts and marquis and the officers of the former court. It would be necessary to snatch the grocers, manufacturers and merchants who, by the excessive price of goods of all kinds, have starved, ruined and made desperate the people and who determined it through many frauds to curse its lot. It would be necessary to snatch all the actors and actresses who have played the role of duke, queen, and emperor; who applauded the royalist maxims inserted into the plays called "*L'Ami des Lois*," "Pamela," etc., etc.

It would be necessary to snatch all those who miss the former government, the deputies who passed tyrannical laws; those who carried them out and violate the sublime constitution that they swore to defend unto death last August 10. And since we're making laws retroactive, it's necessary to grab those who pronounced the death penalty under the reign of the tyrant, against anyone who spoke of abolishing the monarchical constitution or who proposed the republic.

The imagination loses itself in calculating the number of persons who would be subject to arrest, since the number of enemies of liberty is infinitely greater than the number of incorruptible patriots. It is thus evident that the law of last September 17 has an unclear meaning and that it is inexcusable by its too great latitude. Consequently, that law, in the hands of revolutionary committees, is an instrument of oppression and vengeance. I would even say that in the space of two centuries as many *lettres de cachet* haven't been issued as arrest warrants in the last month.

All honor to you virtuous representative of the people, honor to you Boucher Saint-Sauveur* who had the courage to rise up against this new variety of tyranny, to abandon a post where you couldn't make the voice of justice heard. A good man can only blush for belonging to the human race when he considers that liberty and the fate of the republic are in the hands of a few commissioners who are covered in blood, debt and opprobrium; of vile intriguers who formerly swept the ante-chambers of courts; who a hundred times a day pronounced the name "my lord" if they were paid; and who drink with all the former pedants of the *ancien régime* as long as it doesn't cost them anything; of those scoundrels who fight over power, who raise themselves above the National Convention by having arrested those freed by its orders.

Would you like to know who are the ones who are principally stricken with anathema by those infamous committee leaders who are preparing the counter-revolution? It is those energetic men who want real liberty: the republicans who love the fatherland for itself, and not for the positions it grants; the brave sans-culottes who expose themselves to daggers in order to unmask the knaves, hypocrites and conspirators.

I can't understand how those who rose up against the inquisitorial commission of the Twelve three months ago have decreed 44,000 tribunals invested with a power so frightful, such an attack on public freedom. Those deputies faithful to the cause of the people must have foreseen the abuses of so monstrous an authority, subject to the whims of ambitious and cruel commissioners. They should put a brake to their despotism in making them responsible, under pain of death and in conformity with the constitution, for the arrest of citizens who they sacrifice to their barbaric fury. They should declare incapable of ever occupying any employ in the Republic those intriguers who make false denunciations, who render the name Frenchman odious to all peoples by incarcerating patriots who removed themselves from lands of slavery to come breathe among us the pure air of liberty.

Everything must be said here, since we dare to undertake everything. What idea will nations form of our republic when they learn that we everywhere violate the rights of people; that we drag from their homes peaceful and virtuous citizens based on the vague statements of a hypocrite, a knave, a schemer, of a desperate aristocrat; that we exercise in

---

* Antoine Boucher Saint-Sauveur. Member of the Committee of General Safety.

their regard an inquisition more terrible than that in Spain? What taste could a volunteer have to fight the henchmen of tyrants beyond our borders when he has before his eyes the terrible spectacle of patriots groaning in irons? When he sees his father, his mother, his brothers, his children about to be sacrificed to the vengeance of the monopolists they denounced, the ambitious whose pride they wounded, the traitors whose plots they foiled, conspirators they delivered to the sword of the law, and the enemies of liberty whose conduct they constantly keep watch over. And what will be the fate of freedom if its most zealous defenders pitilessly fall beneath the blows of perverted men; if virtue, in prisons, is confused with crime; if those who were among the first to sound the tocsin of insurrection, who overthrew the Bastille, who seized the Tuileries, and who shaped public opinion concerning the crimes of the Tyrant are treated like conspirators and traitors?

These are the measures that circumstances urgently command: That a man who sells his conscience and betrays his obligations be punished with death; that we have public bloodsuckers killed; that we arrest, that we strike those who had criminal intelligence with the scoundrels, with the monsters who brought all possible plagues down on our unfortunate fatherland. But to make it a crime for a man to have exercised this or that estate; to have not always demonstrated the dominant opinion; to have not given himself completely over to revolutionary impulses, to which the average citizen isn't susceptible; to make him bear the penalty for the crimes of his forebears, prejudge his actions, deliver him to public execution, indirectly designate him for the daggers of assassins for having lived so many years a subject of the laws of his country, is an act that proves the corruption of morals in society, and the barbarism of some of the ministers of the law.

For it can't be hidden that we can't arrest so many fathers, soldiers, officers, tailors, workers, and artists without starving an infinite number of citizens, without depriving the Republic of its most zealous defenders, without slowing down public works, without slowing down war operations, and without cursing the Revolution in the eyes of those who served it with the greatest courage. I would even say that we light an inextinguishable flame of discord, we designate victims to posterity; we stifle the seed of social virtues; we furnish powerful weapons to fight us to the enemy within and without and with new occasions to commit terrible massacres on the patriots of departments that they invaded, on soldiers that they took prisoner; on the Frenchmen they have as hostages. We can thus not keep under arrest for too long a time the true sans-culottes, rich men, merchants and artists (I mean to speak here of those against whom there are no proofs) without breaking the chains of commerce, paralyzing the arts, without covering 100,000 families in universal mourning; without assassinating liberty and the Republic; without dishonoring ourselves in the eyes of all peoples.

Gracchus Babeuf
(1760-1797)

Jean-Francois-Noel Babeuf left his native St. Quentin, its endless gray Picard skies and its basilica, and came to Paris. He had been forced to flee his native region where, as the Marat of the Somme, he had pressed revolutionary measures. He brought with him an idea that would germinate for just over a century and would blossom in the form of modern communism. For Babeuf, now Gracchus Babeuf (following the classical mode of the period, he had taken the name of the Roman popular leader who had pushed for land reform and been killed for his beliefs) and the Conspiracy for Equality was the first modern, non-Utopian plan for a world where, as the name of the conspiracy stated, equality would reign.

For Babeuf and his comrades the world would be built by a people who "worn out by the weight of its ills…will rise." The great historian of the French Revolution, Georges Lefebvre was certainly correct when he said that "it is not forbidden to ask oneself if, as is the case for Blanqui, Buonarroti's 'History of the Conspiracy for Equality' didn't give Lenin subjects to think on." Lefebvre thus tied Babeuf's glorious failure not only to the father of the Soviet state, but to Auguste Blanqui, whose desire for the revolutionary struggle was unquenchable and who was the soul of the revolution in nineteenth century France.

The period that gave birth to the Conspiracy was the one that followed the 9th Thermidor and the overthrow of the Robespierrists. Some of the conspirators had been Jacobins, some had suffered under the Jacobin rule as Hébertists or Enragés, but all detested the counter-revolutionary Directory that succeeded Robespierre and which later imprisoned them. As a result, as Conspiracy member Filippo Buonarroti— a descendant of Michelangelo — wrote, "the prisons of Paris…were the centers of a great revolutionary ferment." The reactionary constitution of the year III (1794), which negated the progressive Jacobin constitution of 1793, was the catalyst for the conspiracy.

The uprising planned by the conspirators improved on the improvisatory nature of the equally abortive Hébertist uprising that had preceded it. Committees were formed; plans for a future communist society carefully elaborated, police and economic decrees were prepared. Had the plot not been betrayed and the conspirators arrested, all was foreseen: useful labor was defined, goods to be confiscated laid out, the division of land and labor clearly set out.

Instead the plot was discovered, Babeuf went bravely to the guillotine, Buonarotti took the route of exile and published his account in 1828, while Babeuf's dreams waited until 1917 to be realized.

Manifesto of the Equals (1796)[*]

> Real equality, the final goal of social art
> – Condorcet

People of France!

For fifteen centuries you lived as a slave and, consequently, unhappy. For the last six years you barely breathe, waiting for independence, freedom and equality.

EQUALITY! The first wish of nature, the first need of man, the first knot of all legitimate association! People of France! You were not more blessed than the other nations that vegetate on this unfortunate globe! Everywhere and at all times the poor human race, handed over to more or less deft cannibals, served as an object for all ambitions, as feed for all tyrannies. Everywhere and at all times men were lulled with beautiful words; at no time and in no place was the thing itself ever obtained through the word. From time immemorial they hypocritically repeat: *all men are equal*; and from time immemorial the most degrading and monstrous inequality insolently weighs upon the human race. As long as there have been human societies the most beautiful of humanity's rights has been recognized without contradiction, but was only able to be put in practice once: equality was nothing but a beautiful and sterile legal fiction. And now that it is called for with an even stronger voice we are answered: be quiet, you wretches! Real equality is nothing but a chimera; be satisfied with conditional equality; you're all equal before the law. What more do you want, filthy rabble? Legislators, you who hold power, rich landowners, it is now your turn to listen.

Are we not all equal? This principle remains uncontested, because unless touched by insanity, you can't say it's night when it's day.

Well then! We claim to live and die equal, the way we were born: we want this *real* equality or death; *that's* what we need.

---

[*] From *Ph. Buonarroti. La conspiration pour l'égalité*, Editions Sociales, Paris. 1957. Written by Sylvain Maréchal, one of the conspirators, the Manifesto didn't meet with unanimous support from the leaders of the revolt. Especially contested was Maréchal's "Let the arts perish, if need be, as long as real equality remains."

And we'll have this real equality, at whatever price. Unhappy will be those who stand between it and us! Unhappy will be those who resist a wish so firmly expressed.

The French Revolution was nothing but a precursor of another revolution, one that will be greater, more solemn, and which will be the last.

The people marched over the bodies of kings and priests who were in league against it: it will do the same to the new tyrants, the new political Tartuffes seated in place of the old.

What do we need besides equality of rights?

We need not only that equality of rights written into the Declaration of the Rights of Man and the Citizen; we want it in our midst, under the roofs of our houses. We consent to everything for it, *to make a clean slate so that we hold to it alone.* Let all the arts perish, if need be, as long as real equality remains!

Legislators and politicians, you have no more genius than you do good faith; gutless and rich landowners, in vain you attempt to neutralize our holy enterprise by saying: They do nothing but reproduce that agrarian law asked for more than once in the past.

Slanderers, be silent, and in the silence of your confusion listen to our demands, dictated by nature and based on justice.

The agrarian law, or the partitioning of land, was the spontaneous demand of some unprincipled soldiers, of some towns moved more by their instinct than by reason. We reach for something more sublime and more just: *the common good* or the *community of goods!* No more individual property in land: *the land belongs to no one.* We demand, we want, the common enjoyment of the fruits of the land: *the fruits belong to all.*

We declare that we can no longer put up with the fact that the great majority work and sweat for the smallest of minorities.

Long enough, and for too long, less than a million individuals have disposed of that which belongs to 20 million of their kind, their equals.

Let it at last end, this great scandal that our descendants will never believe existed! Disappear at last, revolting distinctions between rich and poor, great and small, masters and servants, *rulers* and *ruled.*

Let there no longer be any difference between people than that of age and sex. Since all have the same faculties and the same needs, let there then be for them but one education, but one food. They are satisfied with one sun and one air for all: why then would the same portion and the same quality of food not suffice for each of them?

Already the enemies of the most natural order of things we can imagine raise a clamor against us.

They say to us: You are disorganizers and seditious; you want nothing but massacres and loot.

PEOPLE OF FRANCE:

We won't waste our time responding to them; we tell you: the holy enterprise that we are organizing has no other goal than to put an end to civil dissension and public misery.

Never before has a vaster plan been conceived of or carried out. Here and there a few men of genius, a few men, have spoken in a low and trembling voice. None have had the courage to tell the whole truth.

The moment for great measures has arrived. Evil has reached its height: it covers the face of the earth. Under the name of politics, chaos has reigned for too many centuries. Let everything be set in order and take its proper place once again. Let the supporters of justice and happiness organize in the voice of equality. The moment has come to found the REPUBLIC OF EQUALS, this great home open to all men. The day of general restitution has arrived. Groaning families, come sit at the common table set by nature for all its children.

PEOPLE OF FRANCE:

The purest of all glories was thus reserved for you! Yes it is you who should be the first to offer the world this touching spectacle.

Ancient habits, antique fears, would again like to block the establishment of the *Republic of Equals*. The organization of real equality, the only one that responds to all needs, without causing any victims, without costing any sacrifice, will not at first please everyone. The selfish, the ambitious, will tremble with rage. Those who possess unjustly will cry out about injustice. The loss of the enjoyments of the few, solitary pleasures, personal ease will cause lively regret to those heedless of the pain of others. The lovers of absolute power, the henchmen of arbitrary authority, will with difficulty bow their haughty heads before the level of real equality. Their shortsightedness will understand with difficulty the imminent future of common happiness; but what can a few thousand malcontents do against a mass of happy men, surprised to have searched so long for a happiness that they had in their hands.

The day after this real revolution, they'll say with astonishment: What? Common happiness was so easy to obtain? All we had to do was want it? Why oh why didn't we desire it sooner? Did they really have to make us speak of it so many times? Yes, without a doubt, one lone man on earth richer, stronger than his like, than his equals, and the balance is thrown off: crime and unhappiness are on earth.

PEOPLE OF FRANCE:

By what sign will you now recognize the excellence of a constitution? That which rests in its entirety on real equality is the only one that can suit you and fulfill all your wishes.

The aristocratic charters of 1791 and 1795 tightened your chains instead of breaking them. That of 1793 was a great step towards true equality, and we had never before approached it so closely. But it did not yet attain the goal, nor reach common happiness, which it nevertheless solemnly consecrated as its great principle.

PEOPLE OF FRANCE:

Open your eyes and your hearts to the fullness of happiness: recognize and proclaim with us the REPUBLIC OF EQUALS.

Babeuf's last letter to his family before his execution (1797)[*]

To my wife and my children:

Good evening, my friends. I am ready to wrap myself in the eternal night. I express myself better to the friend to whom I addressed the two letters you saw; I better express to him my situation as far as it concerns you than I do to you yourselves. It seems that feeling too much, I feel nothing. I put your fate in his hands. Alas, I don't know if you'll find him in a position to do what I ask of him: I don't know how you can reach him. Your love for me has led you here through all of poverty's obstacles. Your faithful feelings have led you to follow every instant of this long and cruel proceeding which you, like me, have drunk to the dregs; but I don't know how you will return to the place from which you started; I don't know how my memory will be appreciated, though I believe I carried myself in an irreproachable manner; finally, I don't know what will become of the republicans, their families, and even the babies still at their mothers' breasts, in the midst of the royalist fury that the counter-revolution will bring. O my friends! How heart-rending these thoughts are in my final moments! To die for the fatherland, to leave a family, children, a beloved wife, all would be bearable if at the end of this I didn't see liberty lost and all that belongs to sincere republicans wrapped in a horrible proscription. Ah, my tender children! What will become of you? I can't defend myself against the strongest of feelings. Don't think that I feel any regret for having sacrificed myself for the most beautiful of causes; even if all I did for it was useless, I fulfilled my task.

If contrary to my expectations you are able to survive the terrible storm that breaks over the republic and everything connected to it, if you are able once again to find yourselves in a peaceful situation, and find a few friends who can assist you in triumphing over your ill fortune, I suggest that you all live together. I recommend to my wife that she attempt to guide the children with much kindness, and I recommend to my children that they merit the kindnesses of their mother by respecting her and always obeying her wishes. The family of a martyr for freedom must set an example of all the virtues in order to attract the esteem and attach-

---

[*] From Ph. Buonarroti. *La conspiration pour l'égalité*, Editions Sociales, Paris. 1957.

ment of all good people. I would like my wife to do everything possible to give her children an education, by having all her friends assist her in doing everything that is possible for them with this aim in view. I invite Emile to accept this wish on the part of a father who believes he was loved, and who loved in his turn; I invite him to do so without wasting any time, and as soon as possible.

My friends, I hope you'll remember me, and that you'll speak of me often. I hope that you'll believe that I always loved you. I couldn't conceive of any other way to make you happy than through the happiness of all. I failed; I sacrificed myself; it is also for you that I die.

Speak of me often with Camille; tell him thousands and thousands of times that I had him with tenderness in my heart.

Say the same to Caius, when he'll be able to understand it.

Lebois has said that he'll publish our defense separately: You must give mine the widest possible publicity. I recommend to my wife, my good friend, that she never give Baudoin, Lebois, or anyone else a copy of my defense without having another correct one in her possession, in order to be sure that this defense is never lost. You will know, my dear friend, that this defense is precious, and that it will always be dear to the virtuous hearts of the friends of their country. The only property that will be left to you will be my reputation. And I am sure that you and the children will be consoled in having possession of it. You will love hearing all feeling and upright hearts say, in speaking of your spouse: *he was perfectly virtuous.*

Farewell. I hold on to the earth by a thread, which tomorrow shall break. This is certain, I see it clearly. The sacrifice must be made. The evil are the stronger, and I surrender to them. At least it is sweet to die with a conscience as clean as mine; the only thing that is cruel, that is heartrending, is to tear myself from your arms, O my tender friends! O all that is dear to me!!! I tear myself away; the violence is done. ... Farewell, farewell, ten million times farewell...

One more word. Write to my mother and my sisters. Send them, by coach or otherwise, my defense as soon as it's published. Tell them how I died, and try to make *these good people* understand that such a death is glorious and far from being dishonorable. ...

So farewell again, my beloved, my tender friends. Farewell forever. I wrap myself in the breast of a virtuous sleep. ...

Sylvain Maréchal
(1750-1803)

The central idea that the war against the ruling class included—perhaps began with—war against the ruling religion, that the fight was one and the same is borne out by the life of Sylvain Maréchal. The theoretical bases for this fight had been laid down by Jean Meslier. Maréchal, an admirer of the atheist priest and who, like Voltaire and d'Holbach before him, wrote a text under Meslier's name, carried this out in practice as a member of Babeuf's Conspiracy for Equality. Maréchal was the author of its Manifesto—perhaps the foundational document of communism—and in his last decade, dedicated himself to attacking the existing order at all levels, working to destroy everything that sustained it.

The greatest part of his fight was against the ideological pillars of the existing order. The French Revolution developed a new calendar, starting time anew from the declaration of the First Republic in 1791, its months poetically named by Fabre de l'Èglantine, such as Ventose (windy) and Pluviose (rainy). In 1788, before the Great Revolution had even occurred, Maréchal had already had the same idea: the calendar of saints, which subjected time to the church, was to be replaced by a calendar of great men and women, heroes of freedom and free thought. Gone were St. Blaise and St. Cunnegunde; now Spinoza would be celebrated on September 24 and on February 21, and Virgil remembered on September 22. February itself was to be renamed Duodecember.

This early calendar, which was likely an inspiration for the later Republican calendar, was an integral part of Maréchal's war against religion, a war to which he dedicated much of his energy in his last years. His "Dictionary of Ancient and Modern Atheists" was an encyclopedic attempt to establish an historic tie between the heroes of antiquity and the time of the Revolution, to show that atheism had as long and a more glorious history than the religions that blighted humanity, and that the Revolution was the heir to this tradition.

It is certainly not a matter of chance that Maréchal produced works in the form of almanacs, calendars, catechisms ("Of the Curé Meslier"), hymns (for the 36 *décadaire* festivals of the new calendar). A skilled propagandist, Maréchal worked within the modes familiar to a priest-ridden society, turning the arms of the church against the church, using the forms of the past to express the content of the future.

Preliminary discourse, or Answer to the question: What is an atheist? (1799)[*]

Ecce vir

There was not always a God. There was a time when a man, living with his family, knew no other authority than that of his father. He had few needs because he had few desires. He wasn't a brute, a barbarian, or an eater of men, as we have been led to believe. Nor was he a polished and false city-dweller, vain and servile: he was a man in all his plenitude, ignorant of the art of writing, perhaps even that of speaking, but knowing how to live; that is, he loved his father, his wife and his children. He worked for them, with them and died in their embrace. In his eyes his fields were the entire universe. Regulating his occupations by the sun's movements and the earth's fecundity, his arms and his heart comprised his entire fortune and pleasure. Suspecting nothing beneath the vegetal layer of the soil he cultivated, the man of that time was a stranger to sciences and vices, to social virtues and crimes, but was entirely given over to nature, to innocence.

Travelers have found a few faint traces of the golden age: it is not a chimera. Poets have rendered its existence doubtful by loading it with factitious ornaments, but that happy age once shone.

Why should we feel any repugnance about believing such things? Are they in the realm of the possible? Is it so difficult to live in this way? And isn't the current existence of humankind even more astonishing?

At that time man, limited to the surface of heaven and earth, neither had nor could he have had any idea of any power other than that which put him on earth and raised him. Do we think about something we have no need of? And what need do we have of a God when we have a father, a wife, children, a friend, arms, eyes and a heart?

But a true atheist is the man of the golden age. The atheist is he who, retreating into himself and freeing himself from the ties he has been forced to contract, or that were made unbeknownst to him, retreats from civilization to that former state of humanity and, in the forum of his conscience, laying low all prejudices of every color, approaches as nearly

---

[*] From *Dictionnaire des athées anciens et modernes*. Chez Grabit, year VIII (1799).

as possible that fortunate time when there was no suspicion of the divine existence, where all was well, where we contented ourselves strictly with family obligations. The atheist is the man of nature.

Nevertheless, placed today in a more complicated and narrow sphere, he fulfills his obligations as a citizen and resigns himself to the decrees of necessity. While groaning about the vicious foundations of political institutions, while striking with contempt those who so poorly organize them, he submits to the public order of the place he lives. But we don't find him becoming chief of a party or of opinion. We never meet him on the banal road that leads to useful or brilliant posts. Consistent with his principles, he lives among his corrupted or corrupting contemporaries like the voyager who, having to traverse muddy beaches, protects himself from the venom of reptiles. He gets off with only being deafened by their insults. He goes his way among these evil beings without taking on their tortuous and servile allure.

The true atheist is thus not the sybarite who, taking himself for an epicurean when he is nothing but a debauchée, doesn't fear to say deep in his worn-out heart: "There is no God, thus there is no morality, so I can permit myself everything."

The true atheist is not the statesman who, knowing that the divine chimera was imagined to frighten the men of the people, commands them in the name of a God he has no use of.

The true atheist cannot be found among those hypocritical and bloody heroes who, in order to open a path to conquest, announce themselves as the protectors of the cult they profess to the nations they propose to tame, and who when among their families amuse themselves on the subject of human credulity.

The true atheist is not that vile man who, condemned for many years for his indelible character as a sacerdotal imposter, changes his habit and opinions when this infamous vocation ceases to be lucrative, and impudently ranges himself among the sages he persecuted.

The true atheist is not that hot-head who goes around the crossroads smashing all the religious signs he meets and preaching the cult of reason to a plebe graced only with instinct.

The true atheist is not one of those men of the world, or men *comme il faut* who, through snobbery, disdain the use of thought and more or less live like the horse they mount, or the women they keep.

Nor is the true atheist seated in the chairs of those scientific societies, whose members ceaselessly lie to their consciences and agree to hide their thoughts and to inhibit the solemn march of philosophy in order to advance their miserable personal interests or for pitiful political considerations.

The true atheist is not the proud semi-savant who wants there to be no other atheist than himself in the world, and who would cease to be one if most people became so. For him the mania for standing out in the crowd takes the place of a philosophy. Self-love is his God. If he could he'd see to it that enlightenment belonged only to him; to hear him speak, the rest of humanity is not worthy of it.

Nor is the true atheist that timorous philosopher lacking in energy who blushes about his opinion as if it were an evil thought. A cowardly friend of truth, he would sooner compromise it than compromise himself. We see him haunting temples in order to cast aside any suspicion of impiety. An egoist who carries circumspection to the point of pusillanimity, he always finds the time to be premature for the extirpation of the most ancient prejudices. He doesn't fear God, but men frighten him. It makes no difference to him that they destroy each other in civil and religious wars, as long as he lives sheltered from harm and in peace.

Nor is the true atheist that systematic physician who only rejects God in order to have the glory of fabricating the world at his leisure, with no other assistance than that of his imagination.

The true atheist is not he who says: "No, I don't want a God." Rather it is he who says: "I can be wise without a God."

The true atheist doesn't reason with great argumentative skill against divine existence. On the contrary, the weakest theologians could embarrass him if he crossed swords with them. But he could say to them with bonhomie and to close the discussion:

"Doctors, is there a God in heaven? For me that question is no more important than this one: Are there animals on the moon? Here is my motto, in one line, doctors:

'I have no more need of a God than he of me.'
- Sylvain, the French Lucretius

"What difference does a God make to me? My thoughts go no further than that which strikes my senses and I don't push my curiosity so far as to want to find in the heavens yet another master: I already meet enough of them on earth. Believing that there is something beyond the all of which I am a part is repugnant to my reason. But if this object were to exist he would be perfectly foreign to me. What is the relationship between us? Enclosed within the limits of the universe in which I live, that which happens among my neighbors is no concern of mine. It is not my affair. The doorway to my house is for me the columns of Hercules. There is quite a distance between man and what we call a God. I am too near-sighted to see that far. It is difficult to get along at such a great distance. In any event, I have everything I need right at hand: rights to exercise, duties to fulfill, and pleasures, which are the results of my duties and rights. The heart's most tender affections and the sweetest illusions of the sprit find around me, in me, and at every instant of my life, nourishment taken from the nature of things. I don't have a moment to waste. Every season of my existence offers me varied subjects for contentment. Newborn I have my mother's breast; a young man I throw myself into the arms of another me. In my old age my children render me the care they received from me.

"Surrounded, embraced by my parents, my wife, my children, my friend, where is there room for God? He has no place in a united family. We don't at all feel the necessity. A good son, a good husband, a good father lacks for nothing.

"If I meet with no reward I go down into the depths of my heart, close myself in and find there ample recompense for the pains I suffer outside, for the losses I feel at my side, for injustices, for the persecutions of the wicked, who are more to be pitied than I.

"I know how to find all I need within myself, without any effort. All my means are at my disposal. I envelop myself in the memory of my good works and rely on my conscience without begging for help above my head, in the clouds.

"Doctors, if your God exists or not you can see that man, if he knows to question himself and knows how to appreciate his personal and internal resources, has no need to go outside of himself to taste happiness, the fruit of his virtue. The happiness of honest men is always their own work. They owe nothing to anyone.

"Doctors, keep your God. I can do without him."

Some good souls take pity on atheists: "The unfortunates (they say) cannot be well either in this world or the next. Hope, this balm of life, has been taken from them. They have a narrow sprit, a dry soul. They don't know how to love, the unfortunates!"

> The heart that didn't love was the first Atheist.
> - L. Mercier

Good people! Don't fret about the lot of atheists. They don't in the least envy your enjoyments. They have their own that are more real and pure. They don't worry about the past that is no longer, or the future, which is not yet. Limited to the present, which alone belongs to them, their interest is in the best possible use of their time. They take their rule of conduct from nature, which knows no lacunae and is never wrong.

Good people, don't fret on their account. Good, true atheists are more dependable lovers, spouses, and friends than other men. They feel and enjoy with more energy. Present life being all for them they work at getting the most advantage from it. And experience has taught them that that they can't abuse it without first harming themselves.

"Certainly, but leave us our God!"

Good people, what do you want with him? What good is he to you? From what evils does he preserve you? After having left you under royal despotism for twelve centuries was your almighty God able to defend you from anarchy? If your God mixes in your affairs why do they go so poorly? Why do you have altars and no morals? Why so many priests and so few honest men? If your almighty God contents Himself on high in a perfect neutrality, then tell me, good people here below, is it not then as if you have no God? Are atheists so wrong, are they so criminal when they see to their own salvation? Keep your God, but don't find it evil if atheists don't needlessly multiply beings. And above all, rid yourselves of all unjust prejudices in their regard.

Atheists, who they once used to frighten women and big and small children with, and still do today, are the best people in the world. They don't form a corporation, like priests[1]; they don't make propaganda. In fact, they don't offend anyone.

The repertoire of ancient and modern atheists [in the "Dictionary of Ancient and Modern Atheists"] will at last prove that most of them are, of all men, the most tolerant, the most peaceful, the most enlightened, and the most loving. They are also the happiest.

Compare the character and the habits of the man without God to the habits and character of the man of God. Is there a more perfect contrast?

Observe the latter: he continuously lives in fear and humiliation, like a slave kissing the whip that strikes him.

If he carries out a good act, instead of giving himself over to a legitimate pride, he is foolish enough to attribute all the merit, all the honor to a master who dictated it to him. If he proposes a generous resolution he demands the grace and the permission to accomplish it. A weak child, he doesn't dare put a foot in front of the other without looking over at papa God (forgive us the familiarity of the expression, but it is perfectly accurate). Look at how the deist, the theist, the religious man[2] of any sect lowers his head, closes his eyes, joins his hands, extends his arms, bends the knee when he pronounces the word "God." Are there any terms more abject or more foolish than those he uses in his invocations? If he loses his wife or children he thanks his divine creator, for nothing happens without his orders, and it's always for the best. On his deathbed, like a criminal, he trembles at the approach of the supreme judge. The idea of a generous or vengeful God prevents him from giving himself over to nature's final effusions. He coldly casts his family and friends aside in order to prepare himself to appear before the celestial tribunal. Of course such an existence is a perpetual torture and realizes in this life the hell of the other world.

The man without God has and maintains a completely different attitude.

Let us follow him on one of the days of his life. He leaves his wife's arms or wakes up in order to view the rising of the great star, and then he sets his household affairs and labors in order. After having given his children their first lessons he takes the morning meal with his family. Afterwards, each works at his own occupations and commitments. They get together again at midday in order to recuperate the strength worn out by their labors and to gaily prepare themselves for new fatigues. Exercising his natural and acquired faculties, the man without God doesn't know boredom. Every hour procures for him an observation to be made, a service to be rendered. An indispensable part of nature, and as active as it, he coordinates himself with it so as to fulfill the duties imposed on him by his relations with others. The evening come, he passes peaceful moments in the bosom of his family, with a friend, and allows himself to relax, the well-earned salary of a productive and useful day. Gentle rest awaits him during the night. He falls asleep, satisfied that he left no void in his day, modeled on the sun's path.

And when he reaches the term of his existence? He gathers all his strength in order to enjoy the pleasures that remain to him and then closes his eyes forever, but with the certainty of leaving an honorable and cherished memory in the hearts of his kin, from whom he receives the final testimonies of esteem and attachment. His role finished, he peacefully retires from the scene in order to make room for other actors who will take him as their model. He doubtless feels lively regret for the separation from all he loved, but reason tells him that such is the immutable order of things. In any event, he knows that he doesn't entirely die. A father is eternal. He is reborn, he lives again in each of his children, and even in pieces of his body: nothing of him is obliterated. An indestructible link in the great chain of beings, the man without God embraces everything in thought and finds consolation in this, knowing that passing away is nothing but a displacement of matter and a change in form. At the moment he leaves life, he remembers, if he has the time, the good he did, as well as his faults. Proud of his existence, he has only bended his knee before the author of his days. He has walked on the earth, his head high and with a firm step, the equal of every other being and only owing accounts to his conscience. His life is as full as nature: *Ecce Vir* [3].

If the narrow framework in which we are circumscribed allowed us to profit from all the advantages of our subject, we would teach certain people that atheists are trustworthy in commerce, gentle and calm in society, that they alone know how to enjoy with delicacy and in keeping with nature's wishes, which they consult before anything else. Among them it is rare to meet fanatics or hypochondriacs. Happy and content, they are easy to get along with because, knowing how short life is, they prefer to pass it loving each other rather than in disputes or hatred. This is why they don't see anything wrong in one's thinking differently from them. Philosophers without any pretensions, they aren't angered by insults, even those habitually cast at them by men of God. They look upon them as ill-bred children.

If some of the atheists who names are gathered in the "Dictionary" were to return to the world what would we not do to be admitted to their company, to share their easy and remorse-free happiness? Who among us would regret his day if he had passed the first hours of it in the school of Pythagoras or Aristotle, then accepted Anacreon's, Lucretius's or Chaulieu's hospitality. And then, after having strolled in Epicurus's or Helvetius's garden allows himself to be surprised by the night between Aspasian and Ninon.[4]

Without any consideration for these illustrious names, they say to us:

"Nothing less than a God, or the idea of a God, is needed to fill the void in man's heart, to occupy his thoughts. He who doesn't believe is necessarily more ambitious, more boisterous. It's only by achieving honors or material pleasures that he can get by and exist on earth without disgust."

Let us answer this.

He who is an atheist through reason feels more than others the worthlessness of these social distinctions, these vulgar pleasures that most men are so vain and jealous of. A careful observer, an enlightened friend of nature, he needs great objects to feed his imagination. He looks with pity and affliction on those political or religious crises that torment the mass of men for the profit of a handful of wretches whose entire talent lies in the audacity of crime. These are nothing but atrocious and shameful spectacles in which the atheist refuses to play a role.

Sometimes vengeance is taken for his disdain by covering him in insults. It is here that we can admire the influence of liberal opinion on the character and existence of man. The atheist who has come to think in this way by studying the nature of things has necessarily placed himself above them. Filled with his own dignity, he submits his reason to no other authority than that of evidence. Atheism inspires sentiments of elevation and independence to a degree unattainable in any other system.

A God is necessary to the people. The people need one to learn to be docile before their leaders. And these leaders can't do without one in order to ease their tasks of administration.

We answer: God is useful to neither those who are governed nor those who govern. For many years he has made no impression on the spirit of the former. The people aren't so stupid as not to see that God is nothing but a brake used by those who tyrannize them. Daily experience has rudely awakened them to the truth of this.

In any event, in a population of 100,000, there are perhaps not fifty who have taken the trouble to reason out their beliefs. The people accept them without question. They are Catholic, just as they'd be atheist, if their ancestors had been so. God resembles those old articles of furniture which, far from being useful, are only in the way but which are passed on in families and are religiously kept, because the son received it from the father, and the father from his ancestor.

We insist and we say: a God and his priests are as necessary as a police magistrate and his spies.

Whatever the perversity of men in civilization a good correctional tribunal suffices for all causes. Dual employments harm each other, paralyze each other reciprocally. The counter-police of priests is never as good as the active surveillance of spies.[5]

It is at long last time to smash these old politico-religious cogs that everyone agrees are insufficient and so little favorable to human perfectibility.

But here is the most atrocious and most gratuitous of imputations against men without God:

Atheism (they dare to say) demoralizes civil society.

"Holy choler of virtue, guide my pen a moment ..."[6]

Priests of a God, fruit of adultery[7] you dare say to us that atheism demoralizes! ...

And you, theist adorers of an all-powerful providence that has permitted the bloody immoralities of a ten-year long revolution, you too say that atheism demoralizes!

And you too, statesmen, you permit yourselves to become the complacent echoes of priests and you say along with them: "Atheism demoralizes the people." You who every day allow conjugal faith to be ridiculed on all the stages of the land; you who lay a trap for the unfortunate with your lotteries ... This is what truly demoralizes the people. A people loses its morality with priests who sanctify adultery in their liturgy, with semi-philosophers who preach a providence complicit in the crimes he permits ...

Thinkers who are either inconsistent or in bad faith: was it atheism that reigned at the court of our last three monarchical masters, Louis XIV, Louis XV, and Louis XVI?

Was it atheism that dominated the Convention, with Robespierre the persecutor of atheists?

Was it atheism that founded the Inquisition; that covered America with corpses, that ordered the Saint Bartholomew's Day Massacre, and which, in the Vendée, commits all kinds of crimes?

Is it a coalition of atheists, that of the crowned powers that carries the plague of a war of extermination all over Europe?

Were St. Dominic, Charles IX, and Maria de Medicis atheists? Were Ferdinand, George III, Francois II, and Paul I atheists? Was the mother of the latter an atheist? Are Pitt and Maury? Are the French émigrés who turn their swords against their mothers' breasts?

Studious Bayle! Virtuous Spinoza! Wise Fréret! Modest Dumarsais! Honest Helvetius! Sensible d'Holbach! Etc. All of you philosophers who only rejected God so as to bring forth an unalloyed morality! You demoralized the world?

Is the atheist to be looked upon like the scapegoat who the Hebrews charged with all their iniquities?

It is for the amusement of idlers and the education of fools that the coryphées of *bas empire* of French literature enjoy themselves in both prose and verse at the expense of the atheism of those who profess it.

We will only reply to them by burying them in the imposing names and the authority of those in the "Dictionary." These praise-worthy names should at least make them more circumspect. A moral opinion professed by so many great and good men deserves to be spoken of in more measured tones. This mass of suffrages should carry some weight in the scale of the undecided.

We have gathered not only the principal sentiments of known atheists, but also an infinite number of testimonies in their favor. Testimonies worthy of even more credence because they come from the mouths or pens of their adversaries.

We have surprised several theologians stating maxims much more philosophical than they had thought, rendering homage to the purity of conduct and intention of men without God.

It should also be said that many honest citizens and learned men are atheists without believing that they are so. This is because they haven't yet learned to draw the consequences of and apply certain principles that they profess.

Let us add that if there had never been rogues or unfortunates on earth we would never have thought to look for a God in the heavens.

Our descendants will not be able to read certain pages of our annals without asking: were men differently organized than us in those times? What did they do with their reason? What a pity that they placed so much importance on pronouncing the word God!

Regeneration is spoken of, a new order. Great principles are announced, vast plans, and profound insights. Ideologues treat their predecessors as idiots, as shortsighted. And yet these men with their daring concepts don't dare officially publish anything against the most absurd and decrepit of prejudices. They propose the raising of an edifice of the most sublime proportions, yet they seem to respect the Gothic ruins that they fear to deliver a decisive blow to. They allow humanity to remain prostrated at the feet of its ancient fetish instead of saying to it, with all the authority of reason: "Rise up and march with giant steps towards happiness." Following the timid counsels of a false policy they accord public asylum to both sacerdotal imposture and philosophy. Statesmen would be mortified if we thought them religious, but it doesn't bother them that everyone except them be so.

They say: "It is not yet time to take God from the people."

What are you waiting for? Fear the results of semi-enlightenment. Everything must be told the people, or nothing. A people only half enlightened is the most detestable of peoples. You will never make anything of them. But this is perhaps your intention. If all nations have unanimously recognized a God distinct from matter, and dedicated a cult to him, the wise men of all centuries and all countries have only recognized matter working on its own.

Going over our nomenclature we can see these two extremes touch. We see the theologian and the philosopher walk in opposite directions in order to arrive at the same goal. The spiritualist and the materialist draw similar results from their opposing arguments. God is nature to the eyes of the body; nature is God to the eyes of understanding. Matter or abstraction, the divinity is all or it is nothing. And those who speak of it are either Spinozists or Don Quixotes.

It is to be hoped that the reading of the "Dictionary of Ancient and Modern Atheists" will lead its readers to say:

"Why spill so much ink, bile and blood? God can have his moment of utility during the childhood of political bodies. Now that humanity has reached maturity we no longer need that old leash. Freed, we will know how to reduce to their just value those brilliant, vehement speeches. The useful, the good, the true will obtain preference in our spirits over the superb flights of imagination and vanity. Agitated men who meditate on *coups d'état*, deep thinkers who want to carry out revolutions in the empire of ideas, or apply their sublime theories to statistics, will meet sensible men along the way, walking with nature and reason, imperturbable enemies of both political and religious abstractions. With religion, simplified and reduced to filial piety, we will also want to simplify our civil institutions. The entire diplomatic apparatus will appear to us as a gigantic piece of childishness. All of those numerous cogs of social government, which resemble ancient hydraulic machines[8] will be reduced to less complicated movements. We will act in a fashion contrary to our superstitious ancestors, who made little of much. Rid as we will then be of all the petty considerations that were necessary up till now in order not to bump up against venerable and ancient errors, we will say, parodying an expression of Ninon's: 'A government must be quite poor in enlightenment and resources when it thinks it has to come to terms with religious prejudices.'"

Such will be the revolution carried out by atheism. Such, we repeat, will be the influence of that liberal opinion on spirits and institutions. The full and complete destruction of a long and imposing error that penetrated everything[9], that denatured everything, even virtue; that was a trap for the weak, a lever for the powerful, and a barrier before men of genius. The destruction of that long and imposing error will change the face of the world.

While waiting for this great event, which is so feared by those who live on lies, and which the sterile vows of the wise call for but can't hasten, we say to our perplexed contemporaries:

"God has in His favor ignorance and imposture, fear and despotism, and against Him reason and philosophy, the study of nature and the love of independence. God owes His birth to misunderstanding. He only exists through the charm of words: the knowledge of things kills and obliterates Him. Good sense rejects the idea of a corporeal God. An abstract God has no hold on it. And yet God can only be abstraction or matter. It must again be repeated here: God is all or nothing. In order to get along and to be understood, the theologian has to express himself like the philosopher. But if everything is God, then God loses his divinity. On the other hand, ceding to his spirituality, he only exists in the thought of man. We can understand the embarrassment of the schools, constructing on imaginary spaces and with words that have no meaning, or who destroy the ghost when they do. Alas, all the sacred wars that bloody the pages of history are then nothing but grammatical quarrels. Blush for your fathers, who lost themselves in miserable theological questions. Burn those dusty libraries that only attest to the delirium and shame of the human spirit. Life's brevity doesn't leave you enough leisure to waste your fleeting moments in gratuitous conjectures or suppositions.

"Up till the present you have only lived on fictions. Your very laws are still full of them. Man needs something more substantial. Leave aside all that doesn't rest on nature and the evidence of things.

"A modern legislator (Porcher) dared to say, in a moment of openness: 'Opium should be administered to three quarters of men.'

"May this statement dissipate your long sleep. It is only too true: up till today men have only been governed by administering them religious and other soporifics. From here on in, close your ears not only to priests, but also to any statesman who speaks and acts like a priest.

"Three talismanic words[10] were enough to make religions and revolutions. This must no longer occur. You must no longer present—or at least suffer—such spectacles and scandals. Reject all these systems that are the cause or the result of them. Has not everything already been said on the subject of divine science and politics? Pass now to positive objects that truly touch you. Do you not have domestic morality and traditional experience?

"Two books are open to you, your hearts and nature. Think on them above all else. Think about how any other kind of study is petty and pitiful, wasteful and uncertain compared to that of the heart and nature. Only they are real and useful, good and beautiful. Give yourselves over to the results of observation and experience, and to the sweetness of the sentiments of reciprocal benevolence. Place all that has been said and done about God and diplomacy in parallel with the labors of agriculture and family duties. How pitiful and wretched is the profound metaphysician who passes his time in his dusty study in order to make books with other books, compared to the atheist exercising his intellectual and physical faculties under nature's eye and enjoying the purest pleasures, the result of a healthy organization. How thin and ridiculous is the grave publicist next to the laborer, head of a family and having the good sense to be nothing but that, and who relies on the light of his good sense! It is to this that man must sooner or later return.

"Leave God aside. God is of no use to you ... God is of no use to man.

"Learn from your fathers' errors. Don't, like them, sacrifice things to words. Look after your own affairs. Keep an eye on those among you charged with taking care of your external interests. Your agents aren't bothered that the crowd keeps its gaze raised to heaven. While it is looking there, it doesn't see what is going on on earth"

The idea of a God making up in another world for the tyrannies put up with in this one, imprinted on the brain of the ruled, is a comfortable pillow for the head of the rulers.

A republic of atheists would give its supreme administrators less latitude. Atheists are clear-sighted and honest citizens and absolutely refuse to recognize any other power than that of reason. Men like these can't be led with sticks. One fears encountering them. Beautiful exteriors don't impress them; beautiful promises don't satisfy them. It's not to them that we can say: "Be patient, let the evil ones do as they please. God allows them to reach the heights for a moment in order to prepare a greater fall." Atheists don't accept these reasonings. They want to prevent evil; they want justice to be done to the first place holder who does wrong. They want the law, present everywhere at the same time and as prompt as lightning, to replace a hidden and slow-moving God, who allows Cromwell and Monk to die in their beds.

Tolerant by taste and principle, atheists want the magistrate of a great nation, by consecrating a law on the freedom of religion, to nevertheless make felt the absurdity and the inconvenience of all religions in his wise proclamations addressed to fathers and heads of families.

"Citizens! (he could say to them) the freedom of religion is demanded, and we won't refuse it. But is it something good for those who so loudly call for it? We don't think so, and we think it is our obligation to share our doubts with you. We can't forbid the sale of arsenic by pharmacists. But fathers and heads of family, we ask you in the name of good morals and holy truth, in the name of public and private interest, to join your nature to the enlightenment given by all those who were truly wise and preserve the rising generation from the religious contagion.

"Make your children and your dependents feel that they are being fooled, that they owe nothing to a being high above their understanding; that their sole duties are the love of labor and the laws, the recognition of the authors of their days and their instruction. Fathers and heads of family! Accustom your children and your servants to only see in you ministers of morality; to see as their only altars the places where they received life and education, to only confess their faults to you, to only consult you. Finally, to find in you and you alone their God and their priests.

"Heads of family! Reclaim your rights. The only brake a free people requires is laws and morals.

"Good mothers! Be your children's providence. May your daughters' virtues be your work. Don't join strangers to your august functions. A well-born daughter should never leave her mother for an instant. It is indecent to see a young virgin kneel at the feet of a man who is not her father to confess to him her domestics errors. There is a universal religion that is previous to all the others and that will survive them: filial piety. This is the only natural religion. The paternal household is its temple ..."

But such means are slow. Entering into agreement with falsehood, attacking it only with proclamations, promises a victory for truth in a few centuries. I like to think that one day, perhaps soon, a pure man will rise, joining to the sparkle of his intelligence, to the ascendant of his virtues all the strength of a great character.

For many centuries almost all countries have been dissatisfied with their condition. They call on a supernatural being who must come to earth in order to change, or at least ameliorate, the state of things.

At Delphi they prophesied the coming of a son of Apollo who would bring the reign of justice to man.

The Romans waited for a king predicted by their Sybils. The Indians wait for Vishnu, who will appear to them in the form of a centaur. The Persians wait for Ali, the Chinese for Felo. The Japanese wait for Pe'irum and Karbadoxi, and the Siamese for Sammonocodon. The Hebrews think yet about their Messiah. The Christians believe in a second visit from Jesus, in the fearful guise of a severe judge from whom there is no appeal.

The moralists, the philosophers themselves, hope for the appearance of a man daring to openly speak the whole truth.

May he be proclaimed the benefactor of humanity, the wise legislator who will find the secret of erasing from man's brains the word "God," a sinister talisman that has caused so many crimes and so much evil!

What is an atheist?

The true atheist is a modest and peaceful philosopher who doesn't like to make noise and who doesn't show off his principles with a puerile ostentation[10], atheism being of all things in the world the most natural, the most simple.

Without arguing either for or against divine existence, the atheist goes straight to his goal and does for it what others do for their God. It isn't so as to please the divinity that he practices virtue, but in order to be right with himself.

Too proud to obey anyone, even a God, the atheist takes orders only from his conscience.

The atheist has a treasure to guard, and that's his honor. A man who respects himself knows what he must forbid or permit himself and would blush at the idea of taking advice or following a model.

The atheist is an honorable man. He would be ashamed to owe to a God a good work he can do for himself and in his own name. He doesn't like to be pushed to do good, or turned away from evil: he seeks the one and avoids the other of his own will, and we can depend upon him.

How many good acts have been attributed to God that had as their only principle the heart of the great man who produced them?

The most perfect disinterest is the basis for all the resolutions of the atheist. He knows he has rights and obligations. He exercises the first without complaint, and the others without constraint. Order and justice are his divinities, and he makes free sacrifices only to them:

"The wise man alone has the right to be an atheist."

Notes by Maréchal

1. A few years ago a priest put forward a motion that made the most serious men smile: he wanted to submit the priesthood to patent rights.

Such a measure would not be fitting under an order of things that rests entirely on morality. Woe on the republic that would make a resource of the products libertinage and falsehood. Women of ill repute and priests should not be imposed the way we impose useful and honest professions, whose free exercise we protect.

2. For the deist, if he is consistent in his principles, differs but little from a Roman Catholic.

3. The deist, the theist or any other sectarian who admits a religion can be designated under the vulgar expression: *Ecce homo*.

4. We have a false idea of these two women if we see in them only amiable courtesans. One gave lessons to Socrates, the other is celebrated for a rare probity. Both had an anti-religious philosophy superior to their sex and their century.

5. What a happy country would be that which could do without priests or spies.

6. An expression borrowed from the most eloquent of modern writers. See the invocation of the Levite Ephraim.

7. It has been noted that the founders of the three principal religions of the world, Moses, Jesus, and Mohammed were illegitimate children.

8. Marly's machine, for example.

9. It is painful to see how, in the best works, the most thoroughly thought out books, the authors are different, and lower themselves when their pens fall on the word "God." The writer's brain is immediately paralyzed, and that profound brain, so vigorous on every other subject, seems to lose its way and become nothing but the wordy and machine-like echo of soothsayers, principally when these latter have the wind of public opinion going for them. Newton is a deplorable example.

10. All religions are derived from astrology—HORUS ... a German.

Epistle to the Ministers of all Religions (1801)[*]

This treatise for and against the Bible will teach you nothing new. More than anyone, you know the strengths and the weaknesses of your books and the weak point in the armor of your gods. Allow others to cast an impartial eye on the depths of the sanctuary where imposture has long enjoyed the right of asylum. Allow then ...

Or rather, blush for the role you have transmitted from hand to hand for four thousand years. Having left its infancy behind, humanity has reached the age for passing from the regime of wet nurses to that of reason.

It would doubtless be an insult to you to believe you to be the dupes of the fables you traffic in. Of course you aren't, so cease to invent them. Dare to aspire to liberal ideas: it is yet possible for you to take your place among beings worthy of esteem. We will willingly agree to forget what you have been if you sincerely promise us to work at becoming again what you should never have ceased to be. We would like to think that the stain you have contracted is not completely indelible.

Already many among you have removed the theatrical masks and costumes. Follow this example, or be as honest as some of your predecessors of the second century of Christianity: Montanist priests suspended from the vault of their church a bladder full of wind and danced beneath it, singing the hymns to the Holy Spirit, of which this bladder full of wind was a parable.

In the name of reason, which it is never too late to return to, in the name of morality which for so long has suffered and groaned due its alliance with religion; in the name of the pitiless posterity which prepares to punish you if you persist in dragging the people along in your old ruts, have enough respect for yourselves, have enough respect for your kind to put an end to the degradation of humanity. Don't you have reason to be satisfied? Aren't four thousand years of falsehoods enough? Put down the scepter of opinion, which you have allowed to be soiled in your hands. See that eighteen centuries have passed since the second era and the renewal of your boorish, ridiculous, and culpable solemnities: must the XIXth century also be infected by them? As you can see, every day

---

[*] From *Pour et contre la bible*. [n.p.] Jerusalem, 1801.

almost every science takes a step towards the light. Will you alone remain in the shadows?

How would you escape universal derision if some clever chemist were to take it in his head, in the middle of a class, to put your God's blood in their alembic and his body in the crucible, and if he were to repeat the analysis at every crossroads?

Hasten then to abjure a profession that you can no longer exercise without inciting laughter, and without you yourselves laughing behind your altars. Seize the only means that remains to you to deserve pardon by fashioning a justice of your own invention. What are you waiting for? One day the role that you persist in filling will become a historical problem. With all their erudition the future Saumaises will find it difficult to make your current existence appear probable. No one will want to believe them; no one will want to believe that there was a time, a very long time, during which, under the eyes of philosophy, *shameless men*[1] offered from their fingers, for the adoration of the entire earth, *a God made bread*[2]: at the very least, fear the future. In just a short while that plebe, which kneels at your table to eat a God of your fashioning, will want to indemnify itself with violence, with an explosion for having been your plaything for so many years. Fear the awakening of those you have held for so many centuries in the most stupid of slumbers. Realize that you only owe your ascendancy to an old habit. There would long since have been no religions if religions hadn't degenerated into habits, into routines; but everything gets worn out and erased. "But (you will say) we force no one. Everyone is free to come or not every seven days to prostrate himself before our holy stages. Apparently the plebe likes to be fooled[3] and it is perhaps good that they be fooled. ... It is just as well it be us as other, more dangerous charlatans. In a despotic state it isn't the despot who should be reprimanded, but the multitude who suffer him." There are things we should not respond to: they revolt us, or refute themselves. We will continue to say to you:

Ministers of all religions, realize that we don't love you, and that in fact you aren't lovable. Your mythologies are mournful, your ceremonies[4] monotonous and ridiculous, your harangues boring, your books heavy and gloomy. Don't stand against the torrents of the ages, which sweep before them memories and religions. Do better. If the zeal of the House of the Lord still devours you, well then, abandon the profane and the impious to their destiny; go repopulate the Holy Land, that primary theatre of the Bible and the Gospel; bring there your God, your tripods and your books: we don't want them anymore. You are proud of the poetic beauty of your Bible[5] and of the few grand traits spread around your Gospels. But the literary merit of these two religious productions can't save them from the fate that, a little sooner, a little later, puts every book full of indecent fables in its place.

We should add that the books of all religions resemble each other. This is why we address ourselves to the ministers of all religions. If we have lingered more particularly over those of the Catholics it's because we have the spectacle before our eyes, and in this treatise it is not only a question of the Bible and the Gospel, for religions differ among themselves only in their decorations.

Christian priests, you insist:

"For some time several well-known litterateurs have been known to express their admiration with these words: *as beautiful as the Bible*. At least (you add) it can't be denied that we have in our hands the most beautiful of books that exist. No one has yet been able to do better: the Orientals, the Egyptians, Greece, and Rome have produced nothing that has eclipsed the bible. This book occupies the first place, in literature as well as religion."

Ministers of the religion! It is also said, with just as much reason, *beautiful as Homer. Beautiful as Telemachus* has also been said.

This would seem to prove that there are in the Bible, as well as in Homer and the small number of original books, beauties of the first order. But the genius of Homer sometimes falls asleep: *aliquando dormitat Homerus*.[*] The authors of the Old and the New Testaments not only sleep like the author of the Iliad and the Odyssey, they do something worse: they scandalize and revolt their readers with obscene paintings, horrible tableaux, and the defects of the whole.

From which it results that the Bible, written by the hand of God, or inspired by his holy spirit is, like other books composed by men of genius, full of beauty, but is not a book more perfect than them. And yet, according to the great pretensions of its eternal preachers, this should be the case. But there's more: the Bible is beneath many profane works.

To be sure, I would blush to have written certain—in fact, quite numerous—passages, of the Old and New Testaments. Jean Lafontaine

---

[*] sometimes even Homer nods

disavowed his fables. I would think myself more criminal if I were the author of the Bible and the Gospel. I would have shown genius in a few places, but at the same time I would have given a poor opinion of my judgment and my morality.

In a word, if we asked of an enlightened and informed man which of all the famous books he would like to have been the author of, as long as he has a little self-respect he would not answer: the Bible.

Ministers of all religions, you place yourself under the protection of this phrase of Montesquieu's, echoed by many today: "Religion is the best guarantor we can have of men and the stability of states." (*Grand. et Decad. de Rome.*)

Priests! You haven't been able to save the thrones of your very-Christian kings. Your gods and your books couldn't protect the people and their chiefs from a political revolution. Your religions and your books are thus poor guarantors.

In vain as well you boast of the long and showy elegy for Jesus by the most eloquent, but not the wisest of 18th century writers. The "Apology for the Gospels" by J. J. Rousseau, and the "Commentary on the Apocalypse" by Newton only prove that, like other men, men of genius have their weaknesses in judgment.

Let us continue. You are yet spoken of, and you are still feared even today. You still frighten little children and old women. There are even statesmen who say that you are a necessary evil; that you should be used as a bogeyman to frighten and contain the canaille; that religion is a supplement to the police.[6] Too many writers persist in saying that vast states, populous cities cannot do without priests and executioners. These considerations give you pride and assurance; but do you have so little honor as to brag about, to pride yourselves on such an existence. Is there anything here that would lead you to hold your heads high? Never forget that you only owe your credit over weak minds to an ancient political error that is reaching its end.

In just a short while we will dispense with these vain arrangements with you. In just a short while the cobbler will think himself dishonored by touching the hand of a priest.

Don't be insensitive to the contempt, the disgust that you inspire in every honest and reasonable man you find on your path. Skillful as you are, don't imprudently rest on the impunity you enjoy in your corrupting of good morality. You are allowed to do pretty much what you want.

Don't think you've acquired the right to continue your sacred scandals. Adultery, deified for eighteen centuries in your temples has, for all that, not become a virtue. There is no prescription in favor of vice.

We are ready to consent to pass the sponge over the past, but on condition that you respect the present and the future; that you embrace a useful, honest profession, that you leave sons to their parents, young maidens to their mothers, that you no longer incite the hard-working artisans of the two sexes to waste their time and their novice reason to your frequent performances.

Stop staining the most beautiful of life's ages by forcing young girls to engrave in their tender brains[7] the most ridiculously absurd passages of your holy books. Perhaps soon enough some among them will only too well imitate the scandals of Virgin Mary.

If at least the holy letters you profess could lead to some great, profitable or interesting results. Higher mathematics, transcendental geometry, hardly necessary in themselves, have allowed for the most important discoveries in the mechanical arts. What fruits can we draw from the Bible and the Gospels? And what could those who dedicate themselves solely to their study be? Pilgrimages to Mecca or Calvary lead only to the tomb or the void.

Ministers! Your religions are profligate in their spending. You need rich ornaments, shiny costumes, wax, incense, perfumes, golden cups, rugs, vast and sumptuous edifices. This profusion, for all that it's sacred, is not a good example, and in this century, where heads of household must know how to keep accounts, there would be great economy in suppressing religions and the priesthood, even more so because a father, at no cost and with no hindrance, can perfectly well fulfill these functions with his children.[8]

> An honest elder, instructed by the years
> Guiding the destiny of his numerous progeny,
> Can he not, better than a priest, teach virtue?
> Is he not cloaked in a saintly character?
> - S.M.

You will say to us: "But wise and believing Egypt made a gift of a third of its treasury to its priests, so much did it believe itself in debt to us."

That's because Egypt was believing, but wasn't wise.

Ministers of all religions! Glory itself no longer fills us with enthusiasm. Don't brag of lighting the flames of religious fanaticism.[9] From this day forward we will no more have Crusades than civil wars. We will no more fight for priests than we do for masters. We have at least won this, and it is something.

Ministers of all religions! Your good times have passed. This shouldn't be hidden from you and you should expect this: this state could not last forever. Too much was done for you, and you did too little in exchange, for what equivalents did you give for all the goods, all the honors you were covered with? From time immemorial you held the first rank among the orders of the state. The good people of Egypt exempted you from all debts. You had your own separate jurisdiction: your persons, your property, your books were sacred. Even the fines levied against those who dared to doubt aloud the sanctity of your character and the purity of your morals were abandoned to you. You were the censors[10] of kings. For a long time you were the only magistrates, the only judges. On the banks of the Nile and elsewhere you took control of the education of children and the instruction of the people. In Ethiopia things were different: the monarch of this country was chosen by the priests, and consequently always a priest. The magi[11] (the priests of Persia were modestly called thus) were the king's teachers and, later, counselors, and, as in France, monarchs had engraved on their tombs that they had had the honor of being priests before dying. Julius Caesar gloried in the fact of having exercised the high priesthood. In many countries you wore on your head the sovereign's diadem. In Albania, in the east, the first personage after the monarch was the pontiff. In India the Brahmans, who called themselves philosophers and were only priests, didn't even obey the king or the laws. For a long time the Druids brought together in their priestly hands temporal might and sacred power: they judged the princes of the nation and made kings. Among the German people they put in irons whoever they wanted without giving reasons. In Greece the high pontiff several times declared to the first magistrates that they relied not on them, but on God alone. Dennis of Helicanarsus teaches us that in Rome the priests gave account of themselves neither to the people nor the senate. The priests of the time gave the signal for battles and retreats. At all times, in all countries the most beautiful edifices were built for you. The first blooming flowers, the masterpieces of all the arts are piled up on your altars. Mothers confide their children to you, husbands their wives.

Ministers of all religions! How have you responded to so much care? In exchange for so many benefits, what services have you rendered the world? In the petty persecutions you have attracted with your conduct you have inspired the most tender interest in your listeners of both sexes. Women have petted you: what have they received from you in return? Prayers, sermons, ceremonies, panic terrors, servile fears, talismans, rosaries, books full of maxims that are either insolent, immoral, or the cause of perturbations etc. We are tired of spending so much and receiving so little. There is no compensation: the whole benefit in the bargain is on your side. Holy wars, crusades, inquisitions, fasts, the boredom of your solemnity and speeches, feasts lacking in gaiety, yelping hymns, absurd and ridiculous mysteries, old usages that no longer have reason or goal ... Priests! Agree that you discharge poorly all these petty practices for the people, and the people are beginning to realize that you are costing them too much.

I ask you to agree to the justice of the following observation:

If the religion of which you are the ministers had not yet been founded, in order to establish it would you today dare to employ the same methods, the same instruments that were used in the past? Would you not shrug your shoulders at the proposals that would be made to you concerning this? If there were not yet religions it would not be easy to establish one, if we were to judge by the struggle it is for you to maintain those that allow you to barely live.

It costs us to remind you and publish all these harsh truths: it is you yourselves who force us to do this. A marked religious *reaction*[12] characterizes this first year of the 19th Century. Able at seizing on all circumstances, you abuse them with a shamelessness that alarms the friends of reason. But let them be reassured, and be warned that reason will never lose its rights. That its home fires, maintained by a small number of pure hands, will never be extinguished; that its flame sometimes suffers from more or less lengthy eclipses without ever lacking for the sustenance it needs to be re-ignited with even greater brightness; that it has seen all religions pass in succession; that it alone never changes and remains in all centuries. Know also that despite your petty successes, your ephemeral triumphs, your perfumed apologists of both sexes, that most of those who haunt your religious clubs shrug their shoulders on leaving and are surprised that you are allowed to issue so many anarchic[13] and revolutionary maxims in your divine offices. Know that your altars have received a shaking they will always feel, and that they will never recover the original stability of which you were so vain. Know that if it weren't for women[14] your tribunes would be deserted. Know that the farmers, who you count on the most, are finally persuaded that it is neither you, nor your lustrations, nor your psalm singing, but their arms and the sun that make the earth fertile and fill their granges and cellars. Labor is their sole titular divinity; they do without your *God in three* and prefer to give their alms to the truly indigent rather than to you, nourished by a bread that hasn't been watered with the honorable sweat of useful labor.

So abandon an evil cause abandoned by common sense. You have nothing more to do in this world from the moment we know that men in society need, not a religion, but a code written by reason in keeping with the counsels of experience. In a word, we have no more need of you.

Cite one phase of a man's life that requires your presence. When born he has his mother's breast. When young he has his father to mold him. More advanced in age another woman comes to put the final hand to his education and make a man of him. As a spouse, his companion fulfills all his desires. Having in his turn become a father, he passes down the lessons he learned from his father to his children. A citizen, his fatherland calls for his portion of the common labors of the hive. Born sensitive, a friend adds a complement to his happiness. We ask you: is there a sole circumstance in human life, a sole instant where we must deal with a priest? Is there a place for him in the paternal or marital home? So we can very well, without you, be born, live, and die. We have no need of a priest to love and discharge our debt to nature. Does a priest teach a newborn to find its mother's breast and the path to her heart? Does a young maiden need the lessons of a priest to please and make herself adored? Does a young bride have need to consult a priest so as to preserve her husband's esteem and have order and joy reign in their couple?

Ministers of all religions! Your profession is thus perfectly precarious. Your order is a costly and harmful superfluity. You are the parasitical mistletoe of the Druids, which vegetates on the oak at its expense.

"And the salvation of souls!" you will say.

Do we need a priest to pray to God? Isn't the paternal benediction worth as much as the laying on of priestly hands? And can't the great affair of salvation be treated of other than by proxy?

"Read history and geography (you'll say). At all times and everywhere, from Siberia to the isle of Tahiti, from the Ganges to the Amazon we find a God and ministers to serve him. Priests are thus as necessary as

God himself. Why don't you add: we are even more necessary than God, for in fact we can't see God, and we are there to represent him, to recall Him to distracted man."

Ministers of all religions! At all times and everywhere sorcerers were believed in: does this mean that we can't do without them?

No healthy logic can conclude from the fact that there have always been priests that they are still needed. On the contrary, it's because there were that they are no longer needed. The long ordeal we have gone through has disgusted us with them forever, and the people themselves are disenchanted in this regard. If everyone wanted to have his own oven and bake his own bread the profession of baker would no longer exist. In the same way, if everyone were to serve God in his own manner and take communion by his own hand in his own home, at that point there would no longer be any upkeep of the temples and their servants in keeping with the axiom: Beings should not be multiplied without necessity.

This same axiom is the condemnation of the Bible and the Gospels. The good example set by fathers is the best children's book.

Priests! Think by how thin a thread you hold on to your estate.

Once upon a time the multitude exercised its arms for you and you took the trouble to think and pray for it. The time has arrived when each of us will want to simultaneously exercise his intellectual and physical faculties. From that day on you'll have nothing more to do.

Agree with us then that there is nothing on earth more useless than you: even poets are less so. The laborer adds something to nature. The artisan modifies, the banker exchanges and distribute the earth's products. The magistrate preserves order in society. What real services are drawn from you? Panic terrors, imaginary hopes, etc.

If we weigh the authority and suffrage left to you, the decadence of your rule is no longer in doubt. Women without passion, men of a partisan spirit, journalists who Bayle wouldn't have wanted as copyists, a few political Tartuffes, some eager speculating teachers, and finally the routine-ridden plebe: such are your resources.

Ministers of all religions! We are certain that you don't very much like each other and this is as it must be: each of you preaches for his own shop. Well then, if you want to reestablish good relations, don't bear banners or wear livery any longer. Do even better: don't any longer have books. This expiatory sacrifice to good sense, we have no doubt, will cost you, but a beautiful and generous auto-da-fe of the sacred writings of all countries has become indispensable for the peace of all countries. Theology,[15] so sterile yet so fecund, has invaded two thirds of our libraries. It appears that it is only grudgingly that good books, of which there are few, are admitted there. Reason and truth don't take up much room.

If you can't resolve to immediately sacrifice your already printed books, at least don't re-publish them, and especially don't publish new ones: we've had enough of them. We are so full of theology that we're nauseous from it. Remember that Jesus wasn't a maker of books and that far from having the same mania as you, it is claimed that he didn't even know how to read. In certain nations there are certain priests who imitate him in this, and they aren't the worst of them.

But there is another great, and much more general, measure which we exhort you to cooperate in with good grace. In order to put an end to these interminable disputes over words, which have led to the confusion of things and the degradation of men, ministers of all religions, consent to forbid yourselves, along with us, from ever speaking of religion, either for good or ill. We are all tired of forever repeating the same things without ever having attached a meaning to it. This simple measure, once proposed in Switzerland, was successful as long as its execution was watched over. Now that we are a few steps closer to the truth such a resolution would be even less impracticable. So take the only wise position that remains in the current state of spirits: with no regrets, with no exceptions, burn those books in all languages that deal with sacred things: the Bible, the Gospels, the Koran, the Zend Vesta before all others. Tear out the pages in other volumes that even mention them. At the same time we will promise to no longer worry ourselves with all this. Let us no longer stir up these matters whose mephitism has so often asphyxiated the brains of men, but principally let us avoid the idle qualifications of materialists, spiritualists, Catholics, Protestants, Muslims, Jews. ... Let us destroy everything that can maintain or recall these old ideas, which we happily no longer have any need of. Let us return to that great and ancient distinction between men: the good and the evil. Let us simplify as much as possible so as to better understand each other. Misunderstandings, principally in religion, have caused almost all the misfortunes in the world.

Ministers of all religions! How honorable it would be not only for you to adhere in heart and mind to this noble pacific measure, but to even climb to your apostolic pulpits to preach this sublime devotion with your own mouths. How estimable you would again become if, following the example of the Curé Meslier and a few noble spirits before and after this good man, we were to hear you frankly pronounce the following homily: "We confess with truth and repentance that up until today we have not marched correctly before reason. Alas, we have unworthily compromised the dignity of free men and have thought up, through our servility and lying, absurd and evil-doing institutions. But that is all done with: a sudden flash of light has now struck our eyes. Yes, we willingly consent to no longer even pronounce the name of our God. God has no more need of priests to serve Him than He does candles to light His way. Man's religion cannot reach Him: He is too elevated for it. Let Him then enjoy himself at His ease, in His celestial beatitude and for all eternity, without troubling His august leisure and without our importuning Him with indiscreet wishes, with perfectly useless prayers. God doesn't nourish Himself with our incense, any more than we do with His flesh on our holy tables. The moment has arrived to make honorable amends for our having for so many centuries degraded God and misled men by maintaining that at our beckoning and our first request the divine majesty left the heavens to precipitously descend into our narrow chalices and willingly place himself on out lips. We make this confession with all humility and in confusion: such a religion was the height of ridiculousness, foolishness, and impertinence. It must be admitted that never was priestly empiricism carried to such a reversal of all natural ideas.[16] In a word, this religion diminished God without aggrandizing men. In order to expiate so monstrous a scandal we agree to break these factitious ties with our own hands, this magic chain that communicated between heaven and earth. Let each stay in his place: God in the empyrean and men on earth! From this day forward we will no more mix in His affairs than He in ours. We have no quarrel with Him, no more than with the fixed stars. Virtues belong to and suffice for those who practice them. And so, for the repose of the world, let there no longer be any question of God: let's speak no more about it. Statesmen, for their part, are beginning to realize that it is totally useless for them to have the Heavenly One intervene in affairs down below. It would mean provoking the degradation of the primary magistracy of an empire to suspect them of needing priests to administer with wisdom and to be on the watch for materialists and unbelievers. This pusillanimity was part of an old policy whose emptiness and insufficiency we feel today. A government strong enough to be just, similar to the supreme governor of the worlds, remains impassive and indifferent to all religious opinions. It knows neither priests nor atheists: it only sees men born free and graced with reason.

"And so we, ministers of all religions, who imprudently propagated so many errors fatal to public and individual tranquility, are firmly resolved to repair all the harm we have done. We renounce our functions and our books. With pleasure and docility we return to civilian ranks in order to fulfill, to the best of our ability, honest and useful professions.

"We also promise, on our conscience, to never again in the future utter any sacramental words, the bases for all religious sects and the inexhaustible source of animosity and crime. Wanting to recognize but two classes of men, the good and the evil, from this day forward we will do everything possible to deserve a place among the good."

How beautiful will be the day consecrated to this solemn and simultaneous declaration by the ministers of all religions. This will truly mean peace, real peace, universal, lasting peace; the perpetual peace of the good Abbé de Saint-Pierre, which is not the dream of only one man. It waits only for this lone measure.

"But (you will doubtless object), is such an extreme measure not a bit rushed and premature? Let us wait a while; let's not hurry."

Ministers of all religions! We hear you. In your hands religion is Pandora's box, at the bottom of which you always see hope. But know that sooner or later it is necessary that that salutary revolution have its full effect. Every passing day brings it closer. Without looking back, hasten to accomplish it. Assist in the efforts of time. Help us to make a *tabula rasa* of all religious systems. Instead of redecorating the old idol, which for a moment served as a rallying point for our primordial ancestors, let it fall on its own and of its own weight. Don't you see that it's worm eaten? Don't you see that its base is made of clay and sand? Help us to strip your books of this divine character, a misleading varnish that impressed simple souls. Have the merit of assisting in this great work. You must have been among the first to have observed just how much influence religious opinions have lost in relation to enlightenment. They will end up in a short while being completely discredited. Reason's obligations will necessarily get the upper hand over divine service, since they have as foundation the eternal rights and the daily needs of men.

And now, too, we are no longer in the mood to leave for much longer at your disposal, in your hands, this ideal mechanism which you gave the most pompous denominations: in any event, this mechanism becomes weaker with each passing day.

Take away your scaffolding: the edifice has been constructed.

You have felt that the divine religion is only an hors d'oeuvre: in order to make yourselves necessary; you affect to preach a religious morality, but know too that:

> Morality ends where religion begins –
> S.

As long as your holy writings serve as elementary and classic books, don't lay your hands on morality and education. Woe on a people whose primary instruction is confided to priests! Woe on a nation where the priests assume the duties of the father! Woe on fathers who need a priest to inspire virtue in their children! Woe on a city where the priests are legislators!

Men make books. The Bible was written by priests who, to be sure, were not angels. But don't books, in their turn, make men? This question isn't difficult to resolve once we have read the Bible and the Gospels, and once we have observed the Jewish nation and the Christian peoples.

Ministers of religion! It is true that your solemnities are still frequented, though not believed. Religion is nothing but a party affair, and your presence is put up with only in order to oppose you to others who are more feared than you. For many years the people who still attend the divine services have disdained your preaching. Lone women and the elderly stay there to pass their afternoons. Less than ever male sinners present themselves to your tribunals of penitence and your holy tables. Religion is falling into disuse, the scepter is falling from your hands and things are no worse for this.

Has government been less obeyed since maintaining absolute silence on God, giving no religion as an example and commanding only in the name of the law? Does it need you, religious ministers, to sanction its public acts?

Has the French soldier become less patient, less a friend of discipline since we no longer speak of God—either for good or evil—in the French army? Ministers of the religion! Does it need you to say mass before battle in order to carry off victory?

So stop looking upon yourselves as necessary and important citizens. It's a great step towards human perfectibility to have arrived at thinking that we can do without priests, and even their God; that not everything is in the Bible or the Gospels. Our poets aren't worth as much as the prophets, but our books of mathematics and physics have done harm to the holy writings. Nature's marvels take the place of miracles. Ministers of all religions! The naturalists will kill you off, or will at least cut off your supplies. Instead of moping in your chairs and running the risk of dying of hunger at your Lord's holy table, believe us: leave behind a trade that can no longer either nourish or honor its master. Assume again the love of labor, embrace a useful and honest profession, and cease to be priests. Make yourselves men again, and we will see in you only our like and our brothers.

Post-Scriptum

Ministers of all religions! Upon reading this Epistle you will no doubt cry out: "Have we not suffered enough in our property, in our opinions, in our persons? Must we every day see ourselves the subject of reproaches, recriminations, and sarcasm? What can be feared from us at present? We barely have an asylum in which to house our God and to place our altars. How can anyone have the heart to attack people one should rather pity?'

Ministers! To lie every day to one's conscience, to fool the people, to live on charlatanism is, without contradiction, a disagreeable and painful existence. But who forces you to do this? Who forces you, who condemns you to the profession you exercise? Why want to re-tie the strings[17] woven by imposture but worn out by time? Who charged you with, who enjoined you to preach the Gospel instead of morality? Show us the titles for your mission. Finally, why do you remain priests? And since you persist in this job, allow the spectators to boo, to condemn, to hate, and even to punish men who prostitute themselves to the service of profane or sacred stage. You have no right to complain of the treatment you are made to suffer, and, using a banal phrase from your books: those who sow lies harvest degradation: these are your wages, *cuique suum*.*

What is the necessity for this? We could answer like a former statesman (d'Argenson† to the Abbé Desfontaines‡). We will content ourselves with opposing to you the example of one of yours who, in Paris, changed from a God carrier to a water carrier.

---

* to each his own.

† Marc-Pierre de Voyer d'Argenson (1696-1764) Minister of War whose correspondence is widely celebrated.

‡ Pierre Desdontaines (1685-1745) Journalist and translator.

Apostille

We read at the antiquary's that "there were some Greek cities, like Argos, where women exercised the priesthood with authority." In the second century of the church neither the priesthood nor the episcopacy were forbidden to women.

Ministers of all religions! Believe us, put your powers in the hands of women. They know enough to exercise them as well as you. Vaporous and dissimulated, credulous and doubting nothing, friends of the marvelous and of festivals, their vocation is not in doubt. Everyone will gain in this. In any event, if religion were banished from the world it would take refuge in the heads of women.[18] The church has had deaconesses, abbesses, canonesses: let there no longer be anything but priestesses! At least they would be more honest than you. More indulgent, they would make the gentle morality they will preach us more loved. Pass them the censer: it is better that it be in their hands than in yours, and proprieties will be better observed. You complain at seeing your temples abandoned and deserted: let the divine offices be celebrated by young maidens! For the greater glory of the religion, leave the sanctuary, have yourself replaced there by women. Men will come to the feet of the altars and the confessionals when there will only be confessoresses and priestesses.

Notes by Maréchal

1. Honorable readers, please forgive the expression, but only this word can express the idea.

2. It's an important question, knowing whether God is in the bread or around or under it. See the History of the *Impanateurs*.

3. *Mundus vult decipi, ergo decipiatur*—The world loves to be deceived.

4. Short, well-written novels ("Atala," for example, by Auguste Chateaubriand), will not save the mass and the scapular from ridicule. It is deplorable that, in the 19th century, a young man waste his talent rendering lovable the mass and the scapular, priests and Jesuits.

5. The author of "Atala" and that of the "White Swan" promise, the first a "Poetic Dictionary of the Bible for the Use of Artists," two heavy in

octavo volumes, the second three heavy in octavo volumes touching on the "Poetics of Christianity."

6. Certain people say: "I would be quite fond of a police without spies, a religion without priests." These good people are demanding the impossible. A God without priests can no more exist than priests without God.

7. Catechizing young girls is doubtless a lesser evil than slaughtering them, as was done among the ancients (see the sacrifices of Jephtha and Iphigenia.) nevertheless, the one leads to the other.

8. See "Decree regulating a religion without priests," in octavo, Paris, 1790.

9. "Religion can no longer be fanatical," ("*Nouveau Mercure de France*," in octavo) a journalist who should only ever have written poetry said. But it doesn't follow from this, as this wit claims, that philosophy should become religious.

10. Even today the King of Portugal doesn't go hunting without his confessor's permission. See "*Voyage du M. Duchâtel en Portugal*," p 91, vol. I, in octavo, year IX (1801).

11. Mages, synonymous with sages.

12. This word is even more appropriate here in that those of both sexes who showed the most holy zeal for the Lord's mission were once noted for a conduct that was nothing less than profane.

13. In the Old Testament, which is (as everyone knows) the figure of the New, Jewish history on every page breaths the most pronounced *sans-culottisme*. The same goes for the Gospels.

14. Christianity also has its *tricoteuses*. Those who followed the French Revolution will remember this word and its meaning.

15. We read in the old *Encyclopédie française*: "No science requires more subtlety in spirit than theology."—Article on "The Bible," which is why it gives birth to so many volumes.

16. The overturning of natural ideas produced by religions is at least as considerable as the overturning of different parts of the earth caused by volcanic eruptions.

17. *Religio a religiando.*

18. Ancient mythologists gave the elephant as the symbol of religion. Modern iconologists are more fortunate in their imaginings: they represent religion under the parable of a veiled woman, or one blindfolded, carrying under the left arm the Old and New Testaments, and on the right index finger a lovely white dove. A smoking censer is at her feet. She is standing on a cornerstone.

Louis Auguste Blanqui
(1805-1881)

Just reading about the life and political activities of Louis Auguste Blanqui can be exhausting. Perhaps only Giuseppe Garibaldi among nineteenth century revolutionaries—who fought in Italy, France, Argentina, and Uruguay—as totally incarnated the revolution as the man known as *l'Enfermé*—the incarcerated. Blanqui paid the price for his beliefs and activities in full; he spent 37 of his almost 76 years imprisoned, and when not imprisoned he was as often as not on the run from the authorities. In 1872 a former fellow prisoner of Blanqui's wrote: "It appears he was born a prisoner. He knew fifteen minutes of freedom every ten or fifteen years. He commits one act, speaks one word, and then he's back in prison."

Blanqui came by his politics honestly. He was born but 16 years after the great Revolution, and his father, a member of the Convention, voted for the death of Louis XVI. Blanqui *père* eventually drew back from his early radicalism, but for Blanqui himself, compromise was not possible.

By the time he was 17 and a student in Paris, Blanqui was an active revolutionary with a special fondness for small secret societies that carried out the struggle on the people's behalf. The list of these societies is dizzying: the Carbonari, the La Fayette Conspiracy, the Friends of the People, the Schools Committee, the Society of the Families, the Society of the Seasons, the Central Republican Society, and so on. However numerous and short-lived these groups were, they were not mere fantastic creations.

Some of Blanqui's undertakings were however, quixotic: at 22 he suffered his first wound in revolutionary action, and a year later, in 1828, in an attempt to participate in the Greek struggle for independence Blanqui and a friend found themselves stranded in their provincial hometown because they lacked passports.

The overthrow of the Bourbons and their replacement by the July Monarchy did nothing to dampen his revolutionary ardor, and he plotted tirelessly to restore the Republic on a social basis. In the long bitter years between the Revolutions of 1830 and 1848 Blanqui continued his fight, including being part of a group that took possession of Paris's Palais de Justice in May 1839. Each failure brought trials and imprisonment, but he fought on. After a seven-year stretch in prison in the years before the Revolution of 1848, he emerged even more convinced he was right and even more wary of his more moderate comrades.

Blanqui was unable to participate directly in the Paris Commune, for after having led two failed revolts in 1870 within the span of eight months, he then led another group that occupied Paris's Hôtel de Ville, which resulted in his receiving a death sentence. This last adventure kept him in prison and away from an active role in the formation of the Paris Commune, an event he had spent his entire life fighting for. A Blanquist party had come into existence, and though unable to serve in it, he was still elected to the Commune by several of Paris's arrondissements.

In the end, perhaps the most moving element of Blanqui's life was his eternal optimism, his belief in the ineluctable nature of the final victory. His optimism, his faith in his star, his ability to take his wishes for reality were all limitless. In 1866, while head of a *groupuscule*, he wrote a proclamation declaring Napoleon III and his ministers to be public enemies and threatening with death any policeman who appeared in uniform on the streets.

Despite the existence of a party bearing his name, Blanqui himself was not interested in leaving the chance for victory in the hands of the masses or the ballot box. In 1830, in the reception procedure of the Society of the Seasons, one of Blanqui's many secret societies, this was clearly stated: "Can the people govern themselves immediately after the revolution? The social state being gangrened, heroic remedies are required to pass to a healthy state; for a certain period of time the people will need a revolutionary power." Behind the almost comical nature of his many organizations, with their mysterious rites and strange vows, a trait typical of working-class organizations on both sides of the Atlantic during this period, was the idea that only an armed nucleus could take power. As he said in his London Toast of 1851: "who has iron, has food." Will, determination, and sacrifice were what the revolution required. The revolutionaries themselves,

Blanqui wrote, are "superior to the adversary in devotion, they are much more still in intelligence. They have the upper hand over him morally and even physically; in conviction, strength, fertility of resources. No troop in the world is the equal of these elite men." Had there been a hundred people in France who had these qualities in the same measure as Blanqui, French history might have been radically different.

Reception Procedure of the Society of the Seasons (1830)*

The newly-elected member is brought in blindfolded.

The President to the presenter: What is the name of the new brother you bring us ...

To the newly-elected member: Citizen (...) What is your age? Your profession? Your birthplace? Your home? How do you earn a living?

Have you thought through the step you take at this time, the engagement to which you commit yourself? Do you know that traitors are struck down dead?

Swear, Citizen, to reveal to no one what happens in this place.

The President poses the following questions.

- 1 What do you think of royalty and of kings?

   That they are as dangerous to humanity as the tiger is to other animals.

- 2 Who are aristocrats now?

   Aristocracy by birth was abolished in July 1830. It was replaced by the aristocracy of money, which is every bit as voracious as the preceding one.

- 3 Should we be satisfied with overthrowing royalty?

   All aristocrats must be overthrown, all privileges must be abolished.

- 4 What must we put in its place?

   The government of the people by the people, which is to say, the republic.

- 5 Those who have rights without fulfilling obligations, as is the case with aristocrats, are they part of the people?

   They ought not to be part of the people; they are to the social what a cancer is to the human body: the first condition for the re-

---

* From Auguste Blanqui, *Textes choisis, avec préface et notes par V.P. Volguine*, Editions Sociales, Paris, 1971.

turn of the social body to a just state is the wiping out of aristocracy.

- 6 Can the people govern themselves immediately after the revolution?

The social state being gangrened, heroic remedies are required to pass to a healthy state; for a certain period of time the people will need a revolutionary power.

- 7 In summary, what are your principles?

Royalty and all aristocracies must be exterminated; to substitute in their place the republic, which is to say the government of equality; but, to pass to this government, to employ a revolutionary power, which sets the people to exercise its rights.

Citizen, the principles which you have just expressed are the only correct ones, the only ones that can make humanity march towards the goal which is fixed for it; but their realization isn't easy. Our enemies are numerous and powerful; they have at their disposal all of society's forces: we republicans have only our courage and our conviction. You still have time. Think of all the dangers to which you expose yourself in entering our ranks: the sacrifice of fortune, the loss of freedom, perhaps death. Are you determined to brave these dangers?

Your response is the proof of your energy. Rise, Citizen, and take the following vow:

"In the name of the republic, I swear eternal hatred to all kings, all aristocrats, to all of humanity's oppressors. I swear absolute devotion to the people, fraternity to all men, aside from aristocrats; I swear to punish traitors; I promise to give my life, to go to the gallows, if this sacrifice is necessary to bring about the reign of popular sovereignty and equality."

The President puts a dagger in his hand.

"Let me be punished with the death of traitors, let me be stabbed with this dagger if I violate this vow. I agree to be treated as a traitor if I reveal the least thing to anyone at all, even my closest relative, if he is not member of the association."

The President: Citizen, be seated; the Society receives your vow; you are now part of the association; work with others to free the people.

Citizen, your name will not be pronounced among us; here is your registration number in the workshop. You must procure arms, ammunition. The Committee that the Society directs will remain unknown until the moment we take up arms. Citizen, one of your obligations is to spread the principles of the association. If you know any devoted and discreet citizens, you should present them to us.

The newly elected member is returned to the light.

Speech before the Society of the Friends of the People (1832)[*]

The fact shouldn't be hidden that there is a war to the death between the classes that compose the nation. This truth recognized, the truly national party, the ones patriots should rally to, is the party of the masses.

Until now there have been three interests in France: those of the so-called upper classes, those of the middle or bourgeois class, and finally those of the people. I place the people last because they were always the last and because I count on an imminent application of the Gospel maxim that "the last shall be first."

In 1814 and 1815 the bourgeois class, tired of Napoleon not because of despotism (it cares little for liberty, which in its eyes it isn't worth a pound of good cinnamon or a nice fat bill), but because the blood of the people being exhausted, the war was beginning to take its children from it and, even more, because it harmed its tranquility and hindered commerce. The bourgeois class then received the foreign soldiers as liberators and the Bourbons as God's envoys. They were the ones who opened the gates of Paris, who treated the soldiers of Waterloo as brigands, and who encouraged the bloody reaction of 1815.

Louis XVIII rewarded them with the Charter. This Charter established the upper classes as an aristocracy and gave the bourgeois the Chamber of Deputies, called the democratic chamber. With this the émigrés, the nobles, the big landowners who were fanatical partisans of the Bourbons, and the middle class who accepted them from self-interest found themselves in equal part the masters of the government. The people were pushed to the side. Bereft of leaders, demoralized by foreign invasion, having lost faith in liberty, they remained silent and submitted to the yoke while remaining on their guard. You know the consistent support the bourgeois class gave the Restoration until 1825. It loaned its hand to the massacres of 1815 and 1816, to the gallows of Borie and Berton, to the war in Spain, to the arrival of Villèle and the changes in the electoral law; until 1827 it regularly sent majorities submissive to those in power.

---

[*] From *Louis Auguste Blanqui, écrits sur la révolution, Oeuvres completes, Tome 1*. Editions Galilée, Paris, 1977.

In the period 1825-1827, Charles X, seeing that he was succeeding at everything and believing himself strong enough without the bourgeoisie, wanted to proceed to their exclusion, as was done with the people in 1815. He took a daring step towards the *Ancien Régime* and declared war on the middle class by proclaiming the exclusive dominance of the nobility and clergy under the banner of Jesuitism. The bourgeoisie is by essence anti-spiritual: it detests churches, and believes only in double entry bookkeeping. The priests irritated them: they had consented to share with the upper classes in oppressing the people, but seeing its turn arrive as well, full of resentment and jealousy against the high aristocracy, it rallied to that minority of the middle class that had combated the Bourbons since 1815 and that it had sacrificed up till then. It was then that a war of newspapers and elections began, carried out with so much steadfastness and fury. But the bourgeoisie fought in the name of the Charter and nothing but the Charter, and in fact the Charter assured their power. Faithfully executed, it gave them supremacy within the state. Legality was invented to represent this interest of the bourgeoisie's and to serve as its banner. The legal order became a kind of divinity before which constitutional opponents burned their daily incense. This struggle was carried out from 1825-1830, ever more favorably to the bourgeois, who rapidly gained ground and who, masters of the Chamber of Deputies, soon threatened the government with complete defeat.

What were the people doing in the midst of this conflict? Nothing. They remained a silent spectator to the quarrel, and everyone knows that its interests didn't count in the debates of its oppressors. To be sure, the bourgeois cared little about them and their cause, which were looked on as having been lost fifteen years before. You recall that the papers most devoted to the constitutionals regularly repeated that the people had submitted their resignation to their representatives, the only organs of France. It wasn't only the government that considered the masses as indifferent to the debate: the middle classes detested them perhaps even more, and they surely counted on being the only ones to pluck the fruits of victory. That victory didn't go further than the Charter. Charles X and the Charter with an all-powerful bourgeoisie, this was the goal of the constitutionals. Yes, but the people understood the question differently. The people mocked the Charter in execrating the Bourbons. Seeing its masters argue among themselves it spied out in silence the moment to leap onto the battlefield and bring the parties into agreement.

When the classes arrived at such a point that the government no longer had any resource than coups d'état, and that that threat of a coup d'état was suspended over the heads of the bourgeois, then they were gripped with fear! Who doesn't recall the regrets and terrors of the 221 after the order of dissolution that answered their famous address? Charles X spoke of his firm resolve to resort to force, and the bourgeoisie went pale. Already most of them loudly disapproved the 221 for having allowed themselves to be carried away by revolutionary excesses. The most daring placed their hope in the refusal of a tax that would have been paid and in the support of tribunals, almost all of which would gladly have filled the office of summary political courts. If the royalists demonstrated so much confidence and resolution, if their adversaries showed so much fear and uncertainty, it's that both regarded the people as having resigned themselves and expected to find them neutral in the battle. And so on one hand the government depended on the nobility, the clergy and the big landowners, and on the other was the middle class which, after five years of warming up in a war of words, was ready to come to blows with the people, silent for fifteen years and believed resigned.

It was in these conditions that the combat was engaged. The ordinances were issued and the police smashed the newspaper presses. I won't speak of our joy, citizens, we who are shaking off the yoke and who are finally witnessing the reawakening of the popular lion that had slept for so long. July 26 was the most beautiful day of our life*. But the bourgeois! Never has a political crisis offered a spectacle of such frightful, such profound consternation. Pale, frantic, they heard the first shots as the first discharge of a picket that was to shoot them down one by one. You all remember the conduct of the deputies on Monday, Tuesday and Wednesday. They used what presence of mind and faculties fear left to them to ward off, to halt the combat. Preoccupied with their own cowardice, they were unready to foresee popular victory and were already trembling beneath Charles X's knife. But on Thursday the scene changed. The people were the victors. And then another terror seized them, more profound and oppressive. Farewell dreams of the Charter, of legality, of constitutional royalty, of the exclusive domination of the bourgeoisie! The powerless ghost that was Charles X faded away. In the midst of the debris, of flames and smoke, the people appeared standing on the corpse of royalty, standing like a giant, the tricolor flag in hand. They were struck

---

* First of the so-called Three Glorious Days of the Revolution of 1830.

with stupor. It was then that they regretted that the National Guard didn't exist on July 26, that they condemned the lack of foresight and folly of Charles X, who had smashed the anchor of his own salvation. It is too late for regrets! You can see that during these days, when the people were so grand, the bourgeois were tied up between two fears, that of Charles X in the first place, and then that of the workers. A noble and glorious role for these proud warriors who float their high plumes at parades on the Champ de Mars.

But citizens: how is it that so sudden and fearsome a revelation of the force of the masses remained sterile? By what fatality did that revolution made by the people alone, and which should have marked the end of the exclusive reign of the bourgeoisie along with the success of popular interests and power, have as its sole result the establishing of the despotism of the middle class, thus aggravating the poverty of the workers and peasants, and sinking France a bit further into the mud? Alas, the people, like the other old man, knew how to win, but not how to profit from its victory. The fault is not all their own. The combat was so brief that its natural leaders, those who would have led the way to victory, didn't have the time to distinguish themselves from the crowd. They necessarily rallied to the leaders who had figured at the head of the bourgeoisie in the parliamentary struggle against the Bourbons. What is more, they were grateful to the middle classes for their little five year war against their enemies, and you have seen what benevolence, I would almost say what feeling of deference, they showed towards those men in suits they met on the streets after the battle. That cry of "Long Live the Charter!" which was so perfidiously abused was nothing but a rallying cry for proving its alliance with these men. Did they already feel, as if by instinct, that they had just played a nasty trick on the bourgeoisie and, in the generosity of the victor, did they want to make advances and offer peace and friendship to their future adversaries? Whatever the case, the masses hadn't formally expressed any positive political will. What acted on them, what had thrown them into the public square, was the hatred of the Bourbons, the firm resolution to overthrow them. There was both Bonapartism and the Republic in the wishes they formed for the government that was to issue from the barricades.

You know how the people, in its confidence in the chiefs they'd accepted, and which their ancient hostility to Charles X made them consider equally implacable enemies of the entire Bourbon family, retired from the public squares once the battle was finished. At that point the bourgeois came out of their cellars and threw themselves in their thousands onto the streets, which the departure of the combatants had left free. There is no one who doesn't remember with what amazing suddenness the scene changed on the streets of Paris, like at a theatre; the way suits replaced work jackets, in the blink of an eye, as if a fairy wand had made some disappear and others spring up. This was because the bullets were no longer flying. It was no longer a question of receiving blows, but of gathering up loot. To each his role: the men of the workshops disappeared, the men who work behind the counter appeared.

It was then that the wretches who had been given victory as a deposit, after having attempted to place Charles X back on his throne, feeling that their lives were at risk and lacking the courage to brave the dangers of such a treason, stopped at a less perilous treason. A Bourbon was proclaimed king. Under the direction of agents paid with royal gold 10-15,000 bourgeois put in place in the courts of the new palace saluted the master for a few days with their cries of enthusiasm. As for the people, since they have no dividends and lack the means to stroll beneath the windows of palaces, they were in the workshops. But they weren't accomplices in this unworthy usurpation that would not have occurred had they found men capable of guiding their angry and vengeful blows. Betrayed by their chiefs, abandoned by the schools, they remained silent and on their guard, as in 1815. I'll cite you as an example a coachman who drove me last Saturday. After having told me of the part he played in the combats of the three days he added: "On the way to the Chamber I encountered the procession of deputies headed towards the Hôtel de Ville. I followed them to see what they'd do. Then I saw Lafayette appear on the balcony with Louis-Philippe and say, 'Frenchmen, here is your King.' Sir, when I heard that word it was as if I'd been stabbed. I was blinded; I went on my way." That man is the people.

This then was the situation of the parties immediately following the July Revolution. The upper class was crushed; the middle class, which hid itself during the combat and disapproved it, demonstrating as much cleverness as it did prudence, snatched the fruits of victory that were won despite them. The people, who did everything, remained a zero, as before. But a terrible act has been accomplished: like a thunderbolt, the people had suddenly entered a political scene that they took by assault, and though more or less chased from it at the same instant, they nevertheless acted with mastery. They withdrew their resignation. It will henceforth be between them and the middle class that bitter war will be carried out. It's no longer between the upper classes and the bourgeoisie: in order to better resist, the latter will need to call their former enemies to their assistance. In fact, for a long time the bourgeoisie has not hidden its hatred of the people.

If we examine the conduct of the government there is in its policies, the same march, the same progression of hatred and violence as among the bourgeoisie, whose interests and passions it represents.

When the bricks of the barricades were still piled up in the streets all that was spoken of was the program of the Hôtel de Ville, of republican institutions; handshakes, popular proclamations, the grand words of liberty, independence, and national glory were bandied about. And then, when those in power had at their disposal an organized military force, tensions mounted; all the laws, all the ordinances of the Restoration were invoked and applied. Later, the prosecution of the press, the persecutions of the men of July, the people beaten and tracked down with bayonet blows, taxes increased and collected with a rigor unheard of under the Restoration: this entire apparatus of tyranny revealed the government's hatreds and fears. But it felt that the people felt that same hatred for them, and not judging itself strong enough with the support of the bourgeoisie alone it sought to rally the upper classes to its cause in order that, established on this dual base, it would be in a state to more successfully resist the threatened invasion of the proletarians. It is to this maneuver to conciliate the aristocracy that we should attach the system it has developed in the past eighteen months. This is the key to its policy. And this upper class is almost entirely composed of royalists. In order to bring them along it was thus necessary to as nearly as possible approach the Restoration, to follow its meanderings, to continue them. And this is what was done. Nothing was changed except the name of the king. The people's sovereignty was denied, trod upon. The court wore mourning attire for foreign princes, legitimacy was copied in all regards. Royalists were maintained in their places, and all those who had to leave in the first onrush of the revolution found more lucrative positions; the magistracy was preserved in such a way that the whole administration is in the hands of men devoted to the Bourbons. What is more, a part of this upper class, the most rotten part of it, that which above all wants gold and pleasures, deigned to promise to protect public order. But the other part, the one I'll call the least rotted in order not to say "honorable," that which has self-respect and faith in its opinions, which worships its flag and its old memories, these people reject with disgust the caresses of the middle way. They have behind them the largest part of the populations of the south and the west, all those peasants of the Vendée and Brittany who, having remained foreign to the movement of civilization, preserve an ardent faith in Catholicism, and with reason confound in their devotions Catholicism with legitimacy, for these are two things that have lived and must die together.

Do you think that these simple and believing men are open to the seductions of bankers? No, citizens! For the people, whether if in their ignorance they are enflamed with religious fanaticism or if, more enlightened, they allow themselves to be carried away by enthusiasm for liberty, the people are ever great and generous; they don't obey low monetary interests, rather the nobler passions of the soul, the aspirations of elevated morality. But however delicately and deferentially we might handle Brittany and the Vendée, they are still ready to rise at the cry of "God and King" and threaten the government with their Catholic and royal armies, which the first shock will smash. And that's not all: that faction of the upper classes that attached itself to the middle way will abandon it at the first moment. All they promised was to not work to overthrow them. As for devotion, you know it's possible to have it towards coupon clippers. Even more, I'd say that the greatest part of the bourgeoisie, who are pressing, gathering around the government from hatred of the people who they fear, from fright at war, which they have a horror of for they think it'll take their *écus* from them, these bourgeois barely care for the current order; they feel it to be powerless to protect them. Let the white flag [of the Royalists] come along that would guarantee them the oppression of the people and material security and they'd be ready to sacrifice their former political pretensions, for they bitterly regret having, through pride, sapped the power of the Bourbons and prepared their fall. They would abdicate their share of power to the hands of the aristocracy, willingly trading tranquility for servitude.

For the government of Louis-Philippe hardly reassures them. It can copy the Restoration all it wants, persecute patriots, set itself to erasing the stain of insurrection it is soiled with in the eyes of the adorers of public order. The memory of those three terrible days pursues them, dominates them. Eighteen months of successful war against the people were unable to counter-balance one sole popular victory. The battlefield is still theirs, and that already old victory is suspended over the heads of those in power like the sword of Damocles. All are looking to see if the thread is not soon going to break.

Citizens, two principles share France, that of legitimacy and that of popular sovereignty. The first is the ancient organization of the past. This is the framework society lived in for 1400 years, and that some want to preserve by instinct of self-preservation, and others because they fear that the framework won't be able to be promptly replaced and anarchy will follow its dissolution. The principle of popular sovereignty rallies all men of the future, the masses who, tired of being exploited, seek to smash the framework that suffocates them. There is no third flag, no middle term. The middle road is foolishness, a bastard government that wants to give itself airs of legitimacy that one can only laugh at. And so the royalists, who perfectly understand this situation, profit from the tact and indulgence of those in power who seek to bring them over to them so as to more actively work at their destruction. Their many newspapers demonstrate daily that the only possible order is legitimacy, that the middle road is powerless to constitute the country, that apart from legitimacy there is only revolution and once the first has been left behind, there is only the second.

What will then happen? The upper classes are waiting for the moment to raise the white flag. In the middle class the great majority, composed of those men who have no other homeland than their counter or their cash box, who would gladly become Russian, Prussian, or English to earn two *liards* on a piece of cloth or 1/4 % additional profit on discount, will without fail line themselves up behind the white flag. The very names of war and popular sovereignty make them tremble. The minority of that class, made up of intellectual professions and the small number of bourgeois who love the tricolor flag, the symbol of France's independence and freedom, will take the side of popular sovereignty.

What is more, the moment of disaster is rapidly approaching. You see that the Chamber of Peers, the magistracy, and most civil servants are openly conspiring for the return of Henri V, mocking the middle road. Legitimist gazettes no longer hide either the hopes or the projects of the counter-revolution. The royalists in Paris and the provinces are gathering their forces, organizing the Vendée and Brittany, and are proudly planting their banner. They are openly saying that the bourgeoisie is with them, and they aren't wrong. They are only waiting for a signal from foreign lands to raise the white banner, for in foreign countries they would be crushed by the people. They know this and we are counting on their being crushed, even with foreign support.

You can be assured, Citizens that they will not want for this support. This is the place to take a look at our relations with the European powers. It should be noted, in fact, that the external situation has developed in parallel with the political march of the government internally. External shame has grown in the exact same proportion as bourgeois despotism and the poverty of the masses internally.

At the first sound of our revolution the kings lost their heads, and the electric spark of insurrection having rapidly set Belgium, Poland, and Italy aflame, they sincerely thought their last day had arrived. How could it be imagined that the revolution didn't mean a revolution, that the expulsion of the Bourbons didn't mean the expulsion of the Bourbons, that the overturning of the Restoration would be a new edition of the Restoration? Not even the maddest of individuals could believe this. The cabinets saw in the three days the awakening of the French people and the beginning of its vengeance against the oppressors of nations. Nations judged in the same way as cabinets. But for our friends and enemies it was soon obvious that France had fallen into the hands of cowardly merchants who asked only to traffic in its independence and to sell its glory and liberty at the best price possible. While the kings awaited our declaration of war they received begging letters in which the French government implored pardon for its errors. The new master excused himself for having participated against his will in the revolt. He protested his innocence and his hatred for the revolution that he promised to tame, to punish, to wipe out if his good friends the kings promised him their protection, a small place in the Holy Alliance whose faithful servant he would become.

The foreign cabinets understood that the people weren't complicit in this treason and that it wouldn't delay in rendering justice. Their decision was taken: exterminate the insurrections that had broken out in Europe, and when everything returns to order unite their forces against France and come strangle in Paris itself both the revolution and the revolutionary agent. This plan was followed with an admirable consistency and skill. They couldn't go too fast, because the people of July, still full of their recent triumph, would have been too alert to a too direct threat and would have forced its government's hand. In any event, it was necessary to grant time to the middle way to stifle enthusiasm, discourage patriots and instill mistrust and discord in the nation. They also couldn't go too slowly, for the masses could have grown tired of the servitude and poverty that weighed on it internally and for a second time smash the yoke before the foreigners were in shape.

All of these shoals were avoided. The Austrians invaded Italy. The bourgeois who govern us said "Good!" and bowed before Austria. The Russians exterminated Poland. Our government cried "Very good!" and prostrated itself before Russia. During this time the London conference amused the onlookers with its protocols aimed at assuring the independence of Belgium, for a Restoration in Belgium would have opened France's eyes and it would have been in a position to defend its work. The kings are now taking a forward step. They don't want an independent Belgium: it's a Dutch restoration they want to impose on it. The three courts of the north, confronted with the massacre, refuse to ratify the famous treaty that cost the conference sixteen months of labor.

And now will the middle way respond with a declaration of war on this insolent aggression. War! Good God! The word makes the bourgeois turn pale. Listen to them! War means bankruptcy, war means the Republic! War can only be supported with the blood of the people; the bourgeoisie doesn't involve itself in this. Their interests, their passions have to be appealed to in the name of liberty, of the fatherland's independence. The country must be put back into their hands, which alone can save it. It would be a hundred times better to see the Russians in Paris than to unleash the passions of the multitude. At least the Russians are friends of order; they reestablished order in Warsaw. ... These are calculations and the language of the middle way.

The Royalists will keep themselves at the ready, and next spring the Russians, on crossing the border, will find their lodgings prepared for them as far as Paris. For you can be sure that when the time comes the bourgeoisie will not resolve to make war. Its terror will have been increased by all the fear that will be inspired in it by the anger of a people betrayed and sold out, and you'll see the merchants brandish the white rosette and receive the enemy as a liberator, for the Cossacks frighten them less than the mob in work jackets.

First issue of "Le Libérateur" (1834)[*]

Goal of the newspaper

Of all the exclusions that weigh on the citizen without a fortune, the most painful and the one most bitterly felt is that which prohibits him from publishing his thoughts. One can be consoled for not participating in the election of a deputy or a municipal functionary. But we are profoundly wounded by the evil designs of a legislation that restricts thought when that thought doesn't have the insolent pass handed out by wealth. Those men devoted to defending the principle of equality will never forgive the ministers whose popular names served as a cloak for that law of security deposits and franking that makes the press a slave to the opulent classes, for it is they who bear the responsibility for that irreparable fault. And when, carried away by the boiling up of indignation against triumphant iniquity they raise their voices, an iron glove crushes the words on their lips. They are forbidden to take in hand the interests of the oppressed: they don't have the right to that. It's a right that only belongs to the rich; one must be rich in order to better identify with the poor, and riches alone gives the strength to feel and express their sufferings.

This newspaper is a protest against force's insulting derision. A lone citizen, without money, without a *sou* put away, undertakes to brave the prohibition imposed by the aristocracy of the *ecu* against the poor man who dares to think. With his health destroyed, barely out of the prison where a verdict had him expiate the cries he raised up in favor of exploited workers, his hands still marked by the imprint of handcuffs, he today again takes up arms. And he will write, having ceaselessly before his eyes the unfortunate brothers that he left behind in those sad tombs. He is not one of those men who, in the midst of a society torn apart by passions, claims to feel no passion; who in order not to displease selfish dominators protects himself against all convictions as if they were evil things, and affects to maintain a cowardly impartiality between those who suffer and those who cause suffering. The only role appropriate for an honest man is that of loudly avowing his affections and his hatreds. One

---

[*] From *Oeuvres, texts rassemblés et presentés par Dominique de Luz*. Nancy, Presses Universitaires de Nancy, 1993.

should feel sorry for those who boast of the fact that they neither love nor hate anyone, for if they are telling the truth they have nothing in their breasts. And if they lie, what authority remains to their words?

Those of "*Le Libérateur*" will be frank, with neither reticence nor hesitations. On one hand it will make an effort to expose in simple, clear, and precise terms why the people are unhappy and how they can cease to be so. It will explain the nature of the relationships that exist today between the master and the worker, the social question that virtually on its own constitutes all of political economy, and about which professors say barely a word. And at the same time, addressing itself to men whose profound meditations turn them from the hustle and bustle of the moment in order to embrace from on high all of humanity in its past and its future, it will submit to them its critical views on the current organization, or rather, disorganization, as well as ideas on the principles that should preside over the re-composition of the social order.

Who Makes the Soup Should Eat It (1834)[*]

Wealth is born of intelligence and labor. But these two forces can only act with the aid of a passive element—the land, which they put to work by their combined efforts. It thus seems that this indispensable instrument should belong to all men. Such is not the case.

Individuals have taken over common land by ruse or violence, declaring themselves its owners; they have established by law that it will always be theirs, and that the right to property will become the foundation of the social constitution. Which is to say that it will come before and, if need be, absorb all human rights, even that to life, if it has the ill fortune to find itself in conflict with the privilege of a small number.

The right to property has extended itself by logical deduction from the land to other instruments: the accumulated products of labor, designated by the generic name of capital. Since capital, sterile in and of itself can only be made fruitful through labor, and, on the other hand, since it is the primary matter worked on by social forces, the majority, excluded from its possession, finds itself condemned to forced labor, to the profit of the possessing minority. Neither the instruments nor the fruits of labor belong to the workers, but to the idlers. The gluttonous branches absorb the tree's sap, to the detriment of the fertile boughs. The hornets devour the honey created by the bees.

Such is our social order, founded on conquest, which has divided populations into victors and vanquished. The logical consequence of such an organization is slavery. And we didn't have to wait long for its arrival. In fact, with land acquiring value only from cultivation, the privileged have drawn the conclusion that, thanks to the right to own land, they also have that to own the human livestock that makes it fertile. In the first place they have considered it as a complement to their domain but, in the final analysis, they see it as personal property, independent of the land.

Nevertheless, the principle of equality, engraved in the depths of the heart, and which conspires, with the centuries, to destroy the exploitation of man by man in all its forms, delivered the first blow to the sacrilegious right to property by smashing slavery. Privilege was forced to reduce itself

---

[*] From *Auguste Blanqui, Textes Choisis, avec préface et notes par V.P. Volguine*, Editions Sociales, Paris, 1971.

to the possession of men not as movable property, but as real estate auxiliary to, and inseparable from, real estate in the form of land.

In the 16th century a deadly rebirth of oppression brought about the enslavement of blacks; and even today the inhabitants of a land reputed to be French own men in the same way as they do clothing and horses. There is, in fact, less of a difference than meets the eye between our state and that of the colonies. After eighteen centuries of war between privilege and equality the homeland, theatre and principal champion of this struggle, could not put up with slavery in its naked brutality. But the fact exists in name, and the right to property, while more hypocritical in Paris than in Martinique, is neither less inflexible nor less oppressive.

In fact, servitude does not consist solely in being a man's thing, or a lord's serf. He is not free who, deprived of the instruments of labor, remains at the mercy of the privileged that are his owners. This is the state that feeds revolt. In order to exorcise this peril they try to reconcile Cain with Abel. From the necessity of capital as an instrument of labor they go on to conclude with the community of interests, and then to that of solidarity between the capitalist and the worker. How many artistically embroidered phrases there are on this canvas! The lamb is shorn for his own health. It owes thanks. Our Aesculapiuses know how to sugar-coat the pill.

There are still some who are fooled by these homilies, but they are few. Each day the light shines brighter on this so-called association of the parasite and its victim. But the facts are eloquent; they prove the duel, the duel to the death, between revenue and salary. Who will succumb? It's a question of justice and good sense. Let's examine the situation.

There is no society without labor! What's more, there exist no idlers who do not have need of workers. But what need do workers have of idlers? Is capital only productive in the workers' hands on condition that it not belong to them? I imagine the proletariat, deserting *en masse*, taking its tools and its labor to some distant land. Would it by chance die due to the absence of its masters? Can the new society only come about by creating lords of the land and capital, in handing over to a caste of idlers the ownership of all the instruments of labor? Is there no other social mechanism possible but this division of owners and the salaried?

On the other hand, how curious it would be to see the expression on the faces of our proud lords abandoned by their slaves. What would be done with their palaces, their workshops, their deserted fields? Would they die of hunger in the midst of their riches, or would they put on work clothes, take up the pick and, in their turn, humbly sweat on some plot of land? How much would all of them cultivate?

But a people of 32 million souls doesn't retire to Mount Aventine. Let us then take the opposite and more realizable hypothesis. One fine day the idlers evacuate the soil of France, which remains in the workers' hands. A day of happiness and triumph! What an immense relief for so many breasts, relieved of the weight that crushes them! How freely this multitude breathes. Citizens – sing in chorus the song of deliverance!

Axiom: the nation is impoverished by the death of a worker; it is enriched by that of an idler. The death of a wealthy man is a benefit.

Yes! The right of property is in decline. Generous spirits prophesy and call for its fall. The Essenian principle of reality has slowly sapped it over the course of eighteen centuries through the successive abolition of the various servitudes which served as the basis for its power. It will disappear one day, along with the last privileges that serve as its refuge and lair. The past and the present guarantee us this resolution. For humanity is never stationary. It either advances or goes back. Its progressive march led it to equality. Its backward march climbs by privilege's steps to personal slavery, the final word in the right of property. To be sure, before returning there, European civilization would have perished. But through what catastrophe? A Russian invasion? To the contrary, it is the north that will itself be invaded by the principle of equality that the French bring in the conquest of nations. The future is not in doubt.

Let us immediately say that equality doesn't consist in the partitioning of land. The splitting up of land will really change nothing concerning the right of property. With wealth growing from the ownership of the instruments of labor, rather than through labor itself, if the spirit of exploitation is left standing it would soon know, through the reconstruction of large fortunes, how to restore social inequality.

Association alone, in place of private property, will serve as the basis for the reign of justice through equality. This is the foundation of the growing ardor of men of the future to make clear and highlight the elements of association. We, too, will perhaps bring our contingent to the common task.

Appeal of the Committee of the Society of the Seasons—May 12, 1839*

To arms, Citizens!

The fatal hour has rung for the oppressors.

The cowardly tyrant of the Tuileries laughs at the hunger that tears at the guts of the people. But the measure of his crimes is full. They are finally going to receive their punishment.

Betrayed France, the blood of our murdered brothers cries out to you and demands vengeance. Let it be terrible, for it has been delayed too long. Let exploitation perish, and may equality triumphantly assume its seat on the intermingled debris of royalty and aristocracy.

The provisional government has chosen military chiefs for the guiding of the combat. These chiefs come from your ranks. Follow them! They will lead you to victory.

Their names are:

> Auguste Blanqui, Commander-in-Chief; Barbès, Martin-Bernard, Quignot, Meillard, Nétré, Divisional Commanders of the Republican Army.

Arise, People, and your enemies will disappear like dust before a hurricane! Strike, exterminate without pity the vile henchmen, tyranny's voluntary accomplices. But extend your hand to those soldiers who come from your midst and who will never turn their parricidal arms against you.

Forward! Vive la République!
The members of the Provisional Government:
Barbès, Voyer d'Argenson, Auguste Blanqui, Lamennais, Martin-Bernard, Dubosc, Laponeraye.
Paris, May 12, 1839

---

* From *Auguste Blanqui, Textes Choisis, avec préface et notes par V.P. Volguine*, Editions Sociales, Paris, 1971.

Address of the Central Republican Society to the Government—March 2, 1848[*]

We have the firm hope that the government issued from the barricades of 1848 will not, like its predecessor, want to put back in place, along with each paving stone, a law of repression. With this in mind, we offer our assistance to the Provisional Government in the realization of the (beautiful) motto: *Liberté, Egalité, Fraternité.*

We that demand that the government (immediately) decree as a result of the popular victory:

1. The complete and unlimited freedom of the press.
2. The absolute and irrevocable suppression of security deposits and franking and postal rights [for the press].
3. The complete freedom of circulation for works of the intellect through all possible means: through posters, peddlers, public criers, without any restrictions or hindrances, without any need for prior authorization.
4. The freedom of the printing industry and the suppression of all privileges represented by licenses, though with prior indemnification.
5. The holding blameless of printers for any writing whose author is known.
6. The suppression of art. 291 of the Penal Code, of the law of April 9 1834, and the formal abrogation of laws, ordinances, decrees, edicts or rules of any kind, dated previous to February 25, 1848, capable of limiting or inhibiting the absolute and inalienable right to association and gathering.
7. The removal from the standing and sitting magistracy of those from the three last reigns, and their provisional replacement by lawyers, advocates, notaries, etc.
8. The immediate armament and organization in National Guards of all workers not established in a profession and who receive a sal-

---

[*] From Louis Auguste Blanqui, *Ecrits sur la Révolution*, présenté et annoté par A. Munster. Editions Galilee, Paris, 1977.

ary, without any exception in the amount of two francs for each day of active service.
9. The abrogation of art. 415 and 416 of the Penal Code, as well as of all special laws against working-class coalitions.

The Central Republican Society (1848)*

To the Provisional Government

Citizens:

The counter-revolution has just bathed in the blood of the people. Judgment, immediate judgment of the assassins!

For the past two months the royalist bourgeoisie of Rouen has plotted in the shadows a St. Bartholomew's massacre of the workers. It had stocked up on cartridges. The authorities knew of this.

Calls for death had broken out here and there, the premonitory symptoms of the catastrophe. *We have to have done with these scoundrels!* Scoundrels who in February, after three days of resistance, forced the bourgeois guard to submit to the Republic.

Citizens of the Provisional Government, how is it that in two months the working class population of Rouen and the surrounding valleys were not organized into National Guard units?

How is it that only the aristocracy possessed organization and arms?

How is it that at the moment of the execution of its horrible plot it only met unarmed breasts?

How is it that the 28th Regiment of the line, this sinister hero of the faubourg de Vaise, was in Rouen?

How is it that the garrison obeyed the orders of generals who were declared enemies of the Republic, of a General Gerard, creature and henchman of Louis-Philippe?

They were thirsty for a bloody revenge, these hired killers of a fallen dynasty. They needed an April massacre as consolation for a second July. They didn't have to wait long.

April days barely two months after the revolution!

And nothing was missing from these new April scenes! Neither guns, nor bullets, nor destroyed houses, nor state of siege nor the ferocity of the soldiers, nor the insulting of the dead, nor the unanimous insults from the newspapers, these cowardly adorers or might. The rue Trans-

---

* From the original.

nonain* has been surpassed. Upon reading the wretched story of the exploits of these brigands we again find ourselves in the aftermath of the horrible days that once covered France in mourning and shame.

These are exactly the same executioners and the same victims! On one side frenzied bourgeois pushing to carnage imbecilic soldiers that they have filled with wine and hatred. On the other unfortunate workers defenselessly falling under the bullets and bayonets of the assassins.

And as a final sign of resemblance, here comes the royal court, Louis-Philippe's judges, falling like hyenas on the debris of the massacre and filling the prisons with 250 republicans. At the head of these inquisitors is Frank-Carré, the execrable *procureur-general* of the court of peers, this Laubardemont† who asked with rage for the heads of the insurgents of May 1839. The arrest warrants followed those patriots to Paris who fled the royalist proscription.

For it is a royalist terror that reigns in Rouen: do you not know this citizens of the Provisional Government? The bourgeois guard of Rouen furiously rejected the Republic in February. It is the Republic that it blasphemes and that it wants to overthrow.

All that was Republican yesterday has been put in irons. Your very own agents have been threatened with death, removed from office, arrested. The municipal magistrates Lemason and Durand have been dragged through the streets, bayonets at their chests, their clothing in rags. They are being held in secret by authority of the rebels. It is a royalist insurrection that has triumphed in the ancient capital of Normandy, and it is you, republican government, that supports these rebel assassins! Is this treason or is this cowardice? Are you weaklings or accomplices?

You know full well that there was no battle: it was a slaughter! And you let the slaughterers recount their feats of prowess! Is it that in your eyes, like in those of kings, the blood of the people is nothing but water, good for washing down the over-encumbered streets from time to time? If so, then erase from your buildings that detestable lie in three words that you have just inscribed on them: Liberty, Equality, Fraternity!

---

* Site of a massacre of republicans on April 15, 1834 by the forces of the July Monarchy

† After Jean de Laubardemont, Richelieu's agent in the pursuit of the possessed nuns of Loudun in 1633.

If your wives, if your daughters, those brilliant and frail creatures who promenade their idleness in gold and silk in sumptuous equipages, had been thrown at your feet, their breast opened by the fire of pitiless enemies, what cries of pain and vengeance you'd make heard to the ends of the earth!

So go, go see stretched out on the slabs of your hospitals, on cots in mansards the corpses of slaughtered women, their breasts perforated by bourgeois bullets; the very breast that bore and nourished the workers whose sweat fattens the bourgeois!

The women of the people are worth as much as yours, and their blood should not, cannot remain unavenged!

Justice, then, justice for the assassins!

We demand:

> 1. The dissolution and disarmament of the bourgeois guard of Rouen
>
> 2. The arrest and trial of the generals and officers of the bourgeois guard and the troops of the line who ordered and led the massacre
>
> 3. The arrest and trial of the so-called members of the court of appeals, henchmen named by Louis-Philippe who, acting in the name and for the account of the victorious royalist faction, imprisoned the legitimate magistrates of the city and filled the prisons with republicans
>
> 4. Sending far from Paris the troops of the line who at this very moment, at fratricidal banquets, the reactionaries are readying for a St. Bartholomew's massacre of Parisian workers.

For the Central Republican Society, the members of the Bureau:

L-Auguste Blanqui, chairman
C. Lacambre, DMO – vice-chair
Flotte, treasurer
Pierre Beraud, Loroue, secretaries, members of the Bureau
G. Robert
Lachambeaude
Crousse
Pujol
Javelot jeune
Brucker
Fomberteaux

Warning to the People: London Toast—February 25, 1851[*]

What reef menaces tomorrow's revolution?

The reef that broke that of yesterday: the deplorable popularity of bourgeois disguised as tribunes of the people.

Ledru-Rollin, Louis Blanc, Crémieux, Lamartine, Garnier-Pagé, Dupont de l'Eure, Flocon, Albert, Arago, Marrast!

A dismal list! Sinister names written in blood on the paving stones of democratic Europe.

The provisional government killed the Revolution. It is upon its head that the responsibility for all these disasters, for the blood of so many thousands of victims must fall.

Reaction is doing nothing but its job in slitting democracy's throat.

The crime is that of the traitors the trusting people accepted as guides, but who instead gave them reaction.

Miserable government! Despite screams and prayers, it decrees the 45 centime tax that causes the desperate countryside to rise up; it keeps in place the royalist headquarters, the royalist magistrates, the royalist laws. Treason!

It guns down the workers of Paris; April 15 it imprisons those of Limoges; it guns down those of Rouen on the 27th; it sets loose all its executioners; it deceives and tracks down all sincere republicans. Treason! Treason!

To it alone belongs the terrible burden of all of the calamities that have all but wiped out the Revolution.

---

[*] From Mimeographed UCI brochure, 1961. This toast was sent by Blanqui from Belle-Isle to London, in response to a request for a toast for the February 25, 1851 banquet celebrating the anniversary of the 1848 revolution. Engels told the story of the toast; "Barthélemy, calling himself a Blanquiste, convinced Blanqui to send a toast to the congress. Instead, he received a magnificent attack on the Provisional Government, Louis Blanc & Co, among others. Barthélemy, stunned, put the document aside, and it was decided not to publish it."

Oh, these are the real guilty ones, the guiltiest among the guilty; those the deceived people saw as its sword and shield; those it acclaimed with enthusiasm, the judges of its future.

What a misfortune it would be for us if, on the imminent day of the people's victory, the forgetful indulgence of the masses allows a single one of these men who forfeited their mandate to take power! That, for a second time, would be the end of the revolution.

Let the workers always have before their eyes this list of accursed names! And if even one should ever appear in a government that is a product of the insurrection, let them all cry out with one voice: treason!

Speeches, sermons, and programs would only be frauds and lies; the same jugglers will return to perform the same act, with the same bag of tricks; they would form the first link of a new, more furious chain of reaction!

Anathema on them, should they ever dare reappear!

Shame and pity on the imbecilic mass which would again fall into their net!

It's not enough that the February thieves [of 1830] be ejected for good from the Hôtel de Ville; we must be protected against new traitors.

That government would be treasonous which, raised upon the proletarian bulwark, doesn't instantly carry out:

1. The disarmament of the bourgeois guards,
2. The armament and organization of a national militia of all workers.

There are doubtless other indispensable measures, but they will grow naturally from this first act, which is the preliminary guarantee, the only pledge of security for the people.

There must remain not one rifle in the hands of the bourgeoisie. Without this, there is no salvation.

The diverse doctrines which today dispute among themselves for the sympathy of the masses can one day fulfill their promises of betterment and well-being, on condition they not abandon the prey for its shadow.

Arms and organization, these are the decisive elements of progress, *the* serious method for putting an end to misery.

Who has iron, has bread.

We prostrate ourselves before the bayonets; they sweep up the disarmed crowd. France bristling with workers in arms means the advent of socialism.

In the presence of armed workers obstacles, resistances, and impossibilities will all disappear.

But for those workers who allow themselves to be amused by ridiculous strolls in the street, by the planting of liberty trees, by the mellifluous phrases of lawyers, there will first be holy water, then insults, and, finally, the gun. And misery forever.

Let the people choose!

Manual for an Armed Insurrection (1866)[*]

I. Preliminary

This program is purely military and leaves entirely to the side the political and social question, which this isn't the place for: besides, it goes without saying that the revolution must effectively work against the tyranny of the capital, and reconstitute society on the basis of justice.

A Parisian insurrection which repeats the old mistakes no longer has any chance of success today.

In 1830, popular fervor alone was enough to bring down a power taken unaware and terrified by an armed insurrection, an extraordinary event, which had one chance in a thousand.

That worked once. The lesson was learnt by the government, which remained monarchical and counter-revolutionary, although it was the result of a revolution. They began to study street warfare, and the natural superiority of art and discipline over inexperience and confusion was soon re-established.

However, it will be said, in 1848 the people triumphed using the methods of 1830. So be it. But let us not have any illusions! The victory of February [1830] was nothing but a stroke of luck. If Louis-Philippe had seriously defended himself, supremacy would have remained with the uniforms.

The proof is the June days. It is here that one can see how disastrous were the tactics, or rather the absence of tactics of the insurrection. Never had they had such a favorable position: ten chances against one.

On one side, the Government in total anarchy, demoralized troops: on the other, all the workers were solid and almost certain of success. Why did they succumb? Owing to lack of organization. To account for their defeat, it is enough to analyze their strategy.

The uprising breaks out. At once, in the workers' districts, the barricades go up here and there, aimlessly, at a multitude of points.

---

[*] From Auguste Blanqui. *Instruction pour une prise d'armes. L'Éternité par les astres, hypothèse astronomique et autres textes*, Société encyclopédique française, Editions de la tête de feuilles, 1972.

Five, ten, twenty, thirty, fifty men, brought together by chance, the majority without weapons, they start to overturn carriages, dig up paving stones and pile them up to block the roads, sometimes in the middle of a street, more often at intersections. Many of these barriers would present hardly any obstacle to the cavalry.

Sometimes, after the crude beginnings of preparing their defenses, the builders leave to go in search of rifles and ammunition.

In June, one could count more than sixty barricades; about thirty or so alone carried the burdens of the battle. Of the others, nineteen or twenty did not fire a shot. From there, glorious bulletins made much noise about the removal of fifty barricades, where there was not a soul.

While some are tearing the paving stones from the streets, other small bands are disarming the *corps de garde* or seizing gunpowder and weapons from the armories. All this is done without coordination or direction, at the mercy of individual imagination.

Little by little, however, a certain number of barricades, higher, stronger, better built, are chosen by defenders, who concentrate there. It is not calculation, but chance which determines the site of these principal fortifications. Just a few, by a kind of military inspiration rather than design, occupy the large intersections.

During this first period of the insurrection, the troops, on their side, gather. The generals receive and study the police reports. They take good care not to let their detachments venture out without unquestionable data, for fear of failure which would demoralize the soldiers. As soon as they have determined the positions of the insurrectionists, they mass the regiments at various points which from that time on will constitute from the base of their operations.

Both armies are in position. Let us look at their maneuvers. Here will be laid bare the vice of popular tactics, the undoubted cause of the disaster.

Neither direction nor general command, not even coordination between the combatants. Each barricade has its particular group, more or less numerous, but always isolated. Whether it numbers ten or one hundred men, it does not maintain any communication with the other positions. Often there is not even a leader to direct the defense, and if there is, his influence is next to nil. The fighters do whatever comes into their head. They stay, they leave, they return, according to their good pleasure. In the evening, they go to sleep.

In consequence of these continual comings and goings, the number of citizens remaining at the barricades varies rapidly by a third, a half, sometimes by three quarters. Nobody can count on anybody. From this grows distrust of their capacity to succeed and thus, discouragement.

Nothing is known of what is happening elsewhere and they do not trouble themselves further. Rumors circulate, some evil, some rosy. They listen peaceably to the cannons and the gunfire, while drinking at the wine merchant's. As for sending relief to the positions under attack, there is not even the thought of it. "Let each defends his post, and all will be well", say the strongest. This singular reasoning is because the majority of the insurgents fight in their own district, a capital fault which has disastrous consequences, in particular the denunciation by their neighbors, after the defeat.

For with such a system, defeat is certain. It comes at the end in the person of two or three regiments which fall upon the barricade and crush their few remaining defenders. The whole battle is just the monotonous repetition of this invariable maneuver. While the insurrectionists smoke their pipes behind heaps of paving stones, the enemy successively concentrates all his forces against one point, then on to a second, a third, a fourth, and thereby exterminates the insurrection one bit at a time.

The popular fighters do not take care to counter this easy task. Each group awaits its turn philosophically and would not venture to run to the aid of a neighbor in danger. No! "He will defend his post; he cannot give up his post".

This is how one perishes through absurdity!

When, because of such grave faults the great Parisian revolt of 1848 was shattered like glass by the most pitiful of governments, what catastrophe should we not fear if we begin again with the same stupidity, before a savage militarism, which now has in its service the recent conquests of science and technology: railways, the electric telegraph, rifled cannon, the breech-loading rifles?

For example, something we should not count as one of the new advantages of the enemy is the strategic thoroughfares which now furrow the city in all the directions. They are feared, but wrongly. There is nothing about them to be worried about. Far from having created a danger for the insurrection, as people think, on the contrary they offer a mixture of disadvantages and advantages for the two parties. If the troops circulate with more ease along them, on the other hand they are also heavily exposed and in the open.

Such streets are unusable under gunfire. Moreover, balconies are miniature bastions, providing lines of fire on their flanks, which ordinary windows do not. Lastly, these long straight avenues deserve perfectly the name of boulevard that is given to them. They are indeed true boulevards, which constitute the natural front of a very great strength.

The weapon par excellence in street warfare is the rifle. The cannon makes more noise than effect. Artillery could have serious impact only by the use of incendiaries. But such an atrocity, employed systematically on a large scale, would soon turn against its authors and would be to their loss.

The grenade, which people have the bad habit of calling a bomb, is generally secondary, and subject besides to a mass of disadvantages. It consumes a lot of powder for little effect, is very dangerous to handle, has no range and can only be used from windows. Paving stones do almost as much harm but are not so expensive. The workers do not have money to waste.

For the interior of houses, the revolver and the bayonet, sword, saber and dagger. In a boarding house, a pike or eight-foot long halberd would triumph over the bayonet.

The army has only two great advantages over the people: the breech-loading rifle and organization. This last especially is immense, irresistible. Fortunately one can deprive him of this advantage, and in this case ascendancy passes to the side of the insurrection.

In civil disorders, with rare exceptions soldiers march only with loathing, by force and brandy. They would like to be elsewhere and more often look behind than ahead. But an iron hand retains them as slaves and victims of a pitiless discipline; without any affection for authority, they obey only fear and are lacking in any initiative. A detachment which is cut off is a lost detachment. The commanders are not unaware of this, and worry above all to maintain communication between all their forces. This need cancels out a portion of their manpower.

In the popular ranks, there is nothing like this. There one fights for an idea. There only volunteers are found, and what drives them is enthusiasm, not fear. Superior to the adversary in devotion, they are much more still in intelligence. They have the upper hand over him morally and even physically, by conviction, strength, fertility of resources, promptness of body and spirit, they have both the head and the heart. No troop in the world is the equal of these elite men.

So what do they lack in order to vanquish? They lack the unity and coherence which, by having them all contribute to the same goal, fosters all those qualities which isolation renders impotent. They lack organization. Without it, they haven't got a chance. Organization is victory; dispersion is death.

June 1848 put this truth beyond question. What would be the case today? With the old methods, the entire people would succumb should the troops decide to hold out, and they will hold out, so long as they see before them only irregular forces, without direction. On the other hand, the very sight of a Parisian army in good order operating according to tactical regulations would strike the soldiers dumb and make them abandon their resistance.

A military organization, especially when it has to be improvised on the battlefield, is no small business for our party. It presupposes a commander-in-chief and, up to a certain point, the usual series of officers of all ranks. Where to find this personnel? Revolutionary and socialist middle-class men are rare and the few that there are fight only the war of the pen. These gentlemen imagine they can turn the world upside down with their books and their newspapers, and for sixteen years they have scribbled as far as the eye can see, without being tired out by their difficulties; with an equine patience, they suffer the bit, the saddle and the riding crop, and never a kick! Damn that! Return the blows? That's for louts.

These heroes of the inkstand profess the same scorn for the sword as officers for their slices of bread and butter. They do not seem to suspect that force is the only guarantee of freedom; that people are slaves wherever the citizens are ignorant of the art of soldiery and surrender the privilege to a caste or a corporate body.

In the republics of antiquity, among the Greeks and Romans, everyone knew and practiced the art of war. The professional soldier was an unknown species. Cicero was a general, Caesar a lawyer. By taking off the toga and donning the uniform, they would begin as colonel or captain and would acquit themselves ably. As long as it is not the same in France, we will remain civilians fit to be cut down at the mercy of the officer caste.

Thousands of the educated young, working-class and bourgeois tremble under a detested yoke. To break it, do they think of taking up the sword? No! The pen, always the pen, only the pen. Why the one and not the other, as the duty of a republican requires? In times of tyranny, to write is fine, but to fight is better, when the enslaved pen remains powerless. Well then, no! They publish a pamphlet, then go into prison, but they do not think of opening a manual of military tactics, to learn there in twenty-four hours the trade which constitutes all the power of our oppressors, and which would put in our hands our revenge and their punishment.

But what is the good of these complaints? It is the stupid practice of our time to deplore something instead of doing something about it. Jeremiads are the fashion. Jeremiah poses in all possible attitudes, he cries, whips, he dogmatizes, he dominates, he thunders, the plague of all plagues. Let us leave these elegizers, these grave-diggers of freedom! The duty of a revolutionist is the fight, the fight come what may, the fight until death.

Do the cadres lack for the forming of an army? We must improvise them on the ground, even in the course of action. The people of Paris will provide all the elements, former soldiers, ex-national guards. Their scarcity will oblige us to reduce to a minimum the number of officers and NCOs. But no matter. The zeal, the ardor, the intelligence of the volunteers, will make up for this deficit.

The essential thing is to organize. No more of these tumultuous risings, with ten thousand isolated heads, acting at random, in disorder, without any overall design, each in their local area and acting according to their own whim! No more of these ill-conceived and badly made barricades, which waste time, encumber the streets, and block circulation, as necessary to one party as the other. As much as the troops, the Republican must have freedom of his movements.

No useless racing about, hurly-burly, clamoring! Every minute and every step is equally precious. Above all, do not hole up in our own district as the insurrectionists have never failed to do, to their great harm. This mania, after having caused the defeat, facilitates proscriptions. We must cure ourselves of this under penalty of catastrophe.

Proclamation to Parisians (1866)[*]

Parisians:

Sixteen years of gags! Sixteen years of outrages! France scoffed at, pillaged, trampled upon! Wasn't that enough? No! Now hunger tears at the guts of the people!

Bonaparte promised glory and prosperity. Prosperity! Yes, he alone devoured 400 million francs, 25 million a year, 70,000 francs a day. He gorged with gold his Mamelukes, speculators, camp followers, priests. All he left to you to satisfy your hunger was the rubble of demolitions.

Glory! We know it: Mexico, Mentana. And that's only a beginning. From here on out all soldiers between 20 and 30 are soldiers ... soldiers of the Pope.

They'll have the honor of dying for the Jesuits, and Father Hyacinthe promises to hear their confessions on the battlefield.

To those who escape that glory, they'll distribute soup at the doors of churches and barracks.

No more workshops! No more marriages! All of that is revolutionary. Nothing but palaces and prisons, convents and whorehouses!

To arms, Parisians! Enough is enough! You received freedom from your fathers; you will not leave servitude to your sons.

The oppressors have filled the cup to the brim. To arms! Let punishment fall like lightning on their outrages. The hour of the great revolution of the people has sounded! Let us march!

---

[*] From Auguste Blanqui. *Instruction pour une prise d'armes. L'Eternité par les astres, hypothèse astronomique et autres textes*, Société encyclopédique française, Editions de la tête de feuilles, 1972.

Proclamation of February 20, 1866*

Given the declaration by the Minister of War, dated [blank] December 1851, signed Leroy and Saint-Arnaud, which states:

"All individuals taken arms in hand will be executed."

Given that following the criminal attack of December 2, 1851† those prisoners who were defenders of the constitution were put to death during and after combat;

That in diverse places in the capitol a crowd of citizens, inoffensive and without arms, innocent bystanders, were killed at the hands of the Praetorian guards;

That on the boulevard, a mass of peaceful spectators, men, women and children were suddenly and without provocation massacred by Bonaparte's soldiery;

That this same soldiery slaughtered, in their homes, without distinction of either age or sex, the residents of several houses;

That in the departments of the Hérault, Ain and the Nièvre, the defenders of the constitution were not gunned down, but guillotined by sentence of the Councils of War, well after the end of the fight;

Given that in the presence of these crimes the magnanimity which the people has shown over the last forty years during civil wars would now be both a crime and an act of suicide.

The commander-in-chief of the Republican army declares:

> Article 1 – Bonaparte, his ministers, the legislature and the senate are declared public enemies;
>
> Article 2 – All government functionaries are suspended from their duties. All violators will be executed;
>
> Article 3 – All police officers and agents are to remain at home. Those who appear on the streets, in uniform or otherwise, will be executed;

---

* From Auguste Blanqui. *L'Eternité par les astres, hypothèse astronomique et autres textes*, Société encyclopédique française, Editions de la tête de feuilles, 1972.

† Date of Louis Bonaparte's coup d'état.

Article 4 – Those officers who are members of a body that fired on the people will be executed;

Article 5 – Officers, non-commissioned officers and soldiers of any artillery regiment that fired on houses so as to set them on fire, will be executed;

Article 6 – Those non-commissioned officers and soldiers who fired on the people will be sent to the colonies. Those who massacred children, women, or the elderly will be executed;

Article 7 – All soldiers are called upon to shoot down any chief who orders that the people be fired upon;

Article 8 – Those officers who, during the struggle, declare themselves for the Republic, will receive a large reward as a sign of national gratitude;

Article 9 – Those soldiers and non-commissioned officers who, during the struggle, embrace the Republican cause will have a right either to leave the army, or to promotion to a higher rank within the national army. Upon leaving each soldier will receive 300 francs beyond his departure bonus, each non-commissioned officer 500 francs.

The Paris Commune (1871)

The Paris Commune was the full realization of the Great Anger in power. Or perhaps it demonstrated the limitations of the Great Anger, which could only, by its very nature, maintain its grip on the state apparatus for a limited time. Its life span of three months began with the anger and frustration of the working class of Paris caused by the humiliating defeat of the detested Bonapartist government and by the insult to their pride when the Provisional Government demanded the surrender of their artillery. Revolutionary Paris, already defeated in 1830 and 1848 (the socialist Benoit Malon called his book on the Commune "The Third Defeat of the French Proletariat"), embarrassed by the Prussian victory, had had enough and it made a stand.

If the early days of the Great Revolution of 1789 had a certain American slant, with republican ideals of representative democracy and liberty crossing the Atlantic, the Commune from its beginning had no previously marked path to follow. Even the glory days of 1848 couldn't serve as an example: in 1871 the working class was fighting against a government that called itself a Republic. Here for the first time was a working class taking the next step along the revolutionary road to the Social Republic.

As they stepped onto a stage in ruins, the Commune, like the Republic that issued from the Great Revolution, had to carry out two tasks simultaneously: build a better world while arming itself against the one that already existed. The Commune was founded by the working class, striving to remain faithful to their roots and seeking a truer and more direct democracy. They had to build a government and an army from those who had been the *damnés de la terre*—the wretched of the earth—who had been kept not only from power, but from any knowledge of how to make power function.

The *damnés* the Commune had to work with came not only from revolutionary Paris; it included foreigners who had moved to France, inspired by its revolutionary past. Heirs to Baron d'Holbach, the Enragé Anacharsis Cloots, the Babouvist Buonarotti, the Commune placed the Pole Dombrowski and the Hungarian Jew Leo Frankel in positions of responsibility.

The restructuring of the world fought for by the Communards was not only a matter of establishing government on a popular basis, or making working conditions more bearable (by banning night work in bakeries, for example), or suspending rents and liberating pawned goods: the Commune was alert to the symbolism that filled Paris. It confided the task of destroying the Bonapartist Vendôme Column to the great artist Gustave Courbet and widely publicized the event. Monuments to past oppression were destroyed just as the old order was.

Marx, in his "Civil War in France" was not alone in pointing out the many errors and failings of the Commune. But lacking a generalized revolution, it was unlikely the Commune could have survived. And given that the very idea of a Commune, the return to a local and localized power, inhibited its ability to spread the revolution except by example, a communized France was unlikely.

The glory of its failure inspired two diametrically opposed paths: on one path were those who through organized mass activity intended to make the Communards ideas work the next time around, and on the other path were those who, seeing the failure of mass action, tried to seek other, individual ways to bring down the bourgeois state edifice. In the end both groups failed, but the Commune retains a place in the heart of every revolutionary, of whatever stripe. Even today, almost a century and a half later, bouquets are still placed at the wall in Père Lachaise cemetery where the Communards made their last stand.

"Paris Libre"*

April 12, 1871

This morning, April 11 at 7:00, the cannons still rumbled, but the defenders of the Commune, solidly set up in their positions, have nothing to fear from the enemy.

The damages they caused have been repaired.

The well-commanded National Guard is full of confidence.

All worry has ceased.

Formidable barricades are going up from the Porte de Neuilly to the Champs Elysées.

All is calm at our forward positions.

Our lines are stronger than ever and ready to support an attack by the *Versaillais*, if one dared to occur.

*

When on March 18 the people of Paris made a revolution to the cry of "Long Live the Commune" it was in order to re-conquer all civil, political and economic rights, to preserve their weapons, rifles, and cannons that had served to defend Paris against the foreigner and which must, by remaining in their hands, ensure all the conquests of the Revolution.

So let the men of Versailles not come here talking of granting us a municipality of Paris, for that is not what it's a question of.

---

* Edited by Pierre Vésinier (1824-1902), the newspaper *"Paris Libre"* appeared between April 12 - May 24, 1871. Vésinier (who Marx described as "lacking great literary value") had been head of the French Section of London of the First International, which was expelled in 1868. His political activities continued unabated, and he was arrested for his part in seizing the town hall of the 20th arrondissement in October 1870. Exonerated, he was elected to the Commune on April 16, 1871, was a member of the Garibaldi legion, collaborated on several journals, was named editor of *"Le Journal Officiel"* on May 8, and edited *"Paris Libre."* He fled to London after the defeat of the Commune, and remained politically active until his death.

We want, we'll have, we have proclaimed and founded the great Paris Commune. We will maintain it; we know how to defend it, to see it triumph, or to die for it.

April 13, 1871

This morning the royalists began again the attack on Clamart. The fighting is rapidly spreading. Like yesterday, it is the fort of Issy that appears to be the objective of their movements.

MacMahon commands the *Versaillais*; the movement was foreseen yesterday by general Dombrowski. He is carrying out strategic movements that will make the enemy dearly pay for his brazen aggression.

The word had spread in Paris that General Eudes had been wounded. We are in a position to formally deny this information.

General Eudes paid with his person in yesterday's combat, but happily he is safe and sound.

The gendarmes, the police, and the *chouans* of Charette and Cathelinau were less vigorous in this morning's attack. Yesterday's defeat demoralized them a bit.

*

We are actively working at transforming the Place de la Concorde into an entrenched camp. We have already begun digging deep entrenchments at the entries of the main streets, at the Quai Cours-de-la-reine, the Rue Royale, and the Rue de Rivoli, which will be blocked by high and solid barricades.

Other works will be executed around the Champs Elysées.

April 14, 1871

Since last night we are in complete possession of Neuilly, where General Dombrowski yesterday began a full-fledged siege. The *chouans* have been dislodged from all their positions, and our columns, ready to go on the offensive, at the hour we go to press occupy the bridgehead.

*

Decree
The Paris Commune,

> Considering that the Imperial Column is a barbaric monument, a symbol of brute force and false glory, an affirmation of milita-

rism, a negation of international law, a permanent insult on the part of the victors to the vanquished, a perpetual attack on one of the three great principles of the French republic, Fraternity,

Decrees:

Sole article: The Column of the Place Vendôme shall be demolished

The Paris Commune

*

Since yesterday Artillery Captain Caillau has taken command at the Porte de Maillot.

He has excited to the highest degree the zeal of the soldiers in charge of the pieces.

But in another area he is poorly seconded, for having asked for workers to repair during the night the damages caused by the enemy batteries, he didn't obtain what he asked for.

A few engineering officers came, but they established a barricade at the rear of the Porte de Maillot that is ridiculous as a form of defense and at the same time very dangerous for the besieged, for it is entirely made of stone, so when a shell falls on it many pieces of stone are thrown out in all directions.

April 15, 1871

At midnight the enemy attacked the fort of Vanves and was repelled. At the current time all is calm.

– G. Cluseret

The Commune authorizes Citizen Gustave Courbet, president of the Painters, named in General Assembly, to as quickly as possible reestablish the museums of the city of Paris in their normal state, to open the galleries to the public, and to encourage the work usually done there.

To this effect the Commune authorizes 46 delegates, who shall be named tomorrow, Thursday, April 13, at a public session at the School of Medicine (Great Amphitheatre) at exactly 2:00.

In addition, it authorizes Citizen Courbet, as well as the assembly, to reestablish, with the same urgency, the annual exhibit on the Champs Elysées.

Paris April 12, 1871

The Executive Commission
Avrial, F. Cournet, Celescluze, Félix Pyat, G. Tridon, E. Vaillaint, Vermorel

April 16, 1871

April 15 7:30 a.m.: The commandant of the fort of Grand Montrouge and General Eudes announce that they successfully fought all night, that they repelled five enemy attacks.

A large artillery detachment will be joining the garrison of the fort.

*

Yesterday at 1:00 p.m. a Company of *Vengeurs de Paris* passed on the Boulevard Montmartre, escorting a hearse decorated with red flags transporting to Père Lachaise Cemetery the mortal remains of a young man of 17, Duval, who signed up to fight against the Versailles government and was killed in combat the day before yesterday at the advanced positions of Moulin-de-Pierre, before Issy.

Mortally struck by two bullets to the head, this courageous and valiant child of Paris fell while crying out: *Vive la France, Vive la Commune!*

*

The construction has begun on the scaffolding that will be used in dismantling the Vendôme Column.

April 17, 1871

Theatre directors went yesterday to the Commune asking for authorization to open their theatres to organize benefit performances for the widows and orphans of those who have died for the Republic.

The request was favorably received. The Theatre de la Porte Saint Martin will open the march and in a few days will put on a brilliant show with the participation of the principal artists of the capital.

April 18, 1871
Letter from General Dombrowski: April 16, 1871

Citizens:

The siege of Neuilly advances little by little.

We have occupied the whole of a new quarter, taken three barricades.

At one of them we took a flag of the Pontifical Zouaves and from another one that seems to be American.

The parquets of houses taken, covered with large pools of blood, bear witness to the fact that the enemy suffered great losses.

In order to more vigorously carry out the operations I need more men, artillery and munitions.

The troops' sprits are good. The National Guard is making progress, and is getting used to fire, privations, and shows a remarkable enthusiasm.

Salut et Fraternité

Dombrowski

*

Order:

In order to avoid accidents on the streets of Paris the former rule on horsemen is once again in effect.

It is forbidden to all horsemen, military staff officer or civilian, to circulate at a gallop on the streets of Paris.

The National Guard, the civil police, and the population are charged with execution of the present order and the arrest of delinquents.

The commanding general of the place: P-O.

April 19, 1871

Three small attacks on Vanves and Issy

Few losses

All is well

Intermittent fusillade

Very calm night

– Eudes

*

The *Versaillais* were pushed back yesterday at 2:00 in the morning.

They had attempted an attack on the *fédérés** who still occupy Asnières. We had the sorrow of losing a Mexican general who had spontaneously put his sword at the service of the Commune.

April 20, 1871

Order:

The Citizen Delegate for War learns that barricades are being constructed the plans of which haven't been submitted to him, and that promises of high salaries are being made for this work. These high salaries will not be paid.

*

At Neuilly yesterday the affair was heated. But General Dombrowski arrived, and soon everyone was in place, the National Guard assembled, the officers led their men and the positions were retaken.

*

The Professional Chamber of Tailors:

> In order to respond to the decree of the Paris Commune of April 16, the chamber believes itself obliged to make a fraternal appeal to the professional chambers of workers, as well as all the existing workers' societies, in order to immediately convoke a meeting to name delegates charged with carrying out an inquiry on the organization of labor, which is called for by said decree.
> Never has a more favorable occasion been offered by a government to the laboring class. To abstain would be to betray the cause of the emancipation of labor.

The secretaries:
Dupire, Verbeck

April 21, 1871

Yesterday was extremely satisfactory.

The attacks by the *Versaillais* were pushed back at all points.

The National Guard took a magazine of military equipment and provisions at Asnières.

---

* The Communards, who wanted a federation of communes.

The losses of the *Versaillais* were out of all proportion to ours.

*

Versaillais dress as National Guards and fire from houses.

April 22, 1871

8:00 a.m. – Firing begins again with a new fury.

100 shots are fired precipitously. The barricade of the Rue Peronnet, behind which the *Versaillais* are sheltered with machine guns, has just been penetrated.

The boutique of Citizen Claise, dairyman, was set on fire by a cannon ball.

The artillerymen are heroic.

*

The Commune has just published its program, which the reactionary journals have been calling for in the hope that it will be too embarrassed to formulate it.

This program, as simple as it is practical, reasonable, and moderate, will remain in history as the most beautiful moment of good sense and practical capacity that the working class has ever demonstrated.

It would have been impossible to more clearly formulate, with greater precision and clarity, the demands of the Parisian populace, and we are convinced that this program will have the marvelous effect of rallying to the Commune the great majority of the population of Paris. ... From this point on, the cause defended so courageously by Paris has been won in public opinion. And since it is after all the latter that triumphs, we have no doubt in the definitive success of the Commune.

April 23, 1871

The enemy is losing ground with every passing minute. His fire has been extinguished at several points.

We become aware of the retreat of the *Versaillais* by the aim of their projectiles.

The projectiles land further and further from our ramparts.

April 24, 1871

Neuilly: Calm night. 7:30 – a strong fusillade opens the engagement.

The fighting is heated and the melee was about to become general when the 1st Belleville Battery arrived at the theatre of action and fired at a short distance.

The *Versaillais* disperse and flee in all directions.

April 25, 1871

The newspapers have published that the Central Committee, having fulfilled its mission, has dissolved itself. This story is completely false. Like the National Guard, of which it is emanation, it will only disappear along with liberty. It hopes that this response will suffice for its detractors.

April 26, 1871

It is said in the newspaper of Citizen Jules Vallès:

> In the garden of the Legion of Honor more than 500 kilos of silverware were found buried that General Eudes then sent to the mint.

April 27, 1871

7:30: The fusillade begins, the cannon roars and the machineguns crackle.

The fight is engaged from the Porte Maillot to Asnières.

8:00 – The firing becomes more intense, the machine guns play a more active role.

The *fédérés* advance, causing great losses to the enemy.

All is well.

*

Proposed decree:

The Paris Commune:

> Considering that the calumnies that are circulating among a certain public are of a nature to hinder defense and to raise the provinces up against Paris;
> Given that the defenders of Paris are accused of pillage by *agents provocateurs*;

Given that in a well-constituted government police work should be done by the people themselves;

Decrees:

Art. 1 – Any citizen spreading word of pillage without immediately denouncing it to the authorities will be arrested, and if the fact is false, punished as a slanderer.

Art. 2 – Any citizen suspected of knowing of a true case of pillage and who will not have made this known to the competent authorities, shall be arrested as an accomplice and condemned to the same penalty as those truly guilty.

Art. 3 – The National Guard is charged with the execution of the present decree.

April 28, 1871

The Commune was proclaimed at Le Mans.

The garrison fraternized with the people.

Two regiments that were called for from Rennes in order to suppress the people of Le Mans did the same.

Cuirassiers arrived. Surrounded by the people they were forced to lay down their arms.

April 29, 1871

The bombardments from the forts in the south continue.

We respond vigorously and keep at a distance the *Versaillais* who are sheltered behind the woods of Clamart and Châtillon.

*

All night the detonations from both camps rivaled each other in intensity.

April 30, 1871

War to the Executive:

I return from visiting Issy and Vanves. The defense of the fort of Issy is heroic. The fort is literally covered in projectiles. While at the fort of Vanves I witnessed a ferocious musket combat *between Versaillais*. It lasted three quarters of an hour. Meudon is in flames.

*

The Executive Commission,

In execution of a decree relative to night work in the bakeries.

After having consulted the bakers, owners and workers,

Decrees:

> Art. 1 – Night work is forbidden in bakeries effective Wednesday May 3.
> Art. 2 – Work cannot start before 5:00 am.
> Art. 3 – The Delegate for Public Services is charged with the execution of the present decree.

Paris April 28, 1871.

*

The fight continues across the entire line.

Yesterday a heated affair took place at the bridge of Ansières, from which the *Versaillais* were forced to abandon by retreating to the station.

*

8:00 a.m.:

The Freemasons from the suburban communes, banners at their head, passed through the gates to go to the demonstration which is to take place at 10:00 in the courtyard of the Louvre.

Everywhere their passing is saluted.

Their arrival produces an indescribable enthusiasm.

So compact is the crowd that circulation on the Rue de Rivoli is completely halted.

100,000 men are there.

We shall see if Thiers will still say that this is a handful of dissidents.

May 1, 1871

The fire of the *fédérés* destroyed the barricade set up across from the Asnières road.

The *Versaillais* took advantage of the armistice imposed by the Freemasons in order to reconstruct this barricade.

A house situated almost on the quay, near the bridge of Asnières, was caved in by the shells of the *Versaillais*. In collapsing, it buried many inoffensive tenants.

*

Two Freemasons were wounded by the shrapnel from shells.

The Freemasons were received with a sympathetic enthusiasm on the ramparts by the National Guardsmen and he artillerymen.

May 2, 1871

The Executive Commission has removed and had arrested General Cluzeret.

The Commune approved his decision.

Citizen Cluzeret was immediately replaced at War by the Colonel of Engineers Rossel, who will provisionally fulfill the functions of delegate.

The choice of his successor shall be submitted for approval to the Commune.

May 3, 1871

Fort of Issy: The Royalists dared call on the Republicans to surrender. They answered that they should come and try to dislodge them, and that rather than surrender they'd blow up the fort.

Porte Maillot:

8:30 a.m. – The fight continues to be violent. The *Versaillais* are concentrating their efforts against this position. They are constantly repelled with great losses.

*

The bombardment of Ternes continues with the greatest intensity.

Thiers sends incendiary and petrol bombs: this fact has been confirmed.

Not only do these bombs cause fires, but they cause holes 50 centimeters deep and of a width eight times greater than their diameter. These are the famous bombs invented by a non-commissioned officer of the Engineering Corps—Sergeant Toussaint if I remember correctly—and which our generals didn't want to use against the Prussians. It is only natural for them that they try them out against Frenchmen.

May 4, 1871

Porte Maillot: 9:30 —The artillerymen are still at work. The firing is continuous.

This battery has earned the recognition of the Commune.

Yesterday two of them were wounded.

*

Friend MacMahon, doubtless disgusted by his lack of success against the Parisians, has resigned as General in Chief of the army of Versailles.

May 5, 1871

Porte des Ternes: 8:00 a.m. The artillery battery of Belleville is on the alert.

At the least sign of movement from the *Versaillais* the fuse is lit, cannonballs fly and the gendarmes fall.

Recquiescat in pace.

*

The municipal elections that just took place in the departments have almost all been favorable to the Commune.

Republican candidates were elected with a great majority... The provinces know that the legislators from the Assembly at Versailles are the worst reactionaries in the world, that they are more royalist than the king, more ultra-Montain than Veuillot, more intolerant, more cruel than Torquemada. The also know that their ferocious orders, composed of gendarmes, of cops of the vilest kind, of the most abject policemen, of former municipal officers, of Paris guards, of police informants, of hired assassins, of Bonapartist bandits, December assassins, pillagers of China, Mexican buccaneers, butchers of Mentana, cowards of Sedan and Metz, of the capitulators of the National Defense, of Chouans and Vendéens, were the vilest collection of rascals and brigands ever seen on the face of the earth.

*

The *fédérés* are holding up well and their attitude, far from permitting the *Versaillais* to continue their forward march has, on the contrary, forced them to retreat.

Last night at 11:00 there was a strong attack by regular troops, and since this time the fighting hasn't ceased.

*

General Dombrowski, with one of his aides-de-camp, yesterday went to the forts of Vanves and Issy.

The small garrison of the latter is still faithfully at its post and has decided to remain there, whatever the gentlemen of Versailles might say or do.

May 6, 1871

Clichy: Ferocious combat all day yesterday. The firing has slowed down this morning.

Asnières: 8:00 a.m.—terrible cannonades and fusillades since yesterday. The ferocity seems to be growing today. The *Versaillais* are making a great effort to advance, but they are being held in check by the armored machines and the battery of the barricade situated at the bridge of Asnières.

May 7, 1871

Clichy: Calm night.

The *Versaillais* are making attacks on the armored machine that continually harasses them.

Porte Maillot: Calm night.

This morning at 6:00 the cannonade regained its intensity.

The *Versaillais* shells reach the Champs Elysées.

The *chouans* have attacked without success, but not without losses.

*

The Committee of Public Safety:

Considering that the building known as the Expiatory Chapel of Louis XVI is a permanent insult to the first revolution and a perpetual protest of reaction against the people's justice,

Decrees:

> Art. 1 – The so-called Expiatory Chapel of Louis XVI shall be destroyed.

Art. 2 – Its materials shall be sold in public auction for the benefit of the administration of domains.

Art. 3 – The director of Domains shall see to the execution of this decree within the next week.

Paris, 16 Floréal, year 79 (May 5, 1871)
The Committee of Public Safety

Ant. Arnaud, Ch. Gerardin, Leo Melliet, Felix Pyat, Ranvier.

May 8, 1871

Porte Clichy: Calm night.

This morning the *Versaillais* fire a few shells to which we don't even respond.

Neuilly: The *Versaillais* attacked this morning.

We haven't yet answered.

Clamart: 10:30 am Heated fusillade from the trenches and attack on the Clamart station. Victorious *fédérés* occupy the station.

*

Yesterday at Issy forty deserters who had abandoned their posts were brought before Colonel Rossel, accompanied by his aides-de-camp.

Citizen Rossel, who is a soldier in all meanings of the word, lined the deserters up in two rows and announced to them that as punishment he was going to slice the right shoulder of their capotes, and that afterwards they'd be executed.

Their prayers and supplications found the colonel impassible.

The captain, the lieutenant and the sub-lieutenant of the deserters were the first to suffer the degradation.

After this beginning to the process of the execution, Colonel Rossel allowed himself to be swayed by those around him.

He then addressed a few strong and serious words, which had a great effect. The soldiers asked to be immediately returned to the fire, swearing that they'd die for the republic.

This act shows the energy of Col. Rossel and what we can expect of him.

*

The Commune Decrees:

Art. 1 – All pledges pawned at the Mont-de-Pieté dating from prior to April 25, 1871 for clothing, furniture, bedding, and work tools with a price of less than 20 francs can be claimed for free dating from this May 12.

Art. 2 – The abovementioned objects can only be delivered to those bearers who can prove their identity and that they are the original borrowers.

May 9, 1871

Porte des Ternes: At 6:30 the combat picks up again with vigor.

Mont-Valerien answers the fire of the *fédérés* without causing us losses of note.

Montrouge: Night of the 6th, Bas-Fontenay attacks the fort of Montrouge, which vigorously ripostes. *Versaillais* reduced to silence.

3:00 a.m., heated fusillade by the *fédérés* on the *Versaillais* defending a barricade at Châtillon.

*

A new committee has just been formed. It is said it will serve as an intermediary between the Commune and the Central Committee.

All of its members belong to the International. Its seat, it is said, will be at the Hôtel de Ville.

*

Vaugirard is being bombarded. Its residents are beginning to move out.

*

Asnières is becoming a veritable retrenched camp. *Fédérés* and *ruraux*[*] increasingly fortify their positions with each passing day.

---

* Literally: rurals, i.e., those from the countryside.

May 10, 1871

Issy: All day yesterday a frightful cannonade continuously fired projectiles on the houses neighboring on the ramparts.

Shells exploded as far as the Rue de Vaugirard.

Porte Maillot: Continuous bombardment.

It is still on this point that the enemy directs his greatest efforts, but our brave artillerymen don't allow themselves to be intimidated, and the riposte doesn't cede to the attack.

*

In Rochefort 1,389 ballots were found in the ballot boxes with this simple motion:

For the Paris Commune!

What must M. Thiers think of this?

*

[At Issy] the *ruraux* again attacked, but they were pushed back across the line. They tried to take the barricade at the Rue de Paris in order to more easily reach the town hall.

They are ready to blow up the fort at the first signal. Explosives have been put in place with this end in mind.

*

The fusillade at Neuilly could be heard all day.

The *ruraux* attacked at several points and were pushed back everywhere.

Passy is being vigorously bombarded.

*

A red flag floats over Cette.

May 11, 1871

Porte Clichy: Heated fusillade last night. It continues this morning.

The cannon have not been fired.

Porte d'Asnières: Cannonade and fusillade all night the entire length of the Seine from Levallois to Neuilly.

Our artillery believes it caused much damage to the *Versaillais*.

Vanves, Issy: The *ruraux* don't dare advance too far into these areas.

*

The area around Grenelles, like that of Vaugirard, is riddled with shells. The residents are locking themselves in their cellars.

*

Colonel Vetzel bravely fell at his combat post. He didn't have the time to turn his command over to Colonel Brunel, who was to replace him. He was killed at the barricade of the Grand Rue, where the shells fall like hailstones.

*

An attack much like that of the preceding days occurred yesterday at Neuilly. Fighting was furious on the barricades of the park.

The combat lasted three hours. The belligerents still occupy their respective positions.

*

Yesterday's events were very serious. The fort of Issy was evacuated, though according to the opinion of many the position was not yet absolutely untenable.

The *Versaillais*, perhaps fearing that the fort had been mined have not yet occupied it.

May 12, 1871

Vanves: Yesterday evening the *Versaillais* carried out a furious attack. The 1st Battalion of the 1st *arrondissement*, which has been in the trenches for the last two weeks, is conducting itself heroically.

This battalion suffered much yesterday, but it caused the *Versaillais* to suffer three times their own losses.

At 5:00 p.m. it is impossible to remain near the ramparts.

Neuilly: Violent artillery combat since yesterday evening.

The enemy doesn't advance.

*

At today's session, May 10, 1871, at 7:00 p.m., the Commune decided:

> 1 – The Naming of Citizen Delescluze to the functions of Civil Delegate for War.
> 2 – The sending before a court martial of Citizen Rossel, ex-Delegate for War.

*

The two places upon which the *Versaillais* are concentrating are the Pont-du-Jour and the bastions of Auteuil. These unfortunate bastions are literally covered with shells, and the surrounding neighborhoods suffer much from bombardments. The artillerymen posted under the viaduct hardly fire at all.

The shells are falling on the Grenelle Bridge and as far as the roundabout where the bus company's offices were until a few days ago.

The batteries of Mont-Valerien and Courbevoie continue to cause a rain of projectiles to fall on Asnières and Neuilly.

In Neuilly the fire is extremely violent.

At Levallois a fusillade between skirmishers on both sides of the river.

This village, exposed to the fires of the Becon batteries, has been virtually abandoned by its inhabitants.

May 13, 1871

Porte des Ternes: The *Versaillais* are massed on this side.

They have attempted several attacks. Each time repelled.

The 25th *fédéré* battalion had the honors of the day.

It took part in all the attacks and caused great losses to the enemy.

Porte Maillot: Furious cannonade.

The *Versaillais* established defense works, which were promptly destroyed by our artillerymen's fire.

*

MINISTRY OF WAR

To Citizens members of the Commune:

Citizens:

Since our arrival at the ministry we have completed the various positions of defense and attack; we have made sure that the guards on the ramparts were sufficiently established and that a good reserve force was in place in case of surprise.

The position of Issy has hardly changed. That of the fort of Vanves was slightly compromised. At a certain moment it was even evacuated.

At 4:00 a.m. General Wroblewski, accompanied by the chief and several members of his headquarters, placed himself at the head of the 187th and 105th battalions, led by the brave chief of the 11th legion.

They entered the fort at bayonet point and dislodged the *Versaillais*, who believed themselves to already be its master. Reinforcements were directed to this point, and we can without a doubt speak of sure success.

All was quiet at Neuilly, and at Asnières things were relatively calm.

*

The Telegraph Delegation has the honor of informing the public that from this day until further notice, it will not consider applications for employment addressed to it, forced as it is to eliminate much of its too numerous, and consequently useless, personnel.

Paris, May 11, 1871
The Delegates for Telegraphy
Edmond Bizot, Mallet, M. Prost

*

At the Porte Dauphine a woman has just been killed in her bed by a cannonball. The son of this poor woman is a captain in the army of Versailles.

*

A guard of the 137th battalion, Citizen Dufour, informs us that the fort of Issy is not occupied.

The position, it appears, is untenable for everyone.

Marine pieces have thus not been installed there, as several newspapers have affirmed.

*

The ramparts of the Porte d'Issy and Vanves have just been armed with strong marine pieces.

May 14, 1871

Asnières: Horrible din all night.

The firing was at almost point blank range.

The cannons and machineguns add to the horror of the combat.

More exposed than the *fédérés*, the *ruraux* suffer serious losses and are retreating to their last entrenched positions.

Porte d'Issy: The *Versaillais* have failed in an attempt to retake the barricade of the park.

They had many dead and wounded.

*

Citizen Vésinier, member of the Commune, has been delegated to take over the direction of l'Officiel.

*

A Versailles newspaper says that the employees of the ministries have been warned to be ready to take up again their positions in Paris at the end of the month.

I think this is a little premature, my good Thiers; what do you think?

*

Levallois and Clichy was the target of machinegun fire and shells, and it can be presumed that the *Versaillais* will attack on this side.

May 15, 1871

Montrouge: Strong attack by the *Versaillais* repelled. They suffered serious losses.

Issy: Violent combat. Despite the unheard of efforts of the *Versaillais* we have preserved our positions.

Asnières: Violent combat.

The *Versaillais* take refuge behind their entrenchments.

*

The Paris Commune decrees:
> Sole article – In the matter of the separation of bodies, the presiding judge can allocate alimony to the woman requesting separation that will serve her until it has been otherwise decided by the tribunal.

*

Yesterday the public arrested on the Boulevard Denis a priest in civilian clothes who was tearing down posters of the Commune.

The crowd, which doesn't have much sympathy for priests, wanted to roughly handle him.

*

At 4:00 p.m. the Boulevard Sebastopol was much aroused by the arrest of a young couple that was promenading arm in arm.

The appearance of the woman being suspicious to the National Guardsmen, the latter approached and recognized that the so-called maiden was a big strong man preparing to flee in order to escape enlistment.

Upon hearing the howls of the crowd our draft-dodger had the stupid look of the fox of the fable.

*

Once again the *Versaillais* attempted to take our barricades by surprising the *fédérés* during the night. But the latter were on the alert, and when the royalists were a few steps away a heated fusillade forced them to retreat, leaving their dead and wounded on the field.

May 16, 1871

Porte Maillot: Yesterday at 9:00 in the evening an infernal bombardment sent projectiles to the area of the gate.

The detonations are deafening.

One would think it was a Walpurgis Night.

This morning the same din and the same results.

Our artillerymen are still at their pieces, aiming with the same courage, and lighting the fuses with the same ardor.

All blows are returned.

Porte des Ternes: Same situation as at Porte Maillot.

Southern forts: The forts furiously attacked and defended.

Many dead and wounded on both sides.

The same respective positions.

*

In Saint-Quentin all the members of the municipal commission were elected. They passed at the head of the lists. The voters eliminated all the members of the former council, regarded as reactionaries.

*

We expect the greatest service from the cannons of Montmartre that, it appears, are served by 60 artillerymen who deserted the cause of Versailles to come to Paris.

May 17, 1871

The *Versaillais* were beaten yesterday at the Bois de Boulogne.

Southern Forts: The *fédérés* had to evacuate the fort of Vanves, whose position was untenable. But contrary to the assertions of several newspapers, the *Versaillais* didn't dare occupy it.

Solid ramparts were constructed to block the passage of the enemy between the fort and the rampart.

*

The demolition of the Vendôme Column will take place today at 2:00 in the afternoon.

*

The *Versaillais* continue to gather in the Bois de Boulogne in an imposing fashion. The noise of fusillades and the detonations of machineguns are incessant on this side. The bullets reach the interior of Paris. Several chance victims have been cited, among them a child who was wounded in the foot by a bullet when passing through the Avenue d'Eylau.

May 18, 1871

The battle has been ferocious since yesterday. The *ruraux*, who see the provinces trembling understand that they are lost if victory doesn't promptly crown their efforts.

But our brave *fédérés* are holding out. They too know the state of spirits in France and, despite the rage of the royalists, Paris stands for the defense of the Republic and its rights.

*

As we announced yesterday, we evacuated the fort at Vanves, but it is false that it is occupied by the *Versaillais*. On the contrary, the truth is that we could reoccupy the position if it weren't so dangerous. At the very least we have the resources to blow it up, and we hope that this time we won't fail to do so.

May 19, 1871

The battle is general. The fighting is heated everywhere.

The noise of arms fills Paris with courage and resolution.

At Issy as in Vanves, at Neuilly as in Asnières and everywhere our rights are threatened, the enemy finds the National Guard there to defend them.

The defense grows in proportion to the danger.

*

Petrol bombs continue to set alight frequent fires in Neuilly.

*

Montmartre from time to time makes heard its loud voice. It has already reduced several *Versaillais* batteries to silence.

*

For two days a furious fight has been engaged in the Bois de Boulogne, and it continued much of the night. ... at Neuilly the fight was no less heated than at the Bois de Boulogne. There too the fight was hand to hand, but without any results.

May 20, 1871

Porte des Ternes: The fusillade is general, from Clichy to the Porte Maillot.

Asnières: A battle. The machineguns dominate the fight. A great attack is expected from here.

We are ready to welcome them.

Montrouge and Asnières are holding out.

Wherever liberty is threatened, its defenders are there, opposing breast to breast, bayonet to bayonet.

*

The Committee of Public Safety
Decrees:

> Art. 1. – The newspapers "La Commune," "L'Echo de Paris," "L'Indépendance Française," "L'Avenir National," "La Patrie," "Le Pirate," "Le Rèpublicain," "La Revue des Deux-Mondes," "L'Echo de l'Ultramar," and "La Justice" are and remain suppressed.
>
> Art. 2. – No new newspaper or political periodical can appear before the end of the war.
>
> Art. 3. – All articles must be signed by their authors.
>
> Art. 4. – Attacks on the Republic and the Commune shall be referred to the court martial.
>
> Art. 5. – Printers in violation will be pursued as accomplices and their presses put under seal.
>
> Art. 6. – The present decree shall be immediately made known to the suppressed newspapers by Citizen Le Moussu, commissioner delegated to this effect.
>
> Art. 7. – General Security is charged with seeing to the execution of the present decree.

Hôtel de Ville 28 Floreal year 79

The Committee of Public Safety
Ant Arnaud, Eudes, Billioray, F. Gamson, G. Ranvier

*

Yesterday at one in the morning the *Versaillais* attempted an assault, but they were vigorously repelled.

Following the Avenue de la Grande Armée they arrived at the Porte Maillot with considerable forces.

But the *fédérés* held out, and the enemy was obliged to withdraw after having lost many.

The enemy also attempted an assault on the fort of Montrouge yesterday.

It appears this was the order given all along the line, but all along the line the royalists were repelled with losses considerable greater than ours.

*

We read in a letter that Garibaldi wrote to his friends in Nice:

> My dear friends; What which pushes the Parisians to war is a sentiment of justice and human dignity, it's the great family called Commune that wants to make and eat the *pissaladina* (a kind of cake common in Nice) without asking for permission of Peking or Berne. It's not a question of communism, as the black detractors of the proletariat want to define it, that is, partisans of a system that consists of enriching the poor and impoverishing the rich.

May 21, 1871

Yesterday the *Versaillais* suffered a bloody reverse at the Bois de Boulogne.

Exasperated by this defeat, they returned to the charge last night without obtaining the least success.

These combats do honor to our artillerymen, whose precise fire has contributed much to the results.

The combat continues under the same conditions.

*

At Montrouge a troop of soldiers of the line advanced without apparent arms on the forward positions of the fort, announcing their decision to surrender.

Handshakes were exchanged, but suddenly these men fired on our National Guards.

*

At the Severin Club, Citizen Pacotte recounts that a poor woman, wounded at the forward positions and transported to the Hôtel-Dieu, where she still is, received this response from Doctor de Maison-Neuve:

"Do I still have long to live?"

"No," he replied, "but even before that our brave soldiers will have wiped out your husband's battalion along with all the miserable insurgents."

Three citizens were immediately designated to accompany Citizen Pacotte to the Hôtel-Dieu to assure themselves of the truth of this infamous statement.

The indignant hall unanimously voted that the name of this wretch be signaled by the newspapers for public indignation, and informed the Commune of this.

May 22, 1871

Neuilly: The fight continues, terrible, ferocious.

Asnières and Saint-Ouen: The fire of the Montmartre batteries holds the *Versaillais* at a distance.

Vaugirard: The combat around the whole perimeter of the Southern forts has had no advantageous result for the enemy.

*

The *chouans* attempted a decisive assault at the Porte of Versailles. The affair was extremely heated. The *fédérés*, overcome by the numbers and the rain of bullets that fell on them, bent for a moment. But they nevertheless held out until the arrival of reinforcements, who caused the *Versaillais* to flee.

*

The cannonade hasn't ceased across the whole line.

*

From Clichy to Point-du-Jour the combat remains ferocious. The energy of the *fédérés* doesn't flag a single instant.

May 23, 1871

According to the latest information, the *Versaillais* have entered by the Saint-Cloud gate. The *fédérés*, forced to withdraw, retrenched themselves at some distance from their barricades, where the enemy, incidentally not very numerous, didn't dare harass them.

The *Versaillais* have entered! And now? This is precisely where we expected them, as we said yesterday. Their position is critical. They must be confronted with street and barricade fighting, at which Parisians are so redoubtable. Will they dare?

They are master of one point. Very well. But how many forces do they require in order to confront all the attacks that will occur?

From all sides battalions are arriving and massing at the Tuileries.

Full of enthusiasm, they prepare to fight the enemy to that cry a thousand times repeated: *Vive la Commune*!

*

Citizens:

Enough of militarism, no more braided and gilded commanders! Make room for the people, the fighters with bare arms. The hour for revolutionary warfare has sounded.

The people know nothing of studied maneuvers; but when it has a weapon in hand, a paving stone under its feet, it fears none of the strategists of the monarchist school.

To arms, citizens, to arms! You know that it's a matter of winning or falling into the pitiless hands of the reactionaries and the clericals of Versailles who, in a partisan fashion, delivered France to the Prussians and who make us pay the ransom of their treason!

If you want the blood that has flowed for the past six weeks to not be infertile; if you want to live free in a free and egalitarian France, to spare your children your pain and misery, you will rise up as one man and, before your formidable resistance, the enemy who boasts that he is returning you to the yoke will have to pay for the useless crimes with which he has sullied himself for the past two months.

Citizens, your representatives will fight and die with you if necessary, but in the name of this glorious France, mother of all popular revolutions, permanent home of the ideas of justice and solidarity which must and will be the laws of the world, march on the enemy and let your revolutionary energy show him that they can sell Paris, but it can be neither delivered nor defeated.

The Commune counts on you.

Count on the Commune.

The Civil Delegate of War
Ch. Delescluze

The Committee of Public Safety

May 24, 1871

Citizens:

The *Versaillais* must understand that at this moment Paris is as strong today as yesterday.

Despite the shells that they rain as far as the Saint-Denis Gate on an inoffensive populace, Paris is standing, covered in barricades and combatants!

Far from spreading terror, their shells only excite even more the anger and courage of the Parisians!

Paris fights with the energy of great days!

Despite all the enemy's desperate efforts he hasn't been able to gain an inch of ground since yesterday.

He is held in check everywhere. Everywhere he dares show himself our cannons and guns spread death in his ranks.

The people, taken by surprise for an instant by treason, have found themselves again. The defenders of right have made themselves known, and it is in swearing to win or die for the Republic that they have descended en masse on the barricades!

Versailles has sworn to slaughter the Republic: Paris has sworn to save it!

No! A new December 2 is no longer possible for, strengthened by its experience of the past, the people prefer death to servitude!

Let the men of September know this: the people remember. It has had enough of the traitors and cowards who by their shameful defections delivered France to the foreigners.

Already the soldiers, our brothers, retreat before the crime they want them to commit.

A great number of them have passed into our ranks.

Crowds of their comrades will follow their example.

Thiers' army will find itself reduced to its gendarmes. – We know what these men want and why they fight.

Between us and then there is an abyss!

To arms!

Courage, citizens. A supreme effort and victory is ours!

Everything for the Republic!

Everything for the Commune!

The Editorial Committee of *"Paris Libre"*

*

Federation of the National Guard
Central Committee
Soldiers of the army of Versailles:

We are fathers,

We fight to prevent our children from one day living, like you, under military despotism.

One day you will be fathers.

If you fire on the people today your sons will curse you the same way that we curse the soldiers who tore out the guts of the people in June 1848 and December 1851.

Two months ago, on March 18, your brothers of the army of Paris, their hearts full of resentment against the cowards who sold out France, fraternized with the people. Imitate them.

Soldiers, our children, our brothers, listen well to this, and let your conscience decide:

When the order is unspeakable, disobedience is an obligation.

3 Prairial, year 79
The Central Committee

*

We have received from Citizen Paschal Grousset the following letter:

Citizens;

The newspapers from Versailles claim that I have left Paris.

Please reassure my friends and tell them that I am incapable of quitting my post.

Greetings and equality,

Paschal Grousset
At the Hôtel de Ville May 22, 1871

*

The Versailles papers are trying to disorganize the defense by having it believe that the members of the Commune have fled.

And so they spread about the word that citizen Protot was arrested at the advanced posts of the *Versaillais*.

Yesterday at 5:00 we saw Citizen Protot at the Hôtel de Ville.

Citizen Raoul Rigault, who they killed in their newspaper columns, is at the head of his battalion and will probably make more that one royalist bite the dust before falling.

The Propagandists of the Deed (1890s)

A century after the highpoint of *sans-culotterie*, in the years around 1892, a wave of attacks occurred that was the ultimate expression of the confluence of message and medium, of the absence of a break between theory and practice. These attacks were a demonstration of the complete identity of theory and practice, the dissolution of theory into practice: the practice of propaganda by the deed. Individual attacks had occurred periodically in the decades after the crushing of the Commune, but the movement had been marginal, with most workers of the left remaining within the sphere of organized opposition of one kind of another, socialist or anarchist. But the international wave of individual terror, which took much of its inspiration from the Russian Narodniks, whose bomb—fabricated by Victor Serge's uncle—killed Tsar Alexander II in 1882, found fertile ground in France, with its history of acceptance of the purifying, sanctifying benefits of the spilling of blood. It must never be forgotten that the national anthem calls for "impure blood [to] fill our furrows."

Though propagandists of the deed were responsible for the deaths of statesmen, presidents, and royals in the U.S., France, and Italy, in France it was Ravachol, Emile Henry, and Auguste Vaillant who, in the extremity of their violence, captured the public's imagination and became the subjects of a peculiarly French glorification, though perhaps beatification would be a better word. The anarchist writer Victor Barrucand called Ravachol "a kind of violent Christ who will perhaps be likened to that other torture victim Jesus the Galilean who, in several regards, was an anarchist." This was a man who, aside from bombing the offices of prosecutors involved in a case that led to the condemnation of a group of anarchists, also robbed a grave, and killed and robbed a hermit.

It wasn't only on the margins of French politics that this glorification occurred. Paul Adam, one of France's most prolific authors of the period, writing in Bernard Lazare's *Entretiens Politiques et*

Litteraires, explained away Ravachol's grave robbing as an act that "demonstrates the shame of a society that sumptuously garbs its carrion while in one year alone 91,000 individuals die of hunger." And as for the murder of the hermit of Notre Dame de Grace: "Is he more guilty in this than society, which allows to perish in the solitude of a garret a being every bit as useful as the student from the school of Beaux-Arts recently found dead in Paris due to lack of food?"

These anarchists refused to be swayed by the judgment of others, even other anarchists. In August 1892, when Errico Malatesta attacked the propagandists of the deed in Zo d'Axa's "*L'endehors*" saying that anarchists "must strive to never go beyond the limits marked by necessity... must be like the surgeon who cuts when he must, but must avoid causing useless suffering," Emile Henry responded in the same journal's pages a week later, saying that the individual anarchist "alone is judge if he is right or wrong to hate, to be savage, even ferocious. There is thus only one means to strike institutions, and that's to strike men, and we greet with joy all energetic acts of revolt against bourgeois society, for we cannot lose sight of the fact that the revolution will only be the result of all particular acts."

Hatred of the existing order, of the rotten, corrupt Third Republic, goes a long way towards explaining this attitude, as does the strange nobility of Ravachol and Henry, who loudly and proudly proclaimed their guilt, their pride in their acts, their hatred for every accomplice in the maintenance of the status quo. For the Ravachols, the Henrys, the Vaillants, even a bomb in a café killing random bourgeois—bourgeois defined as anyone in that café at that time—was a necessary revolutionary act, since there are no innocents. And if this was the case, how much more defendable was Vaillant's 1893 bombing of the Chamber of Deputies, or Henry and Ravachol's attacks on buildings housing enemies of the working class? In a Third Republic of scandals and political maneuvers, the clarity, the unblemished rage of the propagandists of the deed could not but shine through the blood they shed.

Ravachol (1859-1892)

My Principles (1892)[*]

The above named, after having eaten his fill, spoke to us as follows:

"Gentlemen, it is my habit, wherever I am, to do propaganda work. Do you know what anarchism is?"

We answered 'No' to this question.

"This doesn't surprise me," he responded. "The working class which, like you, is forced to work to earn its bread, doesn't have the time to devote to the reading of pamphlets they're given. It's the same for you.

"Anarchy is the obliteration of property.

"There currently exist many useless things; many occupations are useless as well, for example, accounting. With anarchy there is no more need for money, no further need for bookkeeping and the other forms of employment that derive from this.

"There are currently too many citizens who suffer while others swim in opulence, in abundance. This situation cannot last; we all should profit by the surplus of the rich. But even, we should obtain, like them, all that is necessary. In current society, it isn't possible to arrive at this goal. Nothing, not even a tax on income, could change the face of things. Nevertheless, the bulk of workers think that if we acted in this way, things would improve. It is an error to think this way. If we tax the landlord, he'll increase his rents and in this way will arrange for those who suffer to pay the new charges imposed on them. In any event, no law can touch landlords for, being the masters of their goods, we can't prevent them from doing whatever they want with them. What, then, should be done? Wipe out property and, by doing this, wipe out those who take all. If this abolition takes place, we have to also

---

[*] From Un saint nous est né, edited by Philippe Oriol. L'équipement de la pensée, Paris. 1992. While in prison in 1892, this document was dictated to the police by Ravachol. It remained unpublished until the historian Jean Maitron found it in the Paris Police Archives in 1964.

do away with money, in order to prevent any idea of accumulation, which would force a return to the current regime.

"It is in effect money that is the cause of all discord, all hatred, of all ambitions; it is, in a word, the creator of property. This metal, in truth, has nothing but an agreed upon price, born of its rarity. If we were no longer obliged to give something in exchange for those things we need to live, gold would lose its value and no one would seek it. Nor could they enrich themselves, because nothing they would amass could serve them in obtaining a better life than that of others. There would then no longer be any need of laws, no need of masters.

"As for religions, they'd be destroyed, because their moral influence would no longer have any reason for existence. There would no longer be the absurdity of believing in a God who doesn't exist, since after death everything is finished. So we should hold fast to life, but when I say life I mean life, which does not mean slaving all day to make the bosses fat and, while dying oneself of hunger, become the authors of their well-being.

"Masters aren't necessary, these people whose idleness is maintained by our labor; everyone must make himself useful to society, by which I mean work according to his ability and his aptitude. In this way, one would be a baker, another a teacher, etc. Following this principle, work would diminish, and each of us would have only an hour or two of work a day. Man, not being able to remain without some form of occupation, would find his distraction in work; there would be no lazy idlers, and if they did exist, there'd be so few of them that we could leave them in peace and, without complaint, let them profit from the work of others.

"There being no more laws, marriage would be destroyed. We would unite by inclination, and the family would be founded on the love of a father and mother for their children. For example, if a woman no longer loved the man she had chosen as a companion, she could separate from him and form a new association. In a word, complete freedom to live with those we love. If in the case I just cited there were children, society would raise them, that is to say, those who will love the children will take them in charge.

"With this free union, there will be no more prostitution. Secret illnesses would no longer exist, since these are only born of the abuse of the coming together of the sexes, an abuse to which women are forced to submit, since society's current conditions oblige them to take this up as a job in order to survive. Isn't money necessary in order to live, earned at whatever cost?

"With my principles, which I can't in so little time lay out in full detail, the army will no longer have any reason to exist, since there will no longer be distinct nations; private property would be destroyed, and all nations would have joined into one, which would be the Universe.

"No more war, no more disputes, no more jealousy, no more theft, no more murder, no more court system, no more police, no more administration.

"The anarchists have not yet gone into the details of their constitution: the mileposts alone have been laid out. Today the anarchists are numerous enough to overthrow the current state of things, and if that hasn't yet happened, it's because we must complete the education of the followers, give birth in them to the energy and the firm will to assist in the realization of their projects. All that is needed for that is a shove, that someone put themselves at their head, and the revolution will take place.

"He who blows up houses has as a goal the extermination of all those who, by their social standing or their acts, are harmful to anarchy. If it was permitted to openly attack these people without fearing for the police, and so for one's skin, we wouldn't set out to destroy their homes though explosive devices, which could kill the suffering classes they have at their service at the same time as them."

Ravachol's Forbidden Speech (1892)[*]

If I speak, it's not to defend myself for the acts of which I'm accused, for it is society alone which is responsible, since by its organization it sets man in a continual struggle of one against the other. In fact, don't we today see, in all classes and all positions, people who desire, I won't say the death, because that doesn't sound good, but the ill-fortune of their kind, if they can gain advantages from this. For example, doesn't a boss hope to see a competitor die? And don't all businessmen reciprocally hope to be the only ones to enjoy the advantages that their occupations bring? In order to obtain employment, doesn't the unemployed worker hope that for some reason or another someone who *does* have a job will be thrown out of his workplace. Well then, in a society where such events occur, there's no reason to be surprised about the kind of acts for which I'm blamed, which are nothing but the logical consequence of the struggle for existence that men carry on who are obliged to use every means available in order to live. And since it's every man for himself, isn't he who is in need reduced to thinking: "Well, since that's the way things are, when I'm hungry I have no reason to hesitate about using the means at my disposal, even at the risk of causing victims! Bosses, when they fire workers, do they worry whether or not they're going to die of hunger? Do those who have a surplus worry if there are those who lack the basic necessities?"

There are some who give assistance, but they are powerless to relieve all those in need and who will either die prematurely because of privations of various kinds, or voluntarily by suicides of all kinds, in order to put an end to a miserable existence and to not have to put up with the rigors of hunger, with countless shames and humiliations, and who are without hope of ever seeing them end. Thus there are the Hayem and Souhain families, who killed their children so as not to see them suffer any longer, and all the women who, in fear of not being able to feed a child, don't hesitate to destroy in their wombs the fruit of their love.

---

[*] On trial for murder after a series of bombings, Ravachol attempted to give the following speech, not to deny his guilt, but to accept and explain it. According to contemporary accounts, he was cut off after a few words, and the speech was never delivered. He was guillotined shortly afterwards.

And all these things happen in the midst of an abundance of all sorts of products. We could understand if these things happened in a country where products are rare, where there is famine. But in France, where abundance reigns, where butcher shops are loaded with meat, bakeries with bread, where clothing and shoes are piled up in stores, where there are unoccupied lodgings! How can anyone accept that everything is for the best in a society when the contrary can be seen so clearly? There are many people who will feel sorry for the victims, but who'll tell you they can't do anything about it. Let everyone scrape by as he can! What can he who lacks the necessities when he's working do when he loses his job? He has only to let himself die of hunger. Then they'll throw a few pious words on his corpse. This is what I wanted to leave to others. I preferred to make of myself a smuggler, a counterfeiter, a murderer and assassin. I could have begged, but it's degrading and cowardly and even punished by your laws, which make poverty a crime. If all those in need, instead of waiting, *took,* wherever and by whatever means, the self-satisfied would understand perhaps a bit more quickly that it's dangerous to want to consecrate the existing social state, where worry is permanent and life threatened at every moment.

We will quickly understand that the anarchists are right when they say that in order to have moral and physical peace, the causes that give birth to crime and criminals must be destroyed. We won't achieve these goals in suppressing he who, rather than die a slow death caused by the privations he had and will have to put up with, without any hope of ever seeing them end, prefers, if he has the least bit of energy, to violently take that which can assure his well-being, even at the risk of death, which would only put an end to his sufferings.

So that is why I committed the acts of which I am accused, and which are nothing but the logical consequence of the barbaric state of a society which does nothing but increase the rigor of the laws that go after the effects, without ever touching the causes. It is said that you must be cruel to kill your like, but those who say this don't see that you resolve to do this only to avoid the same fate.

In the same way you, gentlemen of the jury, will doubtless sentence me to death, because you think it is necessary, and that my death will be a source of satisfaction for you who hate to see human blood flow. But when you think it is useful to have it flow in order to ensure the security of your existence, you hesitate no more than I do, but with this difference: you do it without running any risk, while I, on the other hand, acted at the risk of my very life.

Well, gentlemen, there are no more criminals to judge, but the causes of crime to destroy! In creating the articles of the Criminal Code, the legislators forgot that they didn't attack the causes, but only the effects, and so they don't in any way destroy crime. In truth, the causes continuing to exist, the effects will necessarily flow from them. There will always be criminals, for today you destroy one, but tomorrow ten will be born.

What, then, is needed? Destroy poverty, this seed of crime, in assuring to each and all the satisfaction of their needs! How difficult this is to realize! All that is needed is to establish society on a new basis, where all will be held in common and where each, producing according to his abilities and his strength, could consume according to his needs. Then and only then will we no longer see people like the hermit of Notre-Dame-de-Grace and others, begging for a metal whose victims and slaves they become! We will no longer see women give up their charms, like a common piece of merchandise, in exchange for this same metal that often prevents us from recognizing whether or not affection is sincere. We will no longer see men like Pranzini, Prado, Berland, Anastay and others who kill in order to have this same metal. This shows that the cause of all crimes is always the same, and you have to be foolish not to see this.

Yes, I repeat it: it is society that makes criminals and you, jury members, instead of striking, you should use your intelligence and your strength to transform society. In one fell swoop you'll suppress all crime. And your work, in attacking causes, will be greater and more fruitful than your justice, which belittles itself in punishing its effects.

I am nothing but an uneducated worker; but because I have lived the life of the poor, I feel more than a rich bourgeois the iniquity of your repressive laws. What gives you the right to kill or lock up a man who, put on earth with the need to live, found himself obliged to take what he lacks in order to feed himself?

I worked to live and to provide for my family; as long as neither my family nor I suffered too much, I remained what you call honest. Then work became scarce, and with unemployment came hunger. It is only then that the great law of nature, that imperious voice that accepts no reply, the instinct of preservation, forced me to commit some of the crimes and misdemeanors of which I am accused and which I admit I am the author of.

Judge me, gentlemen of the jury, but if you have understood me, while judging *me*, judge all the unfortunate who poverty, combined with natural pride, made criminals, and who wealth or ease would have made honest men.

An intelligent society would have made of them men like any other!

Emile Henry (1872-1894)

The Interrogation of Emile Henry (1894)[*]

Q: On February 12 you entered the Café Terminus.

    A: Yes, at eight o'clock.

Q: Your bomb was in your pants belt.

    A: No, in my overcoat pocket.

Q: Why did you go to the Café Terminus?

    A: I had first gone to Bignon, the Café de la Paix and the Americain but there weren't enough people. So I went to the Terminus and I waited.

Q: There was an orchestra. How long did you wait?

    A: An hour.

Q: Why?

    A: So that there would be a bigger crowd.

Q: And then?

    A: You know full well.

Q: I'm asking you.

    A: I threw away my cigar! I lit the fuse and then taking the bomb in my hand I left and, as I was leaving the café, I threw the bomb from the doorway.

D: You hold human life in contempt.

    A: No, the life of bourgeois.

Q: You did everything you could to save yours.

    A: Yes, so I could start again. I counted on leaving the café, closing the door, getting a ticket at the Saint-Lazare station, escaping, and starting over the next day.

Q: As you left you met a waiter. Further on a certain Etienne detained you saying: "I've got you, you wretch!" You answered: "Not yet." What did you then do?

---

[*] From Jean Maitron, *Ravachol et les anarchistes*. Paris, Julliard, 1964.

A: I fired at him.

Q: He fell. What did you say?

A: That he was lucky that I didn't have a better revolver.

Q: Then you were detained by a hairdresser. What did you do?

A: I shot him with the revolver.

Q; He was hit and hasn't healed. Agent Poisson followed you.

A: At this moment, since a crowd was gathering, I stopped. I waited for Agent Poisson and fired three shots at him with my revolver.

Q: You were then arrested, and the policemen had a hard time tearing you from the fury of the crowd.

A: Which didn't know what I'd done.

Q: You had special bullets on you. Why?

A: To cause more harm.

Q: And a dagger on which there was a preparation.

A: I had poisoned the blade in order to strike an anarchist informer.

Q: You were determined to strike the agent with that weapon?

A: Certainly.

Q: You were seated at a table near the door and had thrown the device in front of you. Why didn't you hit more people with that explosion, since you had aimed at the orchestra?

A: I threw the bomb too high. It hit a lamp and went off course.

Q: A muffled explosion was heard and the café was completely destroyed: tables, mirrors, woodwork were broken. There were many wounded: twenty. One of them, M. Borde has since died. His leg was covered with wounds. Another, M. Van Herreweghen received forty wounds. There were women: Mme. Kingsbourg, who is still suffering from her wounds, many others that you will hear. And these women were so terrified that they have hidden their presence and their wounds. You said that the more bourgeois that die the better it would be.

A: That's just what I think.

Q: At first you said you were called Breton. A little later you revealed yourself and you said that your name is Emile Henry and you gave the design of your device. How was it made?

A: It was a small kettle of tin containing a detonator and a fuse.

Q: You said that you had been relatively unsuccessful. What does that mean?

A: I wanted to kill more, but the kettle wasn't properly closed.

Q: You had put projectiles in it.

A: I had put 120 pellets in it.

Q: Vaillant, who said he wanted to wound and not kill, had put nails and not pellets.

A: Me, I wanted to kill and not wound.

Q: Your domicile wasn't known.

A: I had said that I didn't have a domicile in Paris, I declared that I arrived from Marseilles or Peking.

Q: Soon afterwards a room at the Villa Faucheur was robbed. The police superintendent found explosives and recognized that this was your home.

A: I don't know who robbed my home.

Q: You were warned that your domicile had been discovered and at that point you declared that quantities of explosives must have been found at your home.

A: I had enough to make twelve to fifteen bombs.

Q: (To the jury) You know the crime and the accused, who has just cynically confessed his crime.

A: It's not cynicism, it's conviction.

Q: Did you want to kill the waiter, Etienne?

A: I wanted to kill all those who put themselves in the way of my escape.

Q: Did you want to kill the Agent Poisson?

A: Certainly. His saber was raised and he would have killed me.

Q: Did you want to kill the people at the Hôtel Terminus?

A: Certainly, as many as possible.

Q: Did you want to destroy the building?

A: Oh, I couldn't care less!

The Presiding Judge to the Jury: This would suffice to establish the guilt of the accused. But whatever the crime, justice—and this is our honor—

never deviates form the usual rules. We must examine all the details and pause before another act for which the accused is reproached.

Q: Your father lived at Brevannes, then he went to Spain, took part in the Paris Commune, and your mother found herself a widow with three children. You received a grant at the École J.-B. Say, at seventeen you qualified for admission to the École Polythechnique. You didn't continue.

    A: In order not to be a soldier and be forced to fire on the unfortunate, like at Fourmies.

Q: You found a job with a builder, M. Bordenave, your relative. How much did you earn?

    A: In Venice I earned 100F a month.

Q: Why did you leave?

    A: For reasons foreign to the affair.

Q: You said that he wanted to force you to carry out a secret surveillance, which revolted you. M. Bordenave when questioned protested.

    A: He recognized that there was a misunderstanding.

Q: You then found another job.

    A: I suffered through three months of poverty before this!

Q: In any event, you soon had a position.

    A: A quite mediocre one: 100 to 120 F a month.

Q: At this moment you come under the influence of one of your brothers. A short while later you were arrested after a meeting in honor of Ravachol, and your boss found anarchist works in your desk, most notably a translation of an Italian newspaper indicating how to make nitroglycerine and in which we read: "Long live theft, long live dynamite!" We can see there the rules you put in practice in the attack on the Rue des Bons-Enfants. So then your boss fired you.

    A: I was fired when these papers were found.

Q: You looked for work at a watchmaker's. Then you were employed by "*l'En dehors*", edited by Matha, who was condemned in 1892—the year you arrived at the newspaper—for inciting insubordination among soldiers. You refused to be a soldier.

    A: I had done three years of school battalion and that was all I could do as a soldier.

Q: You avoided the call to military service and your mother disapproved of you.

A: She feared my expatriation.

Q: On the recommendation of Ortiz, a burglar, you went to work for M. Dupuis.

A: I don't know what Ortiz has done since I knew him.

Q: M. Dupuis had increased your salary.

A: I had much affection for him.

Q: Would you like to repeat before the jury the confessions you made during the questioning? I would very much like it to be you that speaks.

A: Certainly. Tomorrow I'll give the motives for my act. The *Société des Carmaux* is represented in Paris by its administration.

After the strike I bought a kettle. I had dynamite, a primer, fuses.

(The questioning continues. The accused refuses to say what he did during 1893. During a difficult period in the questioning the Presiding Judge shouts:)

Q: Beware of your silence!

A: I don't care. I don't have to beware of my silence. I know full well that I'll be condemned to death.

Q: Listen. I think there's a confession that's damaging to your pride. Vaillant admitted that he received 100 F from a burglar. You don't want to recognize that you extended your hand to receive the money from a theft, the hand that we today see covered in blood.

A: My hands are covered in blood, like your red robe is! In any case, I don't have to answer you.

Q: You are accused and it's my duty to interrogate you.

A: I don't recognize your justice.

Q: You don't recognize justice. Unfortunately for you, you are in its hands, and the jury will be able to appreciate this.

A: I know!

(The Presiding Judge): Be seated.

Letter to the Director of the Conciergerie
Emile Henry February 27, 1894[*]

During the visit you made to my cell Sunday, the 18th of this month, we had a quite friendly discussion of anarchist ideas.

You said you were very surprised to learn to see our theories in a different light, and you asked me to summarize our conversation in writing, in order to better know what the anarchists want.

You can easily understand, sir, that in just a few pages one can't expound upon a theory which analyses our current social life in all of its manifestations; that studies these manifestations the way a doctor examines a sick body, and which then condemns them because they're contrary to human happiness and, in place of them, builds an entirely new life, based on principles completely antagonistic to those upon which the old society was built.

Besides, others have already done what you ask of me: Kropotkin, Reclus, Sébastien Faure have set forth their ideas, and pushed their development as far as possible.

Read "*Évolution et Révolution*" by Reclus, "*La morale anarchiste*," "*Les paroles d'un révolté*," "*La conquête du pain*" by Peter Kropotkin; "*Autorité et liberté*," "*Le machinisme et ses consequences*" by Sébastien Faure; "*La société mourante et l'anarchie*" by Grave; "*Entre Paysans*" (Fra Contadini) by Malatesta; read also the numerous pamphlets and manifestoes that have appeared over the last fifteen years, each expounding new ideas, according to whether study or circumstances suggested them to their authors.

Read all of this and then you would form a well-founded judgment about anarchy.

Nevertheless, don't think that anarchism is a dogma, a doctrine that can't be attacked, indisputable, venerated by its followers as the Koran is by Muslims.

No, the absolute freedom that we call for ceaselessly expands our ideas, raises them towards new horizons (following the will of diverse

---

[*] This text was written from jail just two weeks after Henry had thrown a bomb at Paris' Café Terminus, killing one and injuring twenty.

individuals) and removes them from the rigid frameworks of regimentation and codification.

We are not "believers"; we don't bow before Reclus or Kropotkin. We debate their ideas, we accept them when they develop sympathetic impressions in our brains, but we reject them when they don't strike a chord within us.

We are far from possessing the blind faith of the collectivists, who believe in something because Guesde said it had to be believed in, and who have a catechism whose paragraphs it would be sacrilegious to dispute.

This being established, I am going to try to briefly and rapidly expound for you what *I* understand by anarchy, without involving other comrades who, on certain points, could have views different from mine.

You would not dispute the fact that the current social system is evil, and the proof that it is is that everyone suffers from it. From the poor itinerant, with neither bread nor roof, who knows constant hunger, to the millionaire, who lives in fear of a revolt of the poor that would trouble his digestion, all of humanity lives in a state of anxiety.

On what bases does bourgeois society rest? Putting aside the principles of family, fatherland, and religion, which are nothing but corollaries, we can affirm that that the two cornerstones, the two fundamental principles of the current state, are authority and property.

I don't want to go on any longer on this subject: it would be easy for me to prove that all the ills we suffer from flow from property and authority.

Poverty, theft, crime, prostitution, war, revolution are all nothing but the results of these principles.

The two foundations of society being thus evil, there is no reason to hesitate. There's no need to try any of a group of palliatives (e.g. socialism) that serve only to shift the wrong. The two vicious germs must be destroyed, and eradicated from social life.

This is why we anarchists want to replace private property with communism, and authority with freedom.

No more deeds of possession or domination: absolute equality.

When we say absolute equality we don't claim that all men will have the same intelligence, the same physical organization: we know that there will always be the greatest diversity in cerebral and physical aptitudes. It is precisely this variety of capacities that will bring into being the production of all that is necessary for humanity, and we count on this as well to maintain emulation in an anarchist society.

There will be engineers and laborers: this is obvious. But one will not be considered superior to the other, since the work of the engineer is useless without the collaboration of the laborer, and vice versa.

Everyone being free to choose his trade, there will exist only beings who obey, without any constraints, the leanings nature places in them (guarantee of good productivity).

Here a question must be asked: And the lazy? Will everyone want to work?

We answer yes, everyone will want to work, and here is why:

Today, the average workday is ten hours.

Many workers are kept busy at labors that are absolutely useless to society, in particular on armaments for the army and navy. Many are also unemployed. Add to this a considerable number of able-bodied men who produce nothing: soldiers, priests, policemen, magistrates, civil servants, etc.

We can thus say, without being accused of exaggeration, that of a hundred capable of producing some kind of labor, only fifty furnish an effort truly useful to society. It is these fifty who produce all of society's riches.

From this flows the deduction that if everyone worked, instead of ten hours the workday would decrease to only five.

Beyond this we should consider that in the current state of things the total of manufactured products is four times, and of agricultural products three times the amount required to meet humanity's needs; which is to say that a humanity three times more numerous would be clothed, housed, heated, fed; in a word, would have all of its needs satisfied if waste and other causes didn't destroy that overproduction. (You will find these statistics in the little pamphlet: "The Products of the Land and Industry").

From what has gone before, we can draw the following conclusion:

A society where all would work together, and which would be satisfied with productivity not far beyond its consumer needs (the excess of the first over the second would constitute a small reserve), would have to ask of each of its able-bodied members an effort of only two or three hours, perhaps less.

Who would then refuse to give such a small quantity of labor? Who would want to live with the shame of being held in contempt by all and being considered a parasite?

... Property and authority march together, the one supporting the other to keep humanity enslaved.

What is the right to property? Is it a natural right? Is it legitimate that one eats while the other fasts? No. Nature, in creating us, made us with similar organisms, and the laborer's stomach demands the same satisfaction as that of the financier.

Nevertheless, one class today has taken all, stealing from the other class the bread not only of its body, but also of its soul.

Yes, in a century that we call one of progress and of science, is it not painful to think of the millions of intelligences hungry for knowledge and that cannot flourish? How many children of the common man, who could have become men and women of great value, useful to humanity, will never know anything but the few indispensable notions taught in elementary school.

Property! That is the enemy of human happiness, for it alone creates inequality, and in its train hatred, envy, bloody revolt ...

Established authority serves no other purpose than the sanctioning of property. It is there to put force at the service of the act of despoiling.

Work being a natural need you will accept along with me that no one would flee from the demand of as minimal an effort as that which we spoke of above.

(Labor is so natural a need that History shows us several statesmen relieving themselves with joy from the cares of politics to work as simple laborers: To cite two well-known cases: Louis XVI worked with locks, and in our day Gladstone, "The Great Old Man"* profits from his vacations to himself chop down some of the oaks of his forests, like a common lumberjack).

So you see, sir, there would be no reason to have recourse to the law to avoid the problem of idlers.

---

* in English in the original.

But if in some extraordinary case someone wanted to refuse his assistance to his brothers, it would *still* be less costly to feed this unfortunate, who can only be described as sick, than to maintain legislators, magistrates, police and prison wardens to crush him down.

Many other questions arise, but they are of a secondary nature, the most important thing being to establish that the suppression of property would not cause a cessation of production due to the development of laziness, and that anarchist society would know how to feed itself and satisfy all of its needs.

All the other objections that can be raised will be easily refuted by taking inspiration from the idea that an anarchist milieu would cause the love of and solidarity with his like to grow in each of its members, for man will know that in working for others he works for himself.

A seemingly better-founded objection is the following:

> If there is no more authority, if there is no fear of the gendarme to stop the criminal's arm, don't we risk seeing crimes and misdemeanors multiply at a frightening rate?

The answer is easy:

We can categorize the crimes committed today in two principal categories; crimes of interest and crimes of passion.

The first group will disappear on its own, since there can be no attacks on property in a milieu which has done away with property.

As for the second group, no law can stop them. Far from this being the case, the current law—which acquits a husband who kills his adulterous wife—does nothing but favor the frequency of these crimes.

On the contrary, an anarchist milieu would raise the moral level of humanity Man will understand that he has no rights over a woman who gives herself to another man, since that woman does nothing but follow her nature.

Consequently crimes, in a future society, will become increasingly rare, until they disappear completely.

Sir, I am going to summarize for you my ideal of an anarchist society.

> No more authority, which is far more contrary to human happiness than the few excesses that could occur at the beginning of a free society.

In place of the current authoritarian organization, the grouping of individuals by sympathies and affinities without laws or leaders.

No more private property; the gathering in common of products; each one working and consuming according to his needs, which is to say, as he wishes.

No more family, selfish and bourgeois, making man the property of woman and woman the property of man; no more demanding of two beings who loved each other but a moment that they remain attached till the end of their days.

Nature is capricious: it always demands new sensations. It wants free love. This is why we want free unions.

No more fatherlands, no more hatred between brothers, pitting against each other men who have never set eyes on each other.

Replacement of the narrow and petty attachment of the chauvinist for his country by the large and fruitful love of all of humanity, without distinction of race or color.

No more religions, forged by priests to degrade the masses and give them the hope of a better life, while they themselves enjoy life in the here and now.

On the contrary, the continual expansion of the sciences, put within the grasp of every being who will feel attached to their study, little by little bringing all men to a materialist consciousness.

The particular study of hypnotic phenomena, which science is beginning to become aware of, in order to unmask the charlatans who present to the ignorant, in a marvelous and superstitious light, facts which are purely physical.

In a word, absolutely no more hindrances to the free development of human nature.

The free blossoming of physical, cerebral and mental faculties.

I am not so optimistic as to believe that a society built on such foundations will arrive at perfect harmony. But I have the profound conviction that two or three generations will suffice to tear mankind from the influence of the artificial civilization which it submits to today and to return it to the state of nature, which is the state of goodness and love.

But in order to make this ideal victorious, to set anarchist society on a solid foundation, we must begin with the work of destruction. The old, worm-eaten edifice must be torn down.

This is what we are doing.

The bourgeoisie claims that we will never arrive at our goal.

The future, the very near future, will teach them.

Vive l'Anarchie!

Zo d'Axa (1864-1930)

The golden age of French anarchism, the last days of the nineteenth and the beginning of the twentieth centuries, were dominated by figures who issued from the working class. For every scholarly Elisée Reclus there was a struggling Albert Libertad. But the phenomenon of upper-class anarchists that produced Kroptkin in Russia and Malatesta in Italy also produced perhaps the most unique of all those on the left of French politics: Zo d'Axa, born Alphonse Gallaud de la Pérouse. The title of Zo d'Axa's most famous publication clearly expressed his program: "*L'endehors*" (The Outsider). In the writing of Zo d'Axa we can see opposition in a pure state, an opposition that refuses to tie itself to any plan for the future. In his work the evils of the present are enough to justify revolt; let the future decide what will come in its place.

This diffuse, free-floating hatred of the existing order gave Zo d'Axa complete freedom to condemn all that he saw and hated without restraint, since nothing that is will continue to be in the unforeseeable world. "There is," he wrote, "a sure means to pluck joy immediately: Destroy passionately!"

In his 1895 book "From Mazas to Jerusalem" he titled one of the chapters "Without a Goal," and this was the heart of his program, "for the future hasn't yet become clear." If the people were foolish enough to think there is a radiant future and that the voting booth can lead to it, then Zo d'Axa was there to mock the ballot box of their hopes by nominating an ass for office. For if they were "suckers" enough to vote for change, then the ass was their man for, as the candidate is quoted as saying by Zo d'Axa: "I'm no dumber than you."

A Sure Means to Pluck Joy Immediately: Destroy Passionately (1892)*

The Bourse, the Palace of Justice, and the Chamber of Deputies are buildings of which there has been much talk these past few days. These three buildings had been especially threatened by three young men who were fortunately stopped just in time.

Nothing can be hidden from our friends the journalists; they revealed the triple conspiracy, and their colleagues in the prefecture immediately apprehended the conspirators.

Once again the men of the press and the police have earned the gratitude of that part of the population that doesn't yet appreciate the picturesque charm of palaces in ruin, and the strange beauty of collapsed buildings.

The public won't be sparing in its thanks. The services rendered will be recognized with hard cash. Civic virtues must be encouraged. Secret funds will dance, and society's saviors will lead the cotillion.

All the better! For it is edifying to note that if there are, among our adversaries, a small number of clever exploiters, the great mass of them is made up of imbeciles who push the limits of naïveté to the horizon.

How could these uncouth ones believe that the anarchists thought to blow up parliament at this moment?

At a time when the deputies are on vacation!

You have to be lower than the low to think that revolutionaries would choose such a moment.

If only for the sake of common courtesy, we would wait for everyone's return after the vacation season.

Nevertheless, the other morning the storekeepers of Paris, while straightening up their goods, said to themselves, with their robust good sense:

> "There's not the least chance of error. They want to undermine the foundation of our centuries-old monuments. We are confronted with a new plot."

---

* From *L'En-Dehors*, 1892.

Come, come, brave shopkeepers! You wander on the plains of the absurd. This conspiracy you speak of isn't new. If it's a question of tearing down the worm-eaten edifices of the society we hate, well, this has been in preparation for a long time.

This is what we have always plotted.

The temple of the Bourse—where the faithful Catholics and the fervent Jews hold their meetings for the rites and things of petty commerce—the temple of the Bourse must, in fact, disappear, and soon.

The money-handlers will in their turn be handled by the heavy caress of the crumbling stones.

Then the game of the Bourse will no longer be played; those skillful strokes that bring millions to corporations—whose reason for being is to speculate on wheat and to organize famines—will be no more.

Those who work behind the scenes: the brokers, all the bankers—gold's priests—will sleep their last sleep beneath the ruins of their temple.

In this reposeful position the financiers will be pleasing to us.

As for the magistrates, it's well known that they are never so handsome as when they march towards death.

It's a real pleasure to see them.

History is full of striking sketches in honor of prosecutors and judges who the people, from time to time, made suffer. It must be admitted these men had a decorative agony.

And what a superb spectacle it would be: a commotion at the Palace of Justice. Quesnay constrained by a column that will have broken his vertebrae, trying hard to assume the look of a Beaurepaire struck down during the Crusades; Cabot, quoting Balzac with his dying breath; and Anquetil, next to the witty Croupi, crying out:

"Nothing is lost ... we lay below our positions."

The scene would have such grandeur that the good souls that we are would sincerely feel bad for the defeated. We would no longer want to remember the ignominy of the red robes—dyed with the blood of the poor. We will forget that the judiciary was cowardly and cruel.

It will be the ineffable pardon.

And if Atthalin himself—this specialist in political trials—his head slightly cracked, were to ask to be taken to a rest home, we would gallantly accede to this sick man's wish.

In truth, it isn't indispensable to feel oneself an anarchist to be seduced by the coming demolitions.

All those who society flagellates in the very intimacy of their being instinctively want vengeance.

A thousand institutions of the old world are marked with a fatal sign.

Those affiliated with the plot have no need to hope for a far off better future; they know a sure means to pluck joy immediately:

Destroy passionately!

Without a Goal (1895)[*]

"Wait a minute then," people say, "what is their goal?"

And the benevolent questioner suppresses a shrug upon noting that there are young men refractory to the usages, laws and demands of current society, and who nevertheless don't affirm a program.

"What do they hope for?"

If at least these nay-sayers without a credo had the excuse of being fanatics. And no, faith no longer wants to be blind. They discuss, they stumble, they search. Pitiful tactic! These skirmishers of the social battle, these flagless ones are so aberrant as to not proclaim that they have the formula for the universal panacea, the only one! Mangin had more wit.

"And I ask you: what are they seeking for themselves?"

Let's not even talk about it. They don't seek mandates, positions or delegations of any kind. They aren't candidates. Then what? Don't make me laugh. They are held in the appropriate disdain, a disdain mixed with commiseration.

I too suffer from that underestimation.

There are a few of us who feel that we can barely glimpse the future truths.

Nothing attaches us to the past, but the future hasn't yet become clear.

And so we carry on, as misunderstood as foreigners, and it's both here and there, it's everywhere that we are foreigners.

Why?

Because we don't want to recite new catechisms, and we above all else don't want to pretend to believe in the infallibility of doctrines.

We would need to possess a vile form of complacency to admit a group of theories without reserve. And we are not that complacent. There has been no Revelation. We are keeping our enthusiasm virgin in expectation of a fervor. Will it come?

And even if the final term escapes us, we won't skimp on our work. Our era is a transitional one, and the free man has his role to play.

---

[*] From *Zo d'Axa, De Mazas a Jérusalem*. Chamuel, Paris, 1895.

Authoritarian society is odious to us, and we are preparing the experiment of a libertarian society.

Uncertain of its results, we nevertheless long for the attempt, the change.

Instead of stagnating in this aging world where the air is heavy, where the ruins crumble as if to bury us, we hasten to the final demolition.

To do so is to hasten a renaissance.

The Case of the Dog (1896)[*]

It almost happened that the Commissariat of Clichy—this police office that has served as the backdrop for legendary cases of the third degree—met its end in an apotheosis of dynamite.

Two cute little bombs of red copper had been placed in a corridor leading to the Superintendent's office; the fuses had been lit ... everything was going along beautifully, from the special point of view of the depositor arguing for the purification of the place, when a dog, that dog of a dog of a Superintendent, noticed the *al giorno* lighting and began vociferating. It was thus that the alarm was sounded. He barked; he barked and someone came in enough time to extinguish the threatening illumination.

It should be noted that, since the geese of the Capitol, there have always been animals that get involved in things that don't concern them. The vile beasts—this is an image—always cry out: "Watch out!" at the least tumult.

In all fairness, I'd like to specify that the dog's case can be pleaded: whatever the dishonorable function of his master, this faithful quadruped seeks to protect him. One should appreciate a devotion so total, and not cast solemn blame on the puppy who prevented things from totally blowing up.

In any case, it's optional to fear that that the people of the commissariat of Clichy—those worthy representatives of authority who, on May 1 and July 14, conquered a bloody reputation as executioners in the suburbs—only stepped back in order to be better blown up ...

---

[*] From *L'En-Dehors*, 1896.

You Are Nothing But Suckers (1898)[*]

VOTERS:

In presenting myself for your votes, I owe you a few words. Here they are:

> I come from an old French family—I dare to say—and am a pedigreed ass, an ass in the good sense of the word: four paws and hair all over.
>
> My name is Worthless, which is what my competitors in this race are.
>
> I am white, as are many of the votes that have been cast and not counted, but which will now belong to me.
>
> My election is assured.
>
> You will understand that I speak frankly.

CITIZENS:

You are being fooled. It is said that the last Chamber, *made up of imbeciles and thieves,* didn't represent the majority of voters. This is false.

On the contrary, a Chamber made up of deputies who are ninnies and thieves perfectly represents the voters you are. Don't protest; a nation has the delegates it deserves.

Why did you elect them?

Amongst yourselves you don't hesitate to say that the more things change the more they remain the same; that your representatives mock you and think only of their own interests, of vainglory, or of money.

So why would you elect them again tomorrow?

You know full well that the whole lot of those you would send to the legislature would sell their votes for a check, and would sell jobs, functions and tobacco offices.

But who are the tobacco offices, positions and sinecures for if not the Electoral Committees that are also paid?

The shepherds of the Committees are less naïve than the flock.

The Chamber represents the whole.

---

[*] From *La Feuille*, 1898, a document from *La Feuille's* campaign to run an ass named Worthless for the Chamber of Deputies.

Idiots and crafty devils are needed; a parliament of old fools and Robert Macaires* is needed to embody at one and the same time professional voters and depressed workers.

And that's what you are!

You are being fooled, good voters, you are being deceived and fawned over when you are told that you are handsome, that you are justice itself, law, national sovereignty, the people-king, free men. ...Your votes are bought like at a candy store, and you are the candy. ...Suckers.

You continue to be fooled. You are told that France is still France. This isn't true.

With each passing day France loses all meaning in the world, all liberal meaning. It is no longer a hardy, risk-taking, idea-spreading, cult-smashing country. It's Marianne† kneeling before the throne of autocrats. It's *corporalisme* reborn more hypocritically than in Germany: a tonsure under the kepi.

You are being fooled, fooled without cease. They talk to you about fraternity, and never has *the struggle for bread* been sharper or more deadly.

They talk to you—you who have nothing—about patriotism and our sacred patrimony.

They talk to you about integrity, and it's the pirates of the press, the journalists ready to do anything, the master deceivers and blackmailers who sing of national honor.

The supporters of the Republic, the petit-bourgeois, the little lords are tougher on the "rogues" than the masters of the former regimes. *We live under the supervisors' eye.*

The weakened workers—the producers who consume nothing—content themselves with patiently sucking at the bone without marrow that is thrown to them, the bone of universal suffrage. And it's only to tell stories, to engage in electoral discussions, that they move their jaws, the jaws that no longer know how to bite.

And when, on occasion, the children of the people shake themselves from their torpor they find themselves, like at Fourmies,* face to face

---

* Character of a bandit in a popular play by Frederic Lemaître.
† Symbolizes France as a beautiful young woman.
* Site of a May Day rally in 1891 that was brutally put down by the army.

with our brave army ... and the reasoning of the Lebel guns puts lead in their heads.

Justice is the same for all. The honorable thieves of Panama travel in carriages and don't know the cart. But *handcuffs* squeeze the wrists of the old workers who are arrested as vagabonds.

The ignominy of the present moment is such that no candidate dares defend this society. The bourgeois-leaning politicians: the reactionaries, the liberals, the masks, the false noses, the republicans, cry out that in voting for them things will work better, things will work well. Those who have already taken everything from you ask for still more.

Give your votes, Citizens!

The beggars, the candidates, the thieves, the vote-squeezers all have a special way to make and re-make the public good.

Listen to the brave workers, the party quacks; they want to conquer power ... in order to better suppress it.

Others invoke the revolution, and they fool themselves while fooling you. Voters will never make the revolution. Universal suffrage was created precisely to prevent virile action. Charley has a good time voting ...

And even if some incident drew men onto the streets; and even if by some strong act a group went into action, what could we wait and hope for of the crowd we see swarming about, the *cowardly and empty-headed crowd?*

Go ahead men of the crowd! Go ahead, voters! To the urns ... and don't complain. It's enough. Don't try to inspire pity because of the fate you imposed upon yourselves. Afterwards don't insult the *masters* that you gave yourselves.

These masters are your equals as they steal from you. They are doubtless worth more: they're worth 25 francs a day, not counting their small profit. And this is very good.

The voter is nothing but a failed candidate.

The little people—of small savings and small hopes, rapacious small merchants, slow-moving domestic folk—need a mediocre parliament that will mint and synthesize *all that is vile in the nation.*

So vote, voters! Vote! Parliaments emanate from you. A thing is because it must be, because it can't be otherwise. Put in place a Chamber in your image. A dog returns to its vomit. Return to your deputies.

He is Elected (1900)[*]

Listen to the edifying story of a pretty little white ass, candidate in the capital. It isn't a Mother Goose rhyme, or a story from *"Le Petit Journal."* It's a true story for the old kiddies who still vote:

A burro, son of the country of La Fontaine and Rabelais, an ass so white that M. Vervoort gluttonously ate it, aspired—in the electoral game—to a place as legislator. The day of the elections having arrived, this burro, the very type of a candidate, answering to the name of Worthless, pulled off a last minute maneuver.

On this hot Sunday morning in May, when the people rushed to the polling places, the white ass, the candidate Worthless, perched on a triumphal wagon and, pulled along by voters, traversed Paris, his good city.

Upright on his hoofs, ears to the wind, proudly emerging from his vehicle gaudily painted with electoral posters—a vehicle in the shape of a ballot box—his head held high between the water glass and the presidential bell, he passed through the anger, the bravos and the gibes.

The ass looked on a Paris that gazed on him.

Paris! The Paris that votes, the crowd, the people sovereign every four years ... the people sufficiently foolish to believe that sovereignty consists in naming its masters.

As if they were parked in front of the town halls, there were flocks of voters, the dazed, fetishists who held the little cards with which they say: I abdicate.

Mr. Anyone will represent them. He will represent them all the better in that he represents no ideas. And it'll be fine. We'll make laws, we'll balance the budget. The laws will mean more chains; the budget will mean new taxes.

Slowly the ass went through the streets.

Along the way the walls were being covered with posters by members of his committee, while others distributed his proclamations to the crowd:

---

[*] From *La Feuille*, 1900.

"Think carefully, dear citizens. You know that your representatives are fooling you, have fooled you, will fool you—yet still you go to vote. So vote for me! Elect the ass! ... I'm no dumber than you."

This frankness—a tad brutal—wasn't to everyone's taste.

"We're being insulted," some of them said.

"Universal suffrage is being mocked," others more accurately cried out.

Someone angrily brandished his fist at the ass and said:

"Filthy Jew!"

But a sonorous laugh broke out. The candidate was being acclaimed. Bravely, the voters mocked both themselves and their elected representatives. Hats and canes were waved. Women threw flowers ...

The ass passed.

He descended from high in Montmartre towards the Latin Quarter. He crossed the *Grands Boulevards*, the Café Croissant where, without salt, the stuff is cooked up that the gazettes sell. He saw Les Halles where the starving—the Sovereign People—glean piles of rubbish; the quays, where the voters choose bridges as lodgings ...

The heart and the brain! This was Paris! This was democracy!

We are all brothers, old vagabonds! Pity the bourgeois! He's got gout ... and he's your brother, people without bread, man without work, worn out mother who, tonight, will go home tonight to die with the little ones. ...

We are all brothers, young conscript! It's your brother the officer down there, with his girl's corset and forehead covered with bars. Salute! Fix bayonets! In line! The Code awaits you—the military code. Twelve bullets in your skin for a gesture. It's the republican tariff.

The ass arrived before the Senate.

He rolled alongside the palace, where guards jostled each other on leaving. He continued along the outside (alas!) of the too-green gardens. The he reached the Boulevard St-Michel. On the café terraces people clapped. The ever growing crowd grabbed copies of the proclamations. Students hooked themselves to the wagon; a professor pushed the wheels. ...

And as three o'clock sounded, the police appeared.

Since 10:00 am, from post to commissariat, the telegraph and the telephone signaled the strange passage of the subversive animal. The order to bring him in was issued: Arrest the ass! Now the city watchmen blocked the candidate's route.

Near the Place St-Michel, Worthless's faithful committee was summoned by the armed forces to bring the candidate to the nearest commissariat. Naturally, the Committee passed over this order: right over the Seine, where the wagon soon stopped in front of the Palace of Justice.

More numerous, the policemen surrounded the unmoved ass. The candidate was arrested at the gate of the Palace of Justice through which deputies, swindlers and all the great thieves pass as free men.

The wagon lurched from the movements of the crowd. The agents, the brigadier in the lead, seized the shafts and put on the breast-harness. The Committee didn't insist; they harnessed up the policemen.

It was thus that the white ass was released by his most fervent partisans. Like a vulgar politician, the animal went in the wrong direction. The police re-attached him, and Authority guided his route. From that moment on, Worthless was nothing but an official candidate. His friends no longer knew him. The Prefecture opened wide its doors, and the ass entered as if it were his home.

... If we speak about this today it's to let the people know—the people of Paris and the countryside, workers, peasants, bourgeois, proud Citizens, dear lords—that the white ass Worthless has been elected. He has been elected in Paris. He has been elected in the provinces. Add up the blank and the voided ballots, add the abstentions, the voices and the silences that normally gather to signify disgust or contempt. Do some statistics if you please, and you can easily verify that in all districts the *monsieur* who is fraudulently proclaimed deputy didn't receive a quarter of the votes. From this flows the imbecilic locution "relative majority." You might as well say that at night it's relatively day.

And in this way the incoherent, brutal Universal Suffrage, which is based on number—and doesn't even have that—will perish in ridicule. In speaking of the elections in France the gazettes of the entire world, without any malice, brought together the two most notable facts of the day:

> "In the morning, around 9:00, M. Félix Faure went to vote. In the afternoon, at 3:00, the white ass was arrested."

I read this in three hundred newspapers. I was encumbered with clippings from "The Argus" and the *Courrier de la Presse.*" There were reports in English, Wallachian, Spanish ... which I nevertheless understood.

Each time that I read Félix Faure, I was sure that they were speaking of the ass.

Editor's note: During the electoral period the poster-program was really pasted up on the walls, and the day of the vote the satirical candidate really traversed Paris, from Montmartre to the Latin Quarter, cutting through the enthusiastic or scandalized crowd that loudly demonstrated. In Boulevard du Palais, the ass was duly apprehended by the police, who set themselves to drag him to the pound. As the newspapers of the time reported, if there wasn't a fight between the ass's partisans and the representatives of order it's thanks to the editor of *La Feuille* who cried out: "Don't carry on; he's now an official candidate."

Albert Libertad (1875-1908)

It is difficult not to stand in awe and admiration before the life and writings of Albert Libertad, a cripple who could only move about with the aid of crutches and who died at the age of 33. One fact, perhaps, says it best: far from being a hindrance to his life as a militant, Libertad saw his crutches as an addition to his arsenal. Victor Serge said in his memoirs that Libertad loved to brawl, and he freely used his crutches as weapons against the forces of the order he so detested. Indeed, Libertad never hesitated to engage in struggle and saw every forum as a fit one for propaganda. Newly arrived in Paris from his native Bourdeaux, where he had spent his childhood in the care of the public assistance program, he shouted interruptions during a sermon being preached at that symbol of the crushing of the Paris Commune, Sacré Coeur. And he was tireless: Rirette Maitrejean, Serge's companion during his anarchist days, says of Libertad in her *"Souvenirs d'anarchie"* that "what Libertad especially loved was public meetings. Hardly a one was held in Paris or its suburbs without his running there on his crutches. He went to them surrounded by his partisans, few in number but determined. He went to make the Good Word heard. Refusing him access to the tribune was dangerous."

Though he wrote for a variety of anarchist journals, his greatest accomplishment was the three years he spent editing *"l'anarchie,"* the most uncompromising voice on the individualist anarchist left. In its pages he gave his rage free reign, not only against the existing order, but against "the electoral cattle" who deluded themselves that an unjust society could be peaceably changed at the ballot box, as well as others on the left, "collectivists, federalists or centralists, more or less revolutionary communists all [of whom] believe in the need for governmental power. We alone don't believe in this." For Libertad and his comrades the sovereign individual was all.

Following in a direct line from Marat, Libertad—like Zo d'Axa before him, like the propagandists of the deed, and the anarchist criminals who gravitated to *"l'anarchie"*—didn't exempt the people from his rage. Whatever the reasons for their acceptance of the existing order, in one way or another they did accept it. On Bastille

Day 1906 Libertad told his readers that, "the bitterest enemy that is to be fought is within you, is anchored in your brains. He is one, but he has many masks: he is the prejudice Family, the prejudice Property. He is called Authority, the Holy Bastille Authority before which all bodies and minds bow." Libertad had no patience for those who submitted, the "brutes" who cheered on their sons as they joined their regiments. Albert Libertad had seen the enemy and seen the obligation to fight him without ceasing, and he believed every individual had that same obligation, every individual without exception.

He died a week after receiving a kick in the stomach during a brawl. He left his body, worn out by his years of struggle, to the Academy of Medicine.

To the Resigned (1905)[*]

I hate the resigned!

I hate the resigned, like I hate the filthy, like I hate layabouts!

I hate resignation! I hate filthiness, I hate inaction.

I feel for the sick man bent under some malignant fever; I hate the imaginary sick man that a little bit of will would set on his feet.

I feel for the man in chains, surrounded by guards, crushed under the weight of irons on the many.

I hate soldiers who are bent by the weight of braids and three stars; the workers who are bent under the weight of capital.

I love the man who says what he feels wherever he is; I hate the voter seeking the perpetual conquest by the majority.

I love the savant crushed under the weight of scientific research; I hate the individual who bends his body under the weight of an unknown power, of some "X," of a God,

I hate, I say, all those who, surrendering to others through fear or resignation a part of their power as men, not only keep their heads down, but make me, and those I love, keep our heads down too, through the weight of their frightful collaboration or their idiotic inertia.

I hate them; yes I hate them, because me, I feel it. I don't bow before the officer's braid, the mayor's sash, the gold of the capitalist; morality or religion. For a long time I have known that all of these things are just baubles that we can break like glass ... I bend beneath the weight of the resignation of others. O how I hate resignation!

I love life.

I want to live, not in a petty way like those who only satisfy a part of their muscles, their nerves, but in a big way, satisfying facial muscles as well as calves, my back as well as my brain.

I don't want to trade a portion of now for a fictive portion of tomorrow. I don't want to surrender anything of the present for the wind of the future.

---

[*] From *Le Culte de la charogne et autres texts*. Paris, Editions Galilée, 1976; first Published: *l'anarchie* April 13, 1905.

I don't want to bend anything of mine under the words fatherland, God, honor. I too well know the emptiness of these words, these religious and secular ghosts.

I laugh at retirement, at paradises the hope for which holds the resigned, religions, and capital.

I laugh at those who, saving for their old age, deprive themselves in their youth; those who, in order to eat at sixty, fast at twenty.

I want to eat while I have strong teeth to tear and crush healthy meats and succulent fruits. When my stomach juices digest without problem, I want to drink my fill of refreshing and tonic drinks.

I want to love women, or a woman, depending on our common desire, and I don't want to resign myself to the family, law, the Code; nothing has any rights over our bodies. You want, I want. Let us laugh at the family, the law, the ancient form of resignation.

But this isn't all. I want, since I have eyes, ears, and other senses, more than just to drink, to eat, to enjoy sexual love: I want to experience joy in other forms. I want to see beautiful sculptures and painting, admire Rodin or Manet. I want to hear the best opera companies play Beethoven or Wagner. I want to know the classics at the Comédie-Française, page through the literary and artistic baggage left by men of the past to men of the present, or even better, page through the now and forever unfinished oeuvre of humanity.

I want joy for myself, for my chosen companion, for my friends. I want a home where my eyes can agreeably rest when my work is done.

For I want the joy of labor, too; that healthy joy, that strong joy. I want my arms to handle the plane, the hammer, the spade and the scythe.

Let the muscles develop, the thoracic cage become larger with powerful, useful and reasoned movements.

I want to be useful, I want us to be useful. I want to be useful to my neighbor and for my neighbor to be useful to me. I desire that we labor much, for I am insatiable for joy. And it is because I want to enjoy myself that I am not resigned.

Yes, yes, I want to produce, but I want to enjoy myself. I want to knead the dough, but eat better bread; to work at the grape harvest, but drink better wine; build a house, but live in better apartments; make furniture, but possess the useful, see the beautiful; I want to make theatres, but big enough to house their 'me and mine'.

I want to cooperate in producing, but I also want to cooperate in consuming.

Some dream of producing for others to whom they will leave—oh the irony of it—the best of their efforts. As for me, I want, freely united with others, to produce but also to consume.

You resigned, look: I spit on your idols. I spit on God, the Fatherland, I spit on Christ, I spit on the flag, I spit on capital and the golden calf; I spit on laws and Codes, on the symbols of religion; they are baubles, I couldn't care less about them, I laugh at them ...

Only through you do they mean anything to me; leave them behind and they'll break into pieces.

You are thus a force, you resigned, one of those forces that don't know they are one, but who are nevertheless a force, and I can't spit on you, I can only hate you ... or love you.

Above all my desire is that of seeing you shaking off your resignation in a terrible awakening of life.

There is no future paradise, there is no future; there is only the present.

Let us live!

Live! Resignation is death.

Revolt is life.

To the Electoral Cattle (1906)[*]

Under the impetus of interested individuals the political committees are opening the awaited era of electoral quarrels.

As usual, they will insult each other, slander each other, fight each other. Blows will be exchanged for the benefit of a third thief, always ready to profit from the stupidity of the crowd.

Why will you go for this?

You live with your kids in unhealthy lodgings. You eat—when you can—food adulterated by the greed of traffickers. Exposed to the ravages of alcoholism and tuberculosis, you wear yourself out from morning to night at a job that is always imbecilic and useless and that you don't even profit from. The next day you start over again, and so it goes till you die.

Is it then a question of changing all this?

Are they going to give you the means for realizing a flourishing existence, you and your comrades? Are you going to be able to come and go, eat, drink, breathe without constraint, love with joy, rest, enjoy scientific discoveries and their application, decreasing your efforts, increasing your well-being. Are you finally, without disgust or care, going to live the large life, the intense life?

No, say the politicians proposed for your suffrage. This is only a distant ideal. You must be patient ... You are many, but you should also become conscious of your might so as to abandon it into the hands of your 'saviors' once every four years.

But what will they do in their turn?

The make laws! What is the law? The oppression of the greater number by a coterie claiming to *represent* the majority.

In any event, error proclaimed by the majority doesn't become truth, and only the unthinking bow before a legal lie.

The truth cannot be determined by vote.

He who votes accepts being beaten.

So why then are there laws? Because there is property.

---

[*] From *Le Culte de la charogne et autres texts*. Paris, Editions Galilée, 1976; written: February 1906.

So it is from the prejudice of property that all our miseries, all our pain flow.

So those who suffer from it have an interest in destroying property; hence the law.

The only logical means of suppressing laws is not to make them.

Who makes laws? Parliamentary *arrivistes*.

On closer analysis, it is thus not a handful of rulers who crush us, but the thoughtlessness, the stupidity of the herd of those sheep of Panurge who constitute the electoral cattle.

We will fight without cease for the conquest of "immediate happiness" by remaining partisans of the only scientific method and by proclaiming together with our abstentionist comrades:

The voter—that is the enemy!

And now, to the ballot box, cattle.

Down With the Law! (1906)*

"The anarchists find M. de La Rochefoucauld and all those who protest without worrying about legality to be <u>logically consistent</u> with their own ideas," Anna Mahé tells us.

This is obviously not correct, as I am going to show.

All that is needed is one word to travesty the meaning of a phrase, and so the two words underlined suffice to entirely change the meaning of the one I quote.

If Anna Mahé was the leader of a great newspaper she would hasten to accuse the typographers or the proofreader of the phrase and everything would be for the best in the best of all possible worlds.

Or else she would think it wise to maintain an idea that isn't a manifestation of her reasoning, but rather the act of her pen running away with itself.

But on the contrary, she thinks that it is necessary, especially in these lead articles that are viewed as anarchist, to make the fewest errors possible and for us to point them out ourselves when we take note of them.

It is to me that this falls today.

The Catholics, the socialists, all those who at a given moment accept the voting system, are not logically consistent when they rebel against the consequences of a law, when they demonstrate against its agents, its representatives.

Only the anarchists are authorized, are logically consistent *with their ideas* when they act against the law.

When a man deposits his ballot in the ballot box he is not using a means of persuasion that comes from free examination or experience. He is executing the mechanical operation of counting those who are ready to choose the same delegates as he, to consequently make the same laws, to establish the same regulations that all men must submit to. In casting his vote he says: "I trust in chance. The name that will come from this box will be that of my legislator. I could be on the side of the majority, but

---

* From *Le Culte de la charogne et autres texts*. Paris, Editions Galilée, 1976; first published in "*l'anarchie*," February 15, 1906.

there's also the chance of being on the side of the minority. More the better, and too bad."

After having come to agreement with other men, having decided that they will all defer to the mechanical judgment of number, there is on the part of those who are the minority, when they don't accept the laws and regulations of the majority, a feeling of being fooled similar to that of a bad gambler, who wants very much to win, but who doesn't want to lose.

Those Catholics who decided for the laws of exception of 1893-4 through the means of a majority are in no position to rebel when, by means of the same majority, the laws of separation are decided.

Those socialists who, by means of a majority, want to decide in favor of the laws on workers' retirements, are in no position to rebel against the same majority when it decides on some law that goes against their interests.

All parties who accept suffrage, however universal it might be, as the basis for their means of action, cannot rebel as long as they are left the means of affirming themselves by the ballot.

Catholics, in general, are in this situation. The gentlemen in question in the late battles were "great electors," able to vote in Senatorial elections; some were even parliamentarians. Not only had some voted and sought to be the majority in the Chambers that prepare the laws, but the others had elaborated that law, had discussed its terms and articles.

Thus being parliamentarists, voters, the Catholics weren't logically consistent with themselves in their revolt.

The socialists are no more so. They speak constantly of social revolution, and they spend all their time in puerile voting gestures in the perpetual search for a legal majority.

To accept the tutelage of the law yesterday, then reject it today, and take it up again tomorrow, this is the way Catholics, socialists, parliamentarists in general act. It is illogical.

None of their acts has a logical relation to that of the day before, no more than that of tomorrow will have one to that of today.

Either we accept the law of majorities or we don't accept it. Those who inscribe it in their program and seek to obtain the majority are illogical when they rebel against it.

This is how it is. But when Catholics or socialists revolt we don't search for yesterday's acts; we don't worry about those that will be carried out tomorrow: we peacefully look on as the law is broken by its manufacturers.

It will be up to us to see to it that these days don't reoccur.

So the anarchists alone are logical by rebelling.

The anarchists don't vote. They don't want to be the majority that commands; they don't accept being the minority that obeys.

When they rebel they have no need of breaking any contract: they never accept tying their individuality to any government of any kind.

They alone, then, are rebels held back by no ties, and each of their violent gestures bears a relation to their ideas, is logically consistent with their reasoning.

By demonstration, by observation, by experience or lacking these, by force, by violence, these are the means by which the anarchists want to impose themselves. By majority, by the law, never!

The Cult of Carrion (1925)[*]

In a desire for eternal life, men have considered death as a passage, as a painful step, and they have bowed before its "mystery" to the point of veneration.

Even before men knew how to work with stone, marble, and iron in order to shelter the living, they knew how to fashion matter to honor the dead.

Churches and cloisters richly wrapped their tombs under their apses and choirs, while huts were huddled against their sides, miserably sheltering the living.

The cult of the dead has, from the first moments, hindered the forward march of man. It is the original sin, the dead weight, the iron ball that humanity drags along behind it.

The voice of death, the voice of the dead has always thundered against the voice of universal life, which is ever evolving.

Jehovah, who Moses's imagination made burst forth from Sinai, still dictates his laws. Jesus of Nazareth, dead for almost twenty centuries, still preaches his morality. Buddha, Confucius, and Lao Tzu's wisdom still reign. And how many others!

We bear the heavy responsibility of our ancestors; we have their defects and their qualities.

So in France we are the children of the Gauls, though we are French via the Francs and of the Latin race when it comes to the eternal hatred of the Germans. Each of these heredities brings with it obligations.

[We are the oldest children of the church by virtue of who knows which dead, and also the grandchildren of the Great Revolution. We are citizens of the Third Republic and we are also devoted to the Sacred Heart of Jesus. We are born Catholics or Protestants, republicans or royalists, rich or poor. We are always what we are through the dead; we are never ourselves. Our eyes, placed atop our heads, look ahead and, however much they lead us forward, it is always towards the ground

---

[*] From *Le Culte de la charogne et autres textes*. Paris, Editions Galilée, 1976; first published in "*l'anarchie*," 1925. This pamphlet, published in 1925, is taken from articles that originally appeared in "l'anarchie." The sections in brackets were in the original articles but not in the pamphlet.

where our dead repose, towards the past where the dead lived that our education allows us to guide them.]

Our ancestors ... the past ... the dead ...

Whole peoples have died from this triple respect.

China is exactly where it was thousands of years ago because it has guarded the first place in their homes for their dead.

Death is not only a germ of corruption due to the chemical disintegration of man's body, poisoning the atmosphere; it is even more the case because of the consecration of the past, the immobilization of the idea at a certain stage of evolution. Living, it would have evolved, would have been more advanced. Dead, it crystallizes. Yet it is this precise moment that the living choose to admire it, in order to sanctify it, to deify it.

Usages and custom, ancestral errors are communicated from one person to another in the family. One believes in the god of his fathers, another respects the fatherland of his ancestors. Why don't we respect their lighting system, their way of dressing?

Yes, this strange fact is produced that while the externals and the daily economy improve, change, are differentiated, that while everything dies and is transformed, man, man's spirit, remains in the same servitude, is mummified in the same errors.

Just as in the century of the torch, in the century of electricity man still believes in tomorrow's paradise, in the gods of vengeance and forgiveness, in hells and Valhallas as a away of respecting the ideas of his ancestors.

The dead lead us, the dead command us, the dead take the place of the living.

All our festivals, all our glorifications are the anniversaries of deaths and massacres. We celebrate All Saints Day to glorify the saints of the church, the Feast of the Dead so as not to forget a single dead man. The dead go to Olympus or paradise, to the right of Jupiter or God. They fill "immaterial" space and they encumber "material" space with their corteges, their displays, and their cemeteries. If nature didn't take it upon itself to disintegrate their bodies and to disperse their ashes, the living wouldn't today know where to place their feet in the vast necropolis that would be the earth.

The memory of the dead, their acts and deeds, obstruct the brains of children. We only talk to them about the dead; we must only speak to them about this. We make them live in the realm of the unreal and the past. They must know nothing of the present.

If secularism has dropped the story of Mr. Noah or that of Mr. Moses, it has replaced it with those of Mr. Charlemagne or Mr. Capet. Children know the date of death of Madame Feregonde*, but don't have the least notion about hygiene. Some young girls of fifteen know that in Spain a certain Madame Isabelle spent an entire century wearing one blouse, but are strangely upset when their first menstrual period comes.

Some women, who have the chronology of the kings of France at the tip of their fingers without a single mistake don't know what to do with a child who cries out for the first time in its life.

Though we leave a young girl next to a dying man, who is in his final throes, we push her away from a woman whose womb is opening to life.

The dead obstruct cities, streets, and squares. We meet them in marble, in stone, in bronze. This inscription tells us of their birth, and that plaque tells us where they lived. Squares bear their titles or those of their exploits. Street names don't indicate their position, form, altitude or location; they speak of Magenta or Solferino, an exploit of the dead where many were killed. They recall to you Saint Eleuthere or the Chevalier de la Barre; men, incidentally, whose only quality was that of dying.

In economic life it is also the dead who lay out everyone's life path. One sees his entire life darkened by his father's "crime," another wears the halo of the glory, the genius, the daring of his forefathers. This one is born a bumpkin with the most distinguished of spirits, that one is born noble with the most vulgar of spirits. We are nothing through ourselves; we are everything through our ancestors.

And yet ... in the eyes of scientific criticism, what is death? This respect for the departed, this cult of decrepitude, by what argument can it be justified? Few have asked this, and this is why the question is not resolved.

And in the center of cities, don't we see great spaces that the living piously maintain: these are cemeteries, the gardens of the dead.

The living find it good to bury, right next to their children's cradles, piles of decomposing flesh, carrion, the nutritive element of all maladies, the breeding ground of all infections.

---

* *sic* Ferdegonde (543-596) Queen of the Franks.

They consecrate great spaces planted with magnificent trees and depose typhoid-ridden, pestilential, anthracic bodies there, one or two meters deep. And after a few days the infectious viruses roam the city seeking other victims.

Men who have no respect for their living organism, which they exhaust, which they poison, which they put at risk, are suddenly taken with a comic respect for their mortal remains when they should be rid of them as soon as possible, put them in the least cumbersome, the most usable form.

The cult of the dead is one of the most vulgar aberrations of the living. It's a holdover from those religions that promised paradise. The dead must be prepared for the visit to the beyond: give them weapons so they can participate in the hunts of Velleda, some food for the trip, give them the high viaticum, prepare them to present themselves to God. [Religions depart, but their ridiculous formulas remain. The dead take the place of the living.]

Whole groups of workingmen and women employ their abilities and energy at maintaining the cult of the dead. Men dig up the earth, carve stone and marble, forge grilles, prepare a house for all of them in order to respectfully bury in them the syphilitic carrion that has just died.

Women weave the shroud, make artificial flowers, fashion bouquets to decorate the house where the pile in a just-ended tubercular decomposition will repose. Instead of hastening to make these loci of decomposition disappear, of using all the speed and hygiene possible to destroy these evil centers whose preservation and maintenance can only spread death around them, everything possible is done to preserve them as long as possible. These mounds of flesh are paraded around in special wagons, in hearses, through the roads and the streets. When they pass, men remove their hats. They respect the dead.

The amount of effort and matter expended by humanity in maintaining the cult of the dead is inconceivable. If all this force were used to receive children then thousands and thousands of them would be spared illness and death.

If this imbecilic respect for the dead were to disappear and make room for respect for the living, we would increase the health and happiness of human life in unimaginable proportions.

Men accept the hypocrisy of necrophages, of those who eat the dead, of those who live off the dead; from the priest, giver of sacred water, to the merchant of eternal homes; from the wreath seller to the sculptor of mortuary angels. With ridiculous boxes that lead and accompany these grotesque puppets, we proceed to the removal of this human detritus and its distribution in accordance with the state of their fortune, when a good transport service, with hermetically sealed cars and a crematory oven constructed in keeping with the latest scientific discoveries would suffice.

[I will not concern myself with the use of ashes, though it would seem to me more interesting to use them as humus rather then carrying them around in little boxes. Men complain about work, yet they don't want to simplify those gestures that overly complicate the events of their existence, not even to do away with those for the imbecilic—as well as dangerous—preservation of their cadavers. The anarchists have too much respect for the living to respect the dead. Let us hope that some day this outdated cult will have become a road management service, and that the living will know life in all its manifestations.]

As we've already said, it is because men are ignorant that they surround a phenomenon as simple as death with such religious mumbo jumbo. It also worth noting that this is only the case with human death: the death of other animals and vegetables doesn't serve as the occasion for similar demonstrations. Why?

The first men, barely evolved brutes, devoid of all knowledge, buried the dead man with his living wife, his weapons, his furniture, his jewels. Others had the corpse appear before a tribunal to ask him to give an account of his life. Man has always misunderstood the true meaning of death.

And yet, in nature everything that lives dies. Every living organism falls when for one reason or another the equilibrium between its different functions is thrown off. The causes of death, the ravages of the illness or the accident that caused the death of the individual are scientifically determined.

From the human point of view then, there is death, disappearance of life, that is, the cessation of a certain activity in a certain form.

But from the general point of view death doesn't exist. There is only life. After what we call death, the transformative phenomena continue. Oxygen, hydrogen, gas, and minerals depart in different forms and associate in new combinations and contribute to the existence of other living organisms. There is no death; there is a circulation of bodies, modifications in the aspect of matter and energy, endless continuation in time and space of life and universal activity.

A dead man is a body returned to circulation in a triple form: solid, liquid, and gaseous. It is nothing but this, and we should consider and treat it as such.

It is obvious that these positive and scientific concepts leave no room for weepy speculations on the soul, the beyond, the void.

But we know that all those religions that preach the "future life" and the "better world" have as their goals causing resignation among those who are despoiled and exploited.

Rather than kneeling before cadavers it would be better to organize life on better foundations so as to get a maximum amount of joy and well-being from it.

People will be angered by our theories and our disdain: this is pure hypocrisy on their part. The cult of the dead is nothing but an insult to true pain. The fact of maintaining a small garden, of dressing in black, of wearing crepe doesn't prove the sincerity of one's sorrow. This latter, incidentally, must disappear. Individuals should react before the irrevocability and the inevitability of death. We should fight against suffering instead of exhibiting it, parading it in grotesque cavalcades and false congratulations.

This one, who respectfully follows a hearse, had the day before worked furiously at starving the deceased; that one laments behind a cadaver who did nothing to come to his assistance when it would have been possible to save his life. Every day capitalist society spreads death by its poor organization, by the poverty it creates, by the lack of hygiene, the deprivation and ignorance from which individuals suffer. By supporting such a society men are thus the cause of their own suffering, and instead of moaning before destiny they would do better to work at improving their conditions of existence so as to allow human life a maximum of development and intensity.

How could we know life when the dead alone lead it?

How can we live in the present under the tutelage of the past?

If man wants to live, let him no longer have any respect for the dead, let him abandon the cult of carrion. The dead block the road to progress for the living.

We must tear down the pyramids, the tumuli, the tombs. We must bring the wheelbarrows into the cemeteries so as to rid humanity of what they call respect for the dead, but which is the cult of carrion.

Georges Palante (1862-1925)

Nietzsche believed that reading a philosopher's works was equivalent to reading his autobiography. Seldom is this as startlingly true as in the works of Georges Palante. As Michel Onfray said in his preface to the 2004 edition of Palante's collected philosophical works, "Autobiography shows itself in each word, behind each thesis. The writing, the ideas, the composition of all his books, his references, his quotes, everything is mobilized in an attempt to sublimate, in the Freudian sense of the term, an existence dramatically placed under the sign of melancholy, of psychic and physical slowness, of ugliness, of fatigue, of pain and suffering."

Thrown back on himself by his acromegaly, which deformed him physically, Palante produced a philosophy that places the individual at the center of all. A victim of ostracism in life, his philosophy has no place for collective action; in Palante's philosophy we have life as despair. It is a world of great men who will ultimately be laid low, of the ineluctable crushing of any individual who tries to climb out of the enveloping muck. His life was a trail of personal disasters: his dreadful marriage to a woman who misunderstood him and disposed of his unfinished works after his death, his awful disease, whose resultant deformity subjected him to ridicule by those around him (he taught philosophy in high school, where his constant citing of Schopenhauer earned him the nickname of "Schopen," probably the kindest of the names he was called behind his back), his misguided attempt at academic distinction, which ended in bitter failure, and his oversensitivity, which was to lead to a challenge to a duel by a former friend and ultimately to his suicide. All of this fed Palante's genius. His philosophy, founded on his failed personal dreams and miseries, is of a fecundity that touches us even today.

Anarchism and Individualism (1909)[*]

The words anarchism and individualism are frequently used synonymously. Many thinkers vastly different from each other are carelessly qualified sometimes as anarchists, sometimes as individualists. It is thus that we speak indifferently of Stirnerite anarchism or individualism, of Nietzschean anarchism or individualism, of Barrésian anarchism or individualism, etc. In other cases, though, this identification of the two terms is not looked upon as possible. We commonly say Proudhonian anarchism, Marxist anarchism, anarchist syndicalism. But we could not say Proudhonian, Marxist, or syndicalist individualism. We can speak of a Christian or Tolstoyan anarchism, but not of a Christian or Tolstoyan individualism.

At other times the two terms have been melted together in one name: anarchist individualism. Under this rubric M. Hasch designates a social philosophy that he differentiates from anarchism properly so-called, and whose great representative, according to him, are Goethe, Byron, Humboldt, Schleiermacher, Carlyle, Emerson, Kierkegaard, Renan, Ibsen, Stirner and Nietzsche. This philosophy can be summed up as the cult of great men and the apotheosis of genius. It would seem to us to be arguable whether the expression individualist anarchism can be used to designate such a doctrine. The qualification of anarchist, in the etymological sense, can be applied with difficulty to thinkers of the race of Goethe, Carlyle, and Nietzsche, whose philosophy seems on the contrary to be dominated by ideas of hierarchical organization and the harmonious placing of values in a series. What is more, the epithet of individualist can't be applied with equal justice to all the thinkers we have just named. If it is appropriate for designating the egoist, nihilist and anti-idealist revolt of Stirner, it can with difficulty be applied to the Hegelian, optimist, and idealist philosophy of a Carlyle, who clearly subordinates the individual to the idea.

There thus reigns a certain confusion concerning the use of the two terms anarchism and individualism, as well as the systems of ideas and sentiments that these terms designate. We would here like to attempt to clarify the notion of individualism and determine its psychological and sociological content by distinguishing it from anarchism. ...

---

[*] From *La Sensibilité individualiste*. Paris, Alcan, 1909.

Individualism is the sentiment of a profound, irreducible antinomy between the individual and society. The individualist is he who, by virtue of his temperament, is predisposed to feel in a particularly acute fashion the ineluctable disharmonies between his intimate being and his social milieu. At the same time, he is a man for whom life has reserved some decisive occasion, enabling him to note this disharmony. Whether through brutality, or the continuity of his experiences, for him it has become clear that for the individual society is a perpetual creator of constraints, humiliations and miseries, a kind of continuous generation of human pain. In the name of his own experience and his personal sensation of life the individualist feels he has the right to relegate to the rank of utopia any ideal of a future society where the hoped-for harmony between the individual and society will be established. Far from the development of society diminishing evil, it does nothing but intensify it by rendering the life of the individual more complicated, more laborious and more difficult amidst the thousand cogs of an increasingly tyrannical social mechanism. Science itself, by intensifying within the individual the consciousness of the vital conditions made for him by society, arrives only at darkening his intellectual and moral horizons. *Qui auget scientiam augel et dolorem.**

We see that individualism is essentially a social pessimism. In its most moderate form it admits that if life in society is not an absolute evil and completely destructive of individuality, for the individualist it is at the very least a restrictive and oppressive condition, a necessary evil and a last resort.

The individualists who respond to this description form a small morose group whose rebellious, resigned or hopeless words contrast with the fanfares for the future of optimistic sociologists. It is Vigny saying: "The social order is always bad. From time to time it is bearable. Between bad and bearable the dispute isn't worth a drop of blood." It's Schopenhauer seeing social life as the supreme flowering of human pain and evil. It's Stirner with his intellectual and moral solipsism perpetually on his guard against the duperies of social idealism and the intellectual and moral crystallization with which every organized society threatens the individual. It is, at certain moments, an Amiel with his painful stoicism that perceives society as a limitation and restriction of his free spiritual

---

* He who increases knowledge increases suffering.

nature. It's a David Thoreau, the extremist disciple of Emerson, that "student of nature," deciding to stray from the ordinary paths of human activity and to become a "wanderer," worshipping independence and dreams. A "wanderer whose every minute will be filled with more work than the entire lives of many men with occupations." It's a Challemel-Lacour with his pessimistic conception of society and progress. It is perhaps, at certain moments, a Tarde, with an individualism colored with misanthropy that he expresses in one of his works: "It is possible that the flux of imitation has its banks and that, by the very effect of its excessive deployment, the need for sociability diminishes, or rather alters and transforms itself, into a kind of general misanthropy, very compatible, incidentally, with a moderate commercial circulation and a certain activity of industrial exchanges reduced to the strict necessary, but above all appropriate to reinforcing in each of us the distinctive traits of our inner individuality."

Even among those who, like M. Maurice Barrès, through dilettantism and artistic posture are averse to the accents of sharp revolt or discouraged pessimism, individualism remains a sentiment of "the impossibility that exists of harmonizing the private and the general self." It's a determination to set free the primary self, to cultivate it in what it has of the most special, the most advanced, the most rummaged through, both in detail and in depth. "The individualist," says M. Barrès, "is he who, through pride in his true self, which he isn't able to set free, ceaselessly wounds, soils, and denies what he has in common with the mass of men. ... The dignity of the men of our race is exclusively attached to certain tremblings that the world doesn't know and cannot see and which we must multiply in ourselves."

In all of them individualism is a sensibility that goes from hostility and distrust to indifference and disdain vis-à-vis the organized society in which we are forced to live, vis-à-vis its uniformising rules, its monotonous repetitions, and its enslaving constraints. It's a desire to escape from it and to withdraw into oneself. Above all, it is the profound sentiment of the "uniqueness of the self," of that which, despite it all, the self maintains that is unrepressible and impenetrable to social influences. As M. Tarde says, it is the sentiment of the "profound and fleeting singularity of persons, of their manner of being, or thinking, of feeling, which is only once and of an instant."

Is there any need to demonstrate how much this attitude differs from anarchism? There is no doubt that in one sense anarchism proceeds from individualism. It is, in fact, the anti-social revolt of a minority that feels itself oppressed or disadvantaged by the current order of things. But anarchism represents only the first moment of individualism, the moment of faith and hope, of actions courageous and confident of success. At its second moment individualism is converted, as we have seen, into social pessimism.

The passage from confidence to despair, from optimism to pessimism is here, in great part, an affair of psychological temperament. There are delicate souls that are easily wounded on contact with social realities and consequently quick to be disillusioned, a Vigny or a Heine, for example. We can say that these souls belong to the psychological type that has been called "sensitive." They feel that social determinism, insofar as it is repressive of the individual, is particularly tormenting and oppressive. But there are other souls who resist multiple failures, who disregard even experience's harshest examples and remain unshakeable in their faith. These souls belong to the "active" type. Such are the souls of the anarchist apostles: Bakunin, Kropotkin, Reclus. Perhaps their imperturbable confidence in their ideal depends on a lesser intellectual and emotional acuity. Reasons for doubt and discouragement don't strike them harshly enough to tarnish the abstract ideal they've forged and to lead them to the final and logical step of individualism: social pessimism.

Whatever the case, there can be no doubt concerning the optimism of anarchist philosophy. That optimism is laid out, often simplistically and with naiveté, in those volumes with blood red covers that form the reading matter of propagandists by the deed. The shadow of the optimistic Rousseau floats over all this literature.

Anarchist optimism consists in believing that social disharmonies, that the antinomies that the current state of affairs present between the individual and society, are not essential, but rather accidental and provisional; that they will one day be resolved and will give place to an era of harmony.

Anarchism rests on two principles that seem to complement each other, but actually contradict each other. One is the principle that is properly individualist or libertarian, formulated by Wilhelm von Humboldt and chosen by Stuart Mill as the epigraph of his "Essay on Liberty": "The grand, leading principle, towards which every argument unfolded in these pages directly converges, is the absolute and essential importance of human development in its richest diversity." The other is the humanist or altruist principle which is translated on the economic plane by communist anarchism. That the individualist and humanist principles negate each other is proven by logic and fact. Either the individualist principle means nothing, or it is a demand in favor of that which differs and is unequal in individuals, in favor of those traits that make them different, separates them and, if need be, opposes them. On the contrary, humanism aims at the assimilation of humanity. Following the expression of M. Gide, its ideal is to make a reality of the expression "our like." In fact, at the current time we see the antagonism of the two principles assert itself among the most insightful theoreticians of anarchism, and that logical and necessary antagonism cannot fail to bring about the breakup of anarchism as a political and social doctrine.

Whatever the case and whatever difficulties might be met by he who wants to reconcile the individualist and humanist principles, these two rival and enemy principles meet at least at this one point: they are both clearly optimistic. Humboldt's principle is optimistic insofar as it implicitly affirms the original goodness of human nature and the legitimacy of its free blossoming. It sets itself up in opposition to the Christian condemnation of our natural instincts, and we can understand the reservations of M. Dupont-White, the translator of the "Essay on Liberty," had from the spiritualist and Christian point of view (condemnation of the flesh) as concerns this principle.

The humanist principle is no less optimistic. Humanism, in fact, is nothing but rendering divine in man what he has of the general, of humanity, and consequently of human society. As we see, anarchism, optimistic as concerns the individual, is even more so as concerns society. Anarchism supposes that individual freedoms, left to themselves, will naturally harmonize and spontaneously realize the anarchist ideal of free society.

In regard to these two opposing points of view, the Christian and anarchist, what is the attitude of individualism? Individualism, a realist philosophy, nothing but lived life and immediate sensation, equally repudiates these two metaphysics: one, Christian metaphysics, which *a priori* affirms original evil, the other the rationalist and Rosseauist metaphysic, that no less *a priori* affirms the original and essential goodness of our nature. Individualism places itself before the facts. And these latter make visible in the human being a bundle of instincts in struggle with each other and, in human society, a grouping of individuals also necessarily in struggle with each other. By the very fact of his conditions of existence the human being is subject to the law of struggle: internal struggle among his own instincts, external struggle with his like. If recognizing the permanent and universal character of egoism and struggle in human existence means being pessimistic, then we must say that individualism is pessimistic. But we must immediately add that the pessimism of individualism, a pessimism of fact, an experimental pessimism, if you will, pessimism *a posteriori*, is totally different from the theological pessimism that *a priori* pronounces, in the name of dogma, the condemnation of human nature. What is more, individualism to as great a degree separates itself from anarchism. If, with anarchism, it admits Humboldt's principle as the expression of a normal tendency necessary to our nature for its full blossoming, at the same time it recognizes that this tendency is condemned to never being satisfied because of the internal and external disharmonies of our nature. In other words, it considers the harmonious development of the individual and society as a utopia. Pessimistic as concerns the individual, individualism is even more so as concerns society: man is by his very nature disharmonious because of the internal struggle of his instincts. But this disharmony is exacerbated by the state of society which, through a painful paradox, represses our instincts at the same time as it exasperates them. In fact, from the rapprochement of individual wills-to-life is formed a collective will-to-life which becomes immediately oppressive for the individual will-to-life and opposes its flourishing with all its force. The state of society thus pushes to its ultimate degree the disharmonies of our nature. It exaggerates them and puts them in the poorest possible light. Following the idea of Schopenhauer, society thus truly represents the human will-to-life at its highest degree: struggle, lack of fulfillment, and suffering.

From this opposition between anarchism and individualism flows others. Anarchism believes in progress. Individualism is an attitude of thought that we can call non-historical. It denies becoming, progress. It sees the human will-to-life in an eternal present. Like Schopenhauer, with whom he has more than one similarity, Stirner is a non-historical spirit. He too believes that it is chimerical to expect something new and great from tomorrow. Every social form, by the very fact that it crystallizes, crushes the individual. For Stirner, there is no utopian tomorrow, no "paradise at the end of our days." There is nothing but the egoist today. Stirner's attitude before society is the same as that of Schopenhauer before nature and life. With Schopenhauer the negation of life remains metaphysical and, we might say, spiritual (we should remember that

Schopenhauer condemns suicide, which would be the material and tangible negation). In the same way, Stirner's rebellion against society is an entirely spiritual internal rebellion, all intention and inner will. It is not, as is the case with Bakunin, an appeal to pan-destruction. Regarding society, it is a simple act of distrust and passive hostility, a mix of indifference and disdainful resignation. It is not a question of the individual fighting against society, for society will always be the stronger. It must thus be obeyed, obeyed like a dog. But Stirner, while obeying, as a form of consolation, maintains an immense intellectual contempt. This is more or less the attitude of Vigny vis-à-vis nature and society. "A tranquil despair, without convulsions of anger and without reproaches for heaven, this is wisdom itself." And again: "Silence would be the best criticism of life."

Anarchism is an exaggerated and mad idealism. Individualism is summed up in a trait common to Schopenhauer and Stirner: a pitiless realism. It arrives at what a German writer calls a complete "de-idealization" (*Entidealisierung*) of life and society.

"An ideal is nothing but a pawn," Stirner said. From this point of view Stirner is the most authentic representative of individualism. His icy word seizes souls with a shiver entirely different from that, fiery and radiant, of a Nietzsche. Nietzsche remains an impenitent, imperious, violent idealist. He idealizes superior humanity. Stirner represents the most complete de-idealization of nature and life, the most radical philosophy of disenchantment that has appeared since Ecclesiastes. Pessimistic without measure or reservations, individualism is absolutely anti-social, unlike anarchism, of which this is only relatively the case (in relation to current society). Anarchism admits an antinomy between the individual and the state, an antinomy it resolves by the suppression of the state, but it does not see any inherent, irreducible antinomy between the individual and society. This is because in its eyes society represents a spontaneous growth (Spencer), while the state is an artificial and authoritarian organization. In the eyes of an individualist society is as tyrannical, if not more so, than the state. Society, in fact, is nothing else but the mass of social bonds of all kinds (opinions, mores, usages, conventions, mutual surveillance, more or less discreet espionage of the conduct of others, moral approval and disapproval, etc.) Society thus understood constitutes a closely knit fabric of petty and great tyrannies, exigent, inevitable, incessant, harassing, and pitiless, which penetrates into the details of individual life more profoundly and continuously than statist constraints can. What is more, if we look closely at this, statist tyranny and the tyranny of mores proceed from the same root: the collective interest of a caste or class that wishes to establish or to maintain its domination and prestige. Opinion and mores are in part the residue of ancient caste disciplines that are in the process of disappearing, in part the seed of new social disciplines brought with them by the new leading caste in the process of formation. This is why between state constraint and that of opinion and mores there is only a difference in degree. Deep down they have the same goal: the maintenance of a certain moral conformism useful to the group, and the same procedures: the vexation and elimination of the independent and the recalcitrant. The only difference is that diffuse sanctions (opinions and mores) are more hypocritical than the others. Proudhon was right to say that the state is nothing but a mirror of society. It is only tyrannical because society is tyrannical. The government, as Tolstoy remarked, is a gathering of men who exploit others and which favors the wicked and cheaters. If this is the practice of government, this is also that of society. There is conformity between the two terms: state and society. The one is the same as the other. The herd instinct, or the societal instinct, is no less oppressive for the individual than the statist or priestly instincts, which only maintain themselves thanks to and through it.

How strange! Stirner himself, on the question of the relations between society and the state, seems to share the error of Spencer and Bakunin. He protests against the intervention of the state in the acts of the individual, but not against that of society. "The state girds itself with an aureole of sanctity before the individual. For example, it makes laws concerning duels. Two men who agree to risk their lives in order to settle an affair (whatever it might be) cannot execute their agreement because the state doesn't want it. They would expose themselves to judicial pursuit and punishment. What becomes of the freedom of self-determination? Things are completely different in those places, like North America, where society decides to make the duelists suffer certain disagreeable consequences of their act and takes from them, for example, the credit they had previously enjoyed. The refusing of credit is everyone's affair, and if it pleases a society to deprive someone of it for one reason or another, he who is struck by it cannot complain of an attack on his liberty: society has done nothing but exercise its own. The society of which we spoke leaves the individual perfectly free to expose himself to the harmful or disagreeable consequences that result from his way of acting, and leaves full and entire his freedom of will. The state does exactly the contrary: it denies all legitimacy to the will of the individual and only recognizes as legitimate its own will, the will of the state." Strange reasoning. The law doesn't attack me. In what way am I freer if society boycotts me? Such reasoning would legitimize all the attacks against the individual of a public opinion infected by moral bigotry. The legend of individual liberty in Anglo-Saxon countries is built on this reasoning. Stirner himself feels the vice of his reasoning, and a little further along he arrives at his celebrated distinction between society and association. In the one (society) the individual is taken as a means; in the other (association), he takes himself as an end and treats the association as a means of personal power and enjoyment: "You bring to the association all your might, all your riches and make your presence felt. In society you and your activity are utilized. In the first you live as an egoist; in the second you live as a man, i.e., religiously; you work in the Lord's vineyard. You owe society everything you have; you are its debtor and you are tormented with social obligations. You owe nothing to the association. It serves you and you leave it without scruples as soon as you no longer have any advantages to draw from it ..." "If society is more than you then you will have it pass ahead of you and you will make yourself its servant. The association is your tool, your weapon; it sharpens and multiplies your natural strength. The association only exists for you and by you. Society, on the contrary, claims you as its good and can exist without you. In short, society is sacred and the association is your property; society uses you and you use the association."

A vain distinction if ever there was one! Where should we fix the boundary between society and association? As Stirner himself admitted, doesn't an association tend to crystallize into a society?

However we approach it, anarchism cannot reconcile the two antinomic terms, society and individual liberty. The free society that it dreams of is a contradiction in terms. It's a piece of steel made of wood, a stick without a tip. Speaking of anarchists Nietzsche wrote: "We can already read on all the walls and all the tables their word for the future: Free society. Free society? To be sure. But I think you know, my dear sirs, what we will build it with: Wood made of iron ..." Individualism is clearer and more honest than anarchism. It places the state, society, and association on the same plane. It rejects them both and as far as this is possible tosses them overboard. "All associations have the defects of convents," Vigny said.

Antisocial, individualism is openly immoralist. This is not true in an absolute fashion. In a Vigny pessimistic individualism is reconciled with a morally haughty stoicism, severe and pure. Even so, even in Vigny an immoralist element remains: a tendency to de-idealize society, to separate and oppose the two terms society and morality, and to regard society as a fatal generator of cowardice, unintelligence, and hypocrisy. "*Cinq mars,*" "*Stello,*" and "*Servitude et Grandeur militaires*" are the songs of a kind of epic poem on disillusionment. But it is only social and false things that I will destroy and illusions I will trample on. I will raise on these ruins, on this dust, the sacred beauty of enthusiasm, of love, and of honor." It goes without saying that in a Stirner or a Stendhal individualism is immoralist without scruples or reservations. Anarchism is imbued with a crude moralism. Anarchist morality, even without obligations or sanctions, is no less a morality. At heart it is Christian morality, except for the pessimist element contained in the latter. The anarchist supposes that those virtues necessary to harmony will flourish on their own. Enemy of coercion, the doctrine accords the faculty to take from the general stores even to the lazy. But the anarchist is persuaded that in the future city the lazy will be rare, or will not exist at all.

Optimistic and idealistic, imbued with humanism and moralism, anarchism is a social dogmatism. It is a "cause" in the sense that Stirner gave this word. A "cause" is one thing; "the simple attitude of an individual soul" is another. A cause implies a common adherence to an idea, a shared belief and a devotion to that belief. Such is not individualism. Individualism is anti-dogmatic and little inclined to proselytism. It would gladly take as its motto Stirner's phrase: "I have set my affair on nothing." The true individualist doesn't seek to communicate to others his own sensation of life and society. What would be the good of this? *Omne individuum ineffabile.*[*] Convinced of the diversity of temperaments and the uselessness of a single rule, he would gladly say with David Thoreau: "I would not have any one adopt my mode of living on any account; for, beside that before he has fairly learned it I may have found out another for myself, I desire that there may be as many different persons in the world as possible; but I would have each one be very careful to find out and pursue *his own way,* and not his father's or his mother's or his neighbor's instead." The individualist knows that there are temperaments that are refractory to individualism and that it would be ridiculous to want to convince them. In the eyes of a thinker in love with solitude and inde-

---

[*] In every individual, there is something inexpressible.

pendence, a contemplative, a pure adept of the inner life, like Vigny, social life and its agitations seem to be something artificial, rigged, excluding any true and strongly felt sentiments. And conversely, those who by their temperament feel an imperious need for life and social action, those who throw themselves into the melee, those who have political and social enthusiasms, those who believe in the virtues of leagues and groups, those who have forever on their lips the words "The Idea," "The Cause," those who believe that tomorrow will bring something new and great, these people necessarily misunderstand and disdain the contemplative, which lowers the barrier before the crowd of which Vigny spoke. Inner life and social action are two things that are mutually exclusive. The two kinds of souls are not made to understand each other. As antitheses, we should read alongside each other Schopenhauer's "Aphorisms on the Wisdom of Life," that bible of a reserved, mistrustful, and sad individualism, or the *Journal Intime* of Amiel. Or the *Journal d'un Poète* by Vigny. On the other side, we should read a Benoit Malon, an Elisée Reclus or a Kropotkin, and we will see the abyss that separates the two kinds of souls ...

The Relationship Between Pessimism and Individualism (1914)[*]

The century that just passed is without a doubt that in which pessimism found its most numerous, its most varied, its most vigorous and its most systematic interpreters. In addition, individualism was expressed in that century with exceptional intensity by representatives of high quality.

It could be interesting to bring together these two forms of thought, dominant in our era; to ask what is the logical or sentimental connection that exists between them, and to what degree pessimism engenders individualism and individualism engenders pessimism.

But the question thus posed is too general. There are many kinds of pessimism and many kinds of individualism. Among the latter there is one that in no way implies pessimism, and that is the doctrinaire individualism that issues from the French Revolution and to which so many moralists, jurists, and politicians of our century are attached. This individualism could take as its motto the phrase of Wilhelm von Humboldt that Stuart Mill chose as the epigraph of his "Essay on Liberty": "The grand, leading principle, towards which every argument unfolded in these pages directly converges, is the absolute and essential importance of human development in its richest diversity." Individualists of this kind believe that all human individuals can harmonically develop in society, that their very diversity is a guarantee of the richness and beauty of human civilization.

These individualists are rationalists. They have faith in reason, the principle of order, unity, and harmony. They are idealists: they have faith in an ideal of social justice, unitarian and egalitarian, they believe, despite individual differences and inequalities, in the profound and real unity of human kind. These individualists are "humanists" in the sense that Stirner gives to this word: solidarists, socialists, if we take this latter term in its largest sense. Their individualism is turned outwards, towards society. It's a social individualism, in the sense that it doesn't separate the individual from society, which they don't place in opposition to each other. On the contrary, they always consider the individual as a social element that harmonizes with the all and that only exists in function of the all. We will

---

[*] From *Pessimisme et Invidualisme*. Paris, Alcan, 1914.

not insist upon this individualism, which obviously implies a more or less firm social optimism.

The individualism we have in mind here is completely different. This individualism is not a political, juridical and moral doctrine, but a psychological and moral attitude, a form of sensibility, a personal sensation of life and a personal will to life.

It is impossible to fix in a definition all the traits, all the degrees, all the nuances of this psychological disposition. It affects a special tone in every soul in which it makes itself known.

We can say that as a personal sensation of life, individualism is the sentiment of uniqueness, of individuality in what it has of the differential, the private, and the un-revealable. Individualism is an appeal to the interiority of sentiment, to individual inspiration in the face of social conventions and ready-made ideas. Individualism implies a sentiment of personal infallibility, an idea of intellectual and sentimental superiority, of inner artistocratism. Of irreducible difference between an *ego* and an other, the idea of uniqueness. Individualism is a return to the self and a gravitation to the self.

As personal will to life individualism is a desire to "be oneself," according to the wish of a character from Ibsen (Peer Gynt), a desire for independence and originality. The individualist wants to be his own maker, his own furnisher of truth and illusion, his own builder of truth and illusion, his own builder of dreams, his own builder and demolisher of ideals. This wish for originality can, incidentally, be more or less energetic, more or less demanding, more or less ambitious. More or less happy, too, according to the quality and the value of individuality in question, according to the amplitude of the thought and according to the intensity of, the will to, individual strength.

Be it as personal sensation of life or as personal will to life, individualism is or tends to be anti-social: if it is not so from the start, it later and inevitably becomes so. Sentiment of the profound uniqueness of the *ego*, desire for originality and independence, individualism cannot help but provoke the sentiment of a silent struggle between the individual self and society. In fact, the tendency of every society is to reduce the sentiment of individuality as much as possible: to reduce uniqueness through conformism, spontaneity through discipline, instantaneousness of the self through caution, sincerity of sentiment through the lack of sincerity inherent in any socially defined function, confidence and pride in the self through the humiliation inseparable from any kind of social training. This is why individualism necessarily has the sentiment of a conflict between its *ego* and the general *ego*. Individualism becomes here a principle of passive or active inner resistance, of silent or declared opposition to society, a refusal to submit oneself to it; a distrust of it. In its essence, individualism detests and negates the social bond. We can define it as a will to isolation, a sentimental and intellectual, theoretical and practical commitment to withdraw from society, if not in fact—following the examples of the solitaries of the Thebeiad and the more modern one of Thoreau—at least in sprit and intention, by a kind of interior and voluntary retreat. This distancing from society, this voluntary moral isolation that we can practice in the very heart of society can take on the form of indifference and resignation as well as that of revolt. It can also assume the attitude of the spectator, the contemplative attitude of the thinker in an Ivory Tower. But there is always in this acquired indifference, in this resignation or this spectatorial isolation, a remnant of interior revolt.

Sentiment of uniqueness and more or less energetic expression of the will to personal power; will to originality, will to independence, will to insubordination and revolt, will to isolation and to withdrawal into the self. Sometimes also will to supremacy, to the deployment of force on and against others, but always with a return to the self, with a sentiment of personal infallibility, with an indestructible confidence in oneself, even in defeat, even in the failure of hopes and ideals. Intransigence, inaccessibility of internal conviction, fidelity to oneself up to the bitter end. Fidelity to one's misunderstood ideas, to one's impregnable and unassailable will: individualism is all this, either globally or in detail, this element or that, this nuance or that predominating according to the circumstances and the case.

Individualism, understood as we just expressed it, that is, as an internal disposition of the soul, individualism as sensation and will is no longer, like the individualism of which we spoke above, like political and juridical individualism, turned outwards and subordinated to social life, to its constraints, its demands and obligations. It is turned inwards. It places itself at the beginning or seeks refuge in the end in the unbreakable and intangible interior being.

To say that there is a close psychological relationship between the individualist and pessimist sensibilities means almost stating the obvious. Pessimism supposes a basic individualism. It supposes that interiority of sentiment, that return to the self (almost always painful) that is the essence of individualism. While optimism is nothing but an abstract metaphysical thesis, the echo of doctrinal hearsay, pessimism is a sensation of lived life; it comes from the inner, from an individual psychology. It proceeds from what is most intimate in us: the ability to suffer. It predominates among those of a solitary nature who live withdrawn into themselves and see social life as pain. Thoroughbred pessimists, the great artists and theoreticians of suffering, lived solitary and as strangers in the midst of men, retrenched in their *ego* as if in a fortress from which they let fall an ironic and haughty gaze on the society of their kind. And so it is not by accident, but by virtue of an intimate psychological correlation that pessimism is accompanied by a tendency towards egotistic isolation.

Inversely, the individualist spirit is almost fatedly accompanied by pessimism. Does not experience as old as the world teach us that in nature the individual is sacrificed to the species? That in society it is sacrificed to the group? Individualism arrives at a resigned or hopeless noting of the antinomies that arise between the individual and the species on one hand, and between the individual and society on the other.

Life doubtless perpetually triumphs over this antinomy, and the fact that despite it all humanity continues to live can appear to be an unarguable reply that refutes both pessimism and individualism. But this is not certain. For if humanity as a species and as a society pursues its destiny without worrying about individuals' complaints or revolts, individualism does not die for all that. Always defeated, never tamed, it is incarnated in souls of a special caliber, imbued with the sentiment of their uniqueness and strong in their will to independence. Individualism suffers a defeat in every individual who dies after having served ends and surrendered to forces that are beyond him. But he survives himself through the generations, gaining in force and clarity as the human will to life intensifies, diversifies and becomes refined in individual consciousness. It is thus that is affirmed the dual consistency of pessimism and individualism, indissolubly united and interconnected.

Nevertheless, it is possible that this psychological tie that we believe we have discovered between pessimism and individualism is nothing but an *a priori* view. If instead of reasoning about psychological likelihoods we consult the history of ideas of the 19th century we will perhaps see that the relationship of ideas that we have just indicated is neither as simple nor as consistent as at first appears. We must penetrate in detail the different forms of pessimism and individualism and more closely analyze their relationship if we want to arrive at precise ideas.

The Future of Pessimism and Individualism (1914)[*]

Everything in current social evolution indicates an increased reinforcement of society's powers, an increasingly marked tendency towards the encroachment of the collective on the individual.

Everything equally indicates that on the part of most individuals this encroachment will be less and less felt, and will provoke less and less resistance and rebellion. Social conformism and optimism will thus clearly have the last word. Society will emerge victorious over the individual. There will come a moment when social chains will wound almost no one, lacking people sufficiently enamored of independence and sufficiently individualized to feel these chains and suffer from them. Lacking combatants, the combat will come to an end. The small independent minority will become increasingly small.

But however small it might be, it will suffer from the increased social pressure. It will represent, in this time of almost perfect conformism and generalized social contentment, pessimism and individualism.

---

[*] From *Pessimisme et Individualisme*. 1914, Alcan, Paris.

Victor Serge (1890-1947)

Victor Serge traveled many paths and lived many lives, but his goal never varied. The son of exiled Russian revolutionaries in Brussels, whose uncle had manufactured the bomb that killed Alexander II, this wandering (non-) Jew of the revolution was at various times a socialist, an anarchist, a Bolshevik, a Trotskyist, and an ex-Trotskyist. He was at home everywhere there was struggle. From Brussels to Paris to Spain to Moscow to Mexico City, the fight was ever and always for the same thing: freedom. Susan Sontag called him "the most compelling of twentieth century ethical and literary heroes."

His "Memoirs of a Revolutionary" is perhaps the greatest of firsthand accounts of the revolutions of the twentieth century. The autobiography is a work of literary genius (his novels are increasingly coming to be accepted as classics), free of jargon and cant. The "Memoirs" cast a lucid eye on all Serge witnessed and participated in, following his itinerary from the poverty-stricken individualist anarchist in Paris to his end as a poverty-stricken defender of individual liberties in Mexico, ever faithful to the star that had betrayed him. Serge simply shifted his field of action, and from the pages of "*l'anarchie*" to the pages of Emmanuel Mounier's Personalist journal "*Esprit*," he always defended the same essential cause.

Serge's greatest virtue was honor. He assumed the leadership of Libertad's "*l'anarchie*" after the latter's death during the period that led to the valorization of "illegalism," the recourse to robbery and counterfeiting as revolutionary acts. He had already written in 1908 that "we should stand alongside the economic rebel (when he is conscious, of course) the same way we stand beside the political, antimilitarist, or propagandist rebel." All forms of revolt were equally valid, and all revolutionaries must be defended, but the series of killings by the Bonnot Gang shook him.

He knew the men of the Bonnot Gang and, refusing to cooperate with the authorities, he spent five years in prison for his silence. He received no salary from "*l'anarchie*," living on the money he received for his translations, yet, poor as he was, illegalism never tempted him.

Yet he understood the impulse behind it and could not abandon his comrades.

In a certain sad sense, the banditry of Bonnot and his comrades was the logical outgrowth of the unfettered rage and individualism of the circle around "*l'anarchie*," indeed of the entire current that had started with their glorification of Ravachol twenty years earlier. It was the *reductio ad absurdum* of the hatred for all of society's rules, the contempt for those masses who accepted the insult that was daily life under capitalism. In 1892 a friend of Ravachol had written that "the little Ravachols will grow up." When they did, it was to carry out crimes under the cloak of anarchy.

Recognizing the dead end toward which anarchism was headed, Serge, after his release from prison in 1917 and a final brief anarchist period in Spain, returned to his family's homeland after the Bolshevik Revolution. But Stalin's arrival in power represented the end of the liberating dream, and the ossification of Bolshevism found the eternal revolutionary unable to continue along the road to this new dead end. He was imprisoned for being a supporter of Trotsky, but was luckier than many other writers for an international, largely French, campaign for his liberation was able to save him.

He returned to the life of the eternal exile, but even among the oppositionists he was an exile. He was expelled from the Trotskyist movement, and his defeats piled up as his comrade Andres Nin of the Spanish POUM was murdered by the Soviets during the Civil War. In the end he was exiled from everything: from his various homelands, from his languages, from anarchism which had led to crime, from Marxism that had also led to crime. Isolated in distant Mexico, still trying to help comrades in distress, he wrote till the end, striving to find a home for freedom.

The Illegals (1908)[*]

Armand's conviction in Paris for counterfeiting has brought back the old question of the Illegals.

I don't know Armand or the details of his affair. And so without showing any particular interest in his personality—towards which I only feel that sentiment of fraternity that binds all the militants of the idea—I will simply pose questions of principle.

What should our attitude be towards Illegals (in the economic sense of the word, i.e., people living off illicit labor) and particularly towards the comrades in that category?

The answer seems so clear to me that if I hadn't heard numerous discussions on this subject—and even in our circle—the idea of writing this article would never have occurred to me.

We approve and admire the anti-militarist who either by desertion or by some other means refuses to serve the masters' fatherland and in so doing puts himself in open struggle against society, whose law he violates: that of military service, otherwise known as servitude owed the state.

After this, how can we disavow that other comrade, whose temperament bows as little before the regime of the workshop as the anti-militarist bows before that of the barracks and who, by some *illegal* method puts himself in revolt against the law of the slavery of work?

Every revolt is in essence anarchist. And we should stand alongside the economic rebel (when he is conscious, of course) the same way we stand beside the political, antimilitarist or propagandist rebel.

Every rebel, through his acts, is one of ours. Anarchism is a principle of struggle: it needs fighters and not servants the away statist socialism does, a machine with complicated cogs that has only to allow itself to vegetate in order to live in a bourgeois fashion.

But it seems proper to me to trace a limit. I said above "economic rebel," for if the Duvals and the Pinis, who steal because they can't submit to the oppression of the bosses, are our people, it isn't the same for many so-called anarchists who have paraded through the various criminal

---

[*] First Published in *Le Communiste*, No. 14, June 20, 1908, under the pseudonym of Le Rétif; from *Le Rétif, articles parus dans "l'anarchie."* Textes réunis et présentés par Yves Pagés. Paris, Monnier, 1989.

courts over the past few years. Theft is often nothing but an act of cowardice and weakness, for he who commits it has no other goal than that of escaping work, while at the same time escaping the difficulties of social struggle. Before the jury, instead of being a common criminal the burglar or the counterfeiter declares himself an "anarchist" in the hope of being interesting or appearing the martyr to a cause he knows nothing about. He finds nothing better to respond to the judge who condemns him but the traditional and a slightly banal "*Vive l'anarchie!*" But if this cry in other mouths has taken on a powerful resonance, it has here a flimsy title to our solidarity.

For our part these unfortunates deserve neither sympathy nor antipathy. They aren't rebels, but escapists. They have clumsily escaped from the social melee. More clever, more daring, or luckier they would have "arrived" and become bankers, functionaries or merchants—in a word, honest men. They would have legislated against us like vulgar Clemenceaus and without hesitation would have sent their unlucky brethren to the penal colonies. Such shipwrecks denote so much weakness and powerlessness that they can only inspire pity.

Between them and the militant who steals though *revolt* the distance is as great as that between a revolutionary terrorist and the highway murderer who kills a shepherd in order to steal ten *sous* from him. One is a rebel of conscience, the other a rebel by powerlessness or bad luck. The act of the former is an act of revolt; the act of the latter is that of a brute too stupid to imagine better.

To stand alongside economic rebels does not in the least mean preaching theft or erecting it into a tactic. This method has so many drawbacks that preaching it would be madness. It is *admissible* and nothing more. Noting this simply means acting as an anarchist who doesn't fear that what he says will be heard, and having the courage to take his reasoning to its limits.

Admissible, and nothing else. For the anarchist, if he doesn't care about bourgeois legality and honesty, must above all aim at preserving himself for action as long as possible and realizing to the greatest extent possible the life he desires. His work, rather than appearing harmful and destructive, should be a work of life, a long apostolate of stubborn labor, of goodness, of love. In order to partake of the ambiance, the new man, the man of the future must live with goodness, fraternity, and love. In this way, when he will have passed he will have left behind him a trail of sympathy and astonishment that will do more for propaganda than a whole life of petty and shady struggles could have done.

But to work at his labor of life and to preserve himself *all* means are good, for in order to reach the summits of clarity the route is often dark.

Anarchists—Bandits (1909)[*]

Last week the dailies related in detail a tragic incident of the social struggle. In the suburbs of London (in Tottenham) two of our Russian comrades attacked the accountant of a factory and, pursued by the crowd and the police, held out in a desperate struggle, the mere recounting of which is enough to make one shiver ...

After almost two hours of resistance, having exhausted their ammunitions and wounded 22 people, three of them mortally, they reserved for themselves their final bullets. One, our comrade Joseph Lapidus (the brother of the terrorist Stryge, killed in Paris in the Vincennes woods in 1906) killed himself; the other was taken seriously wounded.

Words seem powerless to express either admiration or condemnation before their ferocious heroism. Lips are still; the pen isn't strong enough, sonorous enough.

Nevertheless, in our ranks there will be the timorous and the fearful who will disavow their act. But we, for our part, insist on loudly affirming our solidarity.

We are proud to have had among us men like Duval, Pini, and Jacob.[†] We today insist on saying loudly and clearly: The London "bandits" were at one with us!

Let this be known. Let it be finally understood that in the current society we are the vanguard of a barbarous army. That we have no respect for what constitutes virtue, morality, honesty, that we are outside or laws and regulations. They oppress us, they persecute us, they pursue us. Rebels constantly find themselves before the sad alternative: submit, that is, abolish their will and return to the miserable herd of the exploited, or accept combat against the entire social organism.

---

[*] First Published in "Le Révolté" No. 36, February 6, 1909; from *Le Rétif, articles parus dans 'l'anarchie.'* Textes réunis et présentés par Yves Pagés. Paris, Monnier, 1989.

[†] Clement Duval (1850-1935)—leader of a group of illegalist anarchists called "La Panthère des Batignolles." Pini (1850-189?)—anarchist shoemaker and partisan of "individual expropriation." Marius-Alexander Jacob (1879-1954)—thief and head of a band of anarchist criminals.

We prefer combat. Against us, all arms are good; we are in an enemy camp, surrounded, harassed. The bosses, judges, soldiers, cops unite to bring us down. We defend ourselves—not by all means, for the most peremptory response we can give them is to be better than them—but with a profound contempt for their codes, their morals, their prejudices.

By refusing us the right to free labor society gives us the right to steal. In taking possession of the wealth of the world the bourgeois give us the right to take back, however we can, what we need to satisfy our needs. Anti-authoritarian, we have the burning determination to live free without oppressing anyone, without being oppressed by anyone. Current society, based on the absurd egoism of the strongest, on iniquity and oppression, denies us this. In order not to die of hunger we are forced to have recourse to various expedients: accept the stupefying and demoralizing existence of the wage earner, that is, work, or the dangerous existence of the illegal, that is, steal, and get ourselves out of our mess through means on the margin of the law.

Let this be known! In order to wrest an existence, working—submitting ourselves to the slavery of the workshop—is as much an expedient as stealing. As long as we haven't conquered the ample and large life for which we fight, the various means which the social organization will force us to have recourse to will be nothing to us but a last resort. And so we choose, in keeping with our temperaments and the circumstances, those that are most appropriate to us.

Your codes, your laws, your "honesty": you can't imagine how we laugh at them!

This is why, in the face of the fuming bourgeoisie, in the face of those who judge, of honest brutes, of the prostitutes of journalism, we insist on proclaiming: "We are in solidarity with the bandits of London!"

They are also, incidentally, noble bandits, and we can be proud of them. We won't have vain words of regret, vain tears for them. No! But may their deaths be an example and etch in our memories the sublime motto of the Russian comrades: "Anarchists never surrender!"

Anarchists don't surrender! No more under policemen's bullets than before the shouts of the crowd or the condemnation of those who judge! Anarchists don't surrender!

Resolved to live as rebels and to pitilessly defend themselves to the bitter end, they know, when it's necessary, to accept the epithet of "bandits."

I can guess, dear reader, the sentimental objection that is on your lips: "But the 22 unfortunates wounded by your comrades' bullets were innocent! Have you no remorse?"

No! For those who pursued them could have been nothing but "honest" citizens, believers in the state, in authority. Perhaps oppressed, but oppressed who, by their criminal weakness, perpetuate oppression. Enemies!

Unthinking, you will answer. Yes, but the ferocious bourgeois is also unthinking. For us the enemy is he who prevents us from living. We are under attack, and we defend ourselves.

And so we don't have words of condemnation for our daring comrades fallen in Tottingham, rather much admiration for their peerless bravery, and much sadness this evening to have thus lost, in the fullness of their vigor, men of an exceptional courage and energy.

Our Anti-Syndicalism (1910)[*]

Today, in light of the upcoming anti-parliamentary campaign, the anarchists are divided into two apparently irreconcilable groups: the syndicalists and the anti-syndicalists.

The comrades on the other side, in a brief declaration that it is only right to recognize has the dual merits of clarity and honesty, have said what they want and who they are. Their anti-parliamentary campaign will serve as the basis for syndicalist-revolutionary agitation.

It is thus on this plane that we meet up with them. After Lorulot spelled out our anti-parliamentarism, I think it is right to spell out what our anti-syndicalism should be.

This theme has already been discussed and re-discussed thousands of times among us, and we must recognize that the arguments of both sides have often been of a disconcerting puerility. No later than last week did I not hear friends reproach unions for establishing fixed dues and compare these to taxes? And others defend them by saying that in such and such a professional association they had educational discussions? Ordinarily it is with such futilities that the union movement is attacked and defended. Or else hairs on split about side issues like the functionary-ism of the CGT, the *arrivisme* of the leaders, the authoritarianism of the revolutionary method ...

These are details that are without a doubt interesting to know and useful to criticize. But our anti-syndicalism is based, I believe, on more serious, more profound arguments, and in the upcoming anti-parliamentary battle it is important that we have something other than these clichés to oppose to the theoreticians of working class action.

We shouldn't be declaiming against the demagogues of the rue de la Grange-aux-Belles, nor should we be involved in endless discussions over whether it's advantageous or not to participate in a corporate association; nor should we be elucidating the question of knowing whether we can make anarchist propaganda there. Yes, there is perhaps an interest in taking part in a trade grouping; yes we can sometimes carry out good anarchist work. In the same way there is an interest in being a good sol-

---

[*] First Published in *l'anarchie*, No. 255 February 24, 1910; from *Le Rétif, articles parus dans "l'anarchie."* Textes réunis et présentés par Yves Pagés. Paris, Monnier, 1989.

dier and a good worker. In the same way it is sometimes possible to spread ideas in a barracks. It's the very principle of syndicalism that should be attacked in order to demonstrate its inanity and dangerous consequences.

Let us first look at what syndicalist theory is and what it rests on. We can sum it up thusly:

Two adverse social classes exist and confront each other: idle owners and working non-owners, the latter being far more numerous. All social evil comes from the fact that the ownership of the means of production permits the minority, called "bourgeois," to pressure and exploit the majority, called "proletarian." There is only one remedy for this state of affairs: that the proletarians group together in corporate associations, in a vast confederation—class associations—and that they battle every day to wrest from the enemy caste a few small advantages until such time as, having become numerous and daring enough, they profit from a war or an economic crisis to decree the insurrectionary general strike and take control of the means of production. Once this is accomplished, the unions will organize work. It will be the Social Republic. The fundamental "causes" of human suffering having disappeared, humanity will progress in peace, joy, happiness. Here the field remains open to everyone's imagination, permitting the composition at leisure of the tableaus of universal happiness that, of course, can only ever be way below the reality! This is, with more or less variations, the sales spiels that the syndicalists of all shapes and forms prepare to serve (with, incidentally, much conviction and sincerity) to the good voters. We have to refute this entirely, point by point, omitting nothing. And I say this is quite feasible.

The problem to be solved is this: transforming the existing repellent milieu in order to finally establish a social milieu assuring every individual the greatest amount of happiness. This, in summary, is our objective as reformers, and also that of the syndicalists. Let us then pose the question this way: Given this goal, is it logical to count on the working class for this labor of destruction and construction?

Can we reasonably believe it capable of leading such an enterprise to a successful conclusion?

"Yes," say the *ouvriéristes* (without ever explaining why). "No," we answer them, and we will prove it: The working class has behind it a whole atavism of servitude and exploitation. It is the weakest of the two classes from every point of view. It is above all the less intelligent, and this is the sole cause for its state of subjection. It is within the logic of nature for the stronger to dominate the weaker. By virtue of this law the unaware and cowardly plebe, the imbecilic masses, credulous and fearful, have always been despoiled by more intelligent, healthier, more daring minorities. At present, after nineteen centuries of oppression, the difference between the two classes has been considerably accentuated. Let us repeat it again: *in all areas* impartial science demonstrates to us the inferiority of the working class. Well then, it is foolish to believe it capable of organizing a rational society. The degenerates, the hereditary slaves, the pitiful mass of working stiffs that we know *de visu* are physiologically incapable of living in harmony.

Consequently: organizing the working class in view of a social transformation means wasting time and energy.

Consequently: all the theoretical affirmations flowing from the principle that the working class can and must modify the social regime are false.

Consequently: there is only one urgent, useful, indispensable task; that which, in creating individuals finally worthy of the title of men, little by little improves the milieu, the task of education and anarchist combat.

*

This being established with the assistance of arguments strictly scientific and of an impeccable logic, the very principle of syndicalism having been demonstrated false, let us now pass to a critical examination of the union movement and see if it confirms our deductions. It fully confirms them.

To begin with, let us note a salient contradiction. With the goal of organizing one class against another, the workers are invited to group together in professional associations. Yet the interests of various corporations are often opposed, which renders class cohesion economically impossible, on this basis at least. And which causes a veritable waste ...

Now let's look at the unions. If we examine them closely we see that they come into existence, reproducing to various degrees the defects and blemishes of the bourgeois society they claim to have a mission to destroy. A union is a miniature of the old society. Foolish and complicated administrative cogs galore, regulations restrictive of individual initiative, oppression of minorities by feeble majorities, the triumph of the mediocre on condition that they have the gifts of gab and swindling, everything can be found there, up to and including parasites.

Let us look at the tactics. Far from combating the established social order, it seems that the unions have as a goal their sanctioning. Supposedly anti-statists, they never cease battling for this or that law, to demand another one, thus recognizing the entity Law and, as a corollary, the entity State. These anti-parliamentarians sign duly legalized contracts and call for this to be voted for and that to be rejected ...

In their organization they are a perfect copy of the parliamentary farce. Even the clowns aren't missing. Delegation of power, votes, decisions having force of law, as well as half hidden combinations, personal competition, kitchen squabbles: we can find in the CGT the exact, though miniaturized, transposition of parliamentary hideousness.

As for the unmistakable incoherence of their blather, they pass from a tragic to a comic character by a series of gradations that are amusing to observe. It's the smashing—is it not, Clemenceau—victory of the postal workers transformed a few days later into ... well, you find the diplomatic word. It's the valiant corporation of construction workers who a few months ago naively allowed themselves to be muzzled by a collective contract that was extremely ... clever. It's the CGT today building itself up as defenders of bank employees, as if the valets of the financier were not as repugnant as the financier himself. We could write columns on this theme.

Let us look at the results. Today the CGT is combative: in words more than in acts, but combative all the same. With this as their starting point comrades promise us that in the future its fighting force will grow and will end by ensuring the complete triumph of its demands. We saw above what the reasons were that authorize us—let us be modest—to have some doubts on this subject. A glance at our neighboring countries will be instructive in this regard.

At their beginning all parties, all groups (even all individuals) are combative. Age comes, and with it a potbelly and wisdom. This is the story of many men who we are today permitted to admire raised to the pinnacle of the social machine, the history of the trade union socialist parties. Very revolutionary during the blessed period of their youth, the English trade unions have become what we know them to be. The same thing happened to many German unions, and is now happening to the Belgian worker's movement, which is losing all energy as it grows. In certain places in the United States, in Australia, in New Zealand, in England, where the unions have reached their heights, they have only managed to create a caste of privileged, conservative workers, lined up under the protective shield of the state, and are hardly worth more than the more official bourgeois.

Having seen the evolution of the French unions and observed the incoherence of the CGT, I don't think it's possible to foresee a different destiny for it.

*

We will thus not lack for arguments during the upcoming discussions, for each of these criticisms lends itself to interesting developments and must be backed with proofs drawn from union activity itself—proofs it is not difficult to find cartloads of.

Our critical work thus understood, it remains to define the positive, affirmative part of our propaganda. It is clear and has no need of long developments: the making of anarchists.

In parallel with the tissue of illogic that is syndicalism, and the monument of incoherence that is the union, let us show how, by the transformation of men, society is transformed; how as men become more healthy, more noble, more intelligent, more educated, the air becomes breathable and life appears admirable ...

"Salvation lies within us!" Let us show that the salvation of men is within them and that the route to enlightenment has been laid out for them, if they want to make the effort to free themselves from the old lies ... Let us show it in its fertile intransigence: anarchist action!

And I can't end any better than Lorulot did the other week:

"And now ... to work!"

The Revolutionary Illusion (1910)[*]

"Humanity marches enveloped in a veil of illusions," a thinker—Marc Guyau—said. In fact, it seems that without this veil men aren't capable of marching. Barely has reality torn a blindfold from them than they hasten to put on another, as if their too-weak eyes were afraid to see things as they are. Their intelligence requires the prism of falsehood.

The scandals of Panama, Dreyfus, Syveton, Steinhell, etc.; the turpitudes and incapacities of politicians, and the rifle blows of Narbonne, Draveil, and Villeneuve have, for a considerable minority, torn away the veil of the parliamentary illusion.

We hoped for everything from the ballot. We had faith in the good faith and power of the nation's representatives. And that hope, that faith prevented us from seeing the fundamental idiocy of the system, which consists in delegating one to look after the needs of all. But the ballot revealed itself to be a paper rag. Parliamentarians showed themselves to be ambitious, greedy, corrupt, and most of all, mediocre. Men appeared who were angered by the electoral farce, the comedy of reforms, the reign of republican clowns. A minority was born, which necessarily grows every day and upon which the old illusion has no hold.

Nevertheless, in order to inspire men used to being led, in order to stimulate their activity, images are needed ... and so, replacing the defunct parliamentary illusion the other illusion was forged and was encrusted onto brains: the revolutionary illusion.

Yes, laws are powerless to transform society, parliamentary assemblies are pitiful, and there is nothing to expect from governments. But what legislation can't do demonstrations and strikes will do; and union assemblies will keep the promises of their pitiful predecessors: the Chambers. Finally, we can expect everything from the conscious proletariat which ... and which ... and that ...

The good suckers once thought that sonorous speeches, official texts written and placarded with solemnity were capable of favorably modifying social life. This time has passed. At present it is thought that in order

---

[*] First Published in "*l'anarchie*" April 28, 1910; from *Le Rétif, articles parus dans "l'anarchie."* Textes réunis et présentés par Yves Pagés. Paris, Monnier, 1989.

to do this it suffices to demolish street lamps, burn kiosks, to "knock off" a cop from time to time (on very serious occasions.)

Once, popular hopes were concentrated on deputies. These paunchy gentlemen were capable of some morning decreeing marvelous things. Alas! Now that we've seen them slog through the mud the ideal type of the transformer appears a bit differently. It's the "comrade secretary," influential member of the CGT, whose voice during meetings unleashes waves of enthusiasm. It's Pataud,—his malicious and jovial face, his imperative speech ... and it's also the long-haired revolutionary, with his belligerent hat, and who (his neighbors affirm) never goes out without his two automatic pistols ...

Once the brave voters trusted in parliament—the incarnation of the welfare state—to organize their happiness. Only the "backward masses" today still maintain so foolish a confidence in their representatives. The "advanced," the "conscious," in short: the revolutionaries know what the state and parliament are worth. So they announce to us that after the general strike it will be the CGT that will organize universal felicity and the union committees will deliberate on the measures to be taken for the common welfare. As you can see, this in no way resembles the old parliamentary regime.

As with all errors, it was harmful to be intoxicated by the parliamentary illusion. And it earned for the good citizens of this country the admirable democratic regime, so well illustrated by the Russian alliance— O! Most advantageous of alliances, along with the great and small affairs and, finally, the reign of Clemenceau and Briand ... while waiting for that of Jaurès. M. Viviani—today His Excellency—once said a propos of I don't know which legislature: "There was the Lost Chamber, and there is the Infamous Chamber," and this could equally be said of all the legislatures that have followed, vainly striving to surpass each other in buffooneries. Illusions cost dearly.

And yet, though it's been costly to the poor buggers who have benevolently had their heads shaved, been whipped and shot down, the parliamentary illusion has not done half as much harm as the other illusion can do.

Oh, don't worry. We'll get over this. We'll end up by seeing that the little game of shake-ups doesn't help at all. And we won't see the bloody dawn rise that M. Méric announces to us. Illusions don't last forever. But men will have died for the Cause, died stupidly, uselessly. But one or two generations will have wasted their strength in foolish efforts. We would have wasted life—that's all.

We'll get over this. The great day isn't ready to shine, and probably never will shine, except in the feverish imaginings of its prophets.

And yet, since this dream makes the crowd drunk let's look and see what it presages for us. Let's see what these efforts tend to, what they will manage to do if an impossible victory was to crown them.

Not too long ago a pamphlet came out that shows us what this will be. Our old friend, Citizen Méric*, aka Flax, is the author. It is titled: "How We Will Make the Revolution." This pamphlet is serious, like the program of a future party. In certain places it is as enthralling as the novels of Captain Danrit. In its general appearance it recalls the writings of Mark Twain, the phlegmatic and impassible humor of the Americans.

Citizen Méric—who knows what he's about—demonstrates that when all is said and done a revolution is an easy thing. Our Russian friends can have no doubts on this subject. And then, a few words on the organized proletariat. But without a doubt the most interesting chapter is the one that shows us what will happen after the triumphant insurrection. Here it is possible to see just how far intelligences in the throes of an illusion can be led astray. For if it is possible that Citizen Méric doesn't believe a single word of what he says, it is certain that many people sincerely conceive what he has formulated.

On the day after the great event Citizen Méric announces the revolutionary dictatorship, backed by the Terror. Woe to the adversaries of the new social order (read: The Federal Committee). "Violence alone could give us our momentary victory; terror alone can preserve that victory ... we must not fear being ferocious! We'll speak of justice, goodness and liberty afterwards." And so, dear anti-authoritarian friends, we have been warned.

From these lines we can understand the little enthusiasm among individualists inspired by M. Méric's revolution. The present order crushes us, tracks us down, kills us. The revolutionary order will crush us, will track us down, will kill us. The party can count on our collaboration.

---

* Victor Méric. (1876-1933) Anarchist journalist.

But Citizen Méric gets better and better. On page 22 we note the existence of two committees, and a revolutionary army and police. The rebels will be executed (sic, sic, sic). Isn't this interesting?

The unions "will order everyone to get to work," or else watch out. After this a workers parliament (sic) will be named, which "will have nothing in common with the odious parliamentarism of today." Yeah, sure. Even more as we've already noted, this charming little regime will have nothing in common with the abominable bourgeois oppression.

There will also be a permanent labor council. And the comrade ends by saying forthwith: "The current CGT already gives an approximate idea of the future working class organization." Won't that be lovely!

In order to defend the new fatherland thus constructed, and which will certainly be the gentlest of fatherlands, oh ineffable Meric, militias will be formed. For war is inevitable ...

And after talking about a "new morality imposing heavy obligations and sacrifices," after having told us of revolutionary prisons and tribunals, in short, of what he himself calls worker tyranny, Citizen Méric tranquilly concludes: "This isn't for today, or for tomorrow." Didn't I tell you he had the impassible humor of the Anglo-Saxons!

*

Citizen Méric is perhaps a joker or a refined humorist knowing how to push a joke to an extreme. I'd like to think so. But the fact is that there are simple souls who accept these writings as gospel.

The harmful illusion is that of the belief in this redemptive revolution, when there is no other redemption than that of the human personality, when we can build nothing without having made better and stronger men.

The evil illusion is that of waiting for the revolt of the crowd, of the organized, disciplined, regimented masses. In fact, the only fertile acts are those committed by individuals knowing clearly what they want and advancing without let or hindrance, needing neither chiefs nor discipline. In fact, the only good rebellions are the immediate rebellions of individuals, refusing to wait any longer and determined to immediately grab their share of joy.

The imbecilic illusion is that of imagining that by violence alone, by terror, by bombs and rifles we can create the new society. Violence employed by brutes will be absurd and harmful. A society founded on gibbets, maintained by the force of chains, will always be ignobly oppressive. The revolution of anger and hatred, the revolution of unionized fanatics can only make vainly flow torrents of blood and prepare the arrival of new filibusterers.

In 1789 Robespierre's dictatorship prepared the way for the Empire. The *guillotinades* were the prelude to the Napoleonic carnage. The Terror, by decreasing the value of human life, allowed free rein to the bloody folly of the "Little Corsican." This, brutally, is history's response to revolutionary illusions.

*

To be sure, society does not evolve without bumps, crises, bloody shocks. Often, angry revolts, dictated by sentimental indignation or instilled with faith in the salutary power of violence, break out and are quickly repressed in the horrors of bourgeois reaction. They have their use. They are inevitable. But we should have no illusions as to their fate. Above all, we should not fool ourselves as to the transformative value of force—of the blind force of fanaticized crowds.

In certain circumstances acts of violence can be precious: when they complete the work already accomplished by the revolution in mentalities. And it's a right, a right that sometimes becomes a duty, to rebel by force against the crushing weight of authoritarian institutions. But to deduce from this that the Terror is panacea is a lamentable error in reasoning.

To think that through disordered shake-ups and with the savage energy of worker cohorts we can abolish a power, establish a bit of harmony, is infantile.

To imagine the ideal actor in the form of an individual quick with the fist—or the gun—is naive.

In order to act fruitfully—in whatever way—it is indispensable to know how to reflect, calculate, appreciate an action, to know how to accomplish it with a vigorous hand. The actor—the individual whose revolt, violent or not, is a factor in progress—must be a strong personality, conscious, clear-headed and proud, not clouded with hatred or illusions.

To think that impulsive, defective, ignorant crowds will do away with the morbid illogic of capitalist society is a vulgar illusion. It is precisely the defects of these crowds that must be destroyed so that life can be ample and good for all. Bestial violence, hatred, the sheep-like spirit of leaders, the credulity of the crowds, these are what must be wiped out in order to transform society. Improving individuals, purifying them, making them strong, making them ardently love and desire life, making them capable of salutary revolts: these are the only results that matter. There is no salvation outside the renewal of man!

The Individualist and Society (1911)*

The word society is synonymous with a group. Today most men constitute an immense grouping that, though subdivided into an infinite number of sub-groups (races, nationalities, social classes, ideological groups) can nevertheless be considered as a whole. It is this whole, this formidable collectivity that we designate with the word society.

To consider society as an assemblage of individuals and to deny this any importance, as some do, is simplistic, too simplistic. It means failing to understand social psychology, the psychology of crowds and, what is most surprising, the results of the most elementary observations. In truth, observation shows us and study confirms that from the fact that they find themselves brought together through interests, aspirations, or shared heredity, men are modified. A new psychology is created, common to all the members of the association. From this point they constitute a crowd, and that crowd has a mentality, a life, a destiny distinct from the individuals that compose it.

The existence of a society is thus ruled by laws as immutable as those of biology that rule the existence of individuals.

Let us now pose the question: are these laws favorable to the individual? Are they in harmony with his instincts?

In a excellent little *"Précis de Sociologie"* M. G. Palante wrote: "A society, once formed, tends to maintain itself," by virtue of which, "in all domains—economic, political, legal, moral—individual energies will be narrowly subordinated to common utility. Woe on those energies that do not bow before that discipline. Society breaks or eliminates them with neither haste nor pity. It brings the most absolute contempt of the individual to this execution. It acts like a blind instinct, irresistible and implacable. In a terribly concrete form it represents that brutal force that Schopenhauer described: 'The will to life separated from the intellect.'

"Despite all the optimistic utopias, every society is and will be exploitative, dominating, and tyrannical. It is so not by accident, but by essence."

---

* From *l'anarchie*, No. 323, June 15, 1911.

This is even more the case because we feel the "general law of social preservation," admitted by almost all contemporary sociologists, weighing painfully upon our shoulders.

And if we add the "law of social conformity, which consists in every organized society demanding of its members a certain similarity of conduct, appearance, and even of opinions and ideas," and which "consequently brings with it a law of the elimination of individuals rebellious to this conformism," the conflict between the individual and society appears to us to its full extent.

A glance around us strikingly confirms the conclusion that we arrived at theoretically.

What is more iniquitous in fact than the so-called social contract, in the name of which each is crushed by all? You will be a worker, you will be a soldier, you will be a prostitute, for social necessities demand this, and because a contract that no one will ever asked you to agree to forces you be so. You will obey the law, you will be tradition's servant; you will live according to usage and custom. And yet tradition, law, and usage restrict you, hinder your development, make you suffer. Obey, bow, abdicate, otherwise your neighbors will condemn and pursue you. Public opinion will deride you and will call for the worst punishments for your insolence; the law will attack you. Starved, defamed, cursed, dishonored you will be the rebel who they implacably strangle.

Such is the reality. "I" have neither fatherland, nor money nor property to defend. What difference do my interests make to society? It needs soldiers, and so it imposes on me the fatherland, the barracks, a uniform …

"I" am no longer the dupe of the outdated morality that rules the life of the crowd. I aspire to love freely. But the social body needs loves that are respectful of the law, and if I don't marry before the mayor the law and opinion reserve their rigors for me.

I love work. But I want to do it freely. The wage system presents me with the alternative of being a slave, a thief, or of dying of hunger.

And we shouldn't condemn one form of social organization— authoritarian capitalism—more than other. To be sure, it isn't difficult to conceive of a society incomparably less bad, more logical, more intelligently organized. But aside from the fact that its more or less distant realization is an arguable hypothesis, we shouldn't hide from ourselves that it will always present serious obstacles to the development of the individual.

The hypothesis of a collectivist tomorrow presages a ferocious struggle between the state and the few individualities desirous of preserving their autonomy. Even understood in the broadest sense—that of our anarcho-communist friends—a social grouping will inevitably tend to impose one ideological credo on its members. There will still be the struggle between the individual and society, but instead of disputing his liberty and his material life it will dispute his intellectual and moral independence. And nothing says that for the men of the future—if that future is ever realized—the course of that struggle will not be every bit as painful as the fight for bread, love, and fresh air is today!

In every social grouping the individualist will remain a rebel.

Just because we take note of the antagonism between the individual and society we shouldn't be thought to be unsociable. Yet on several occasions adversaries have sought to create that confusion.

Life in society has advantages that none among us would think of contesting. But as egoists, desirous of living in accordance with our ideas, we don't want to accept even the unavoidable inconveniences. This is one of the characteristic traits of an individualist: "He doesn't resign himself, even to what is fated."

If by a sociable individual we mean he who doesn't disturb his neighbor—or disturbs as little as possible — the individualist is the soul of sociability. Above all, this is the case through interest: to disturb more often than not opens one to being disturbed. He thus lets others live as they wish, as long as they grant him the same right. He doesn't ignore the advantages of "association freely consented to," a temporary association of good wills, with a practical goal in mind. But he doesn't want to be the dupe of the idol of solidarity and allow himself to be absorbed by a coterie, a chapel, or a sect.

If he is strong—and we think that it is impossible to affirm yourself without being strong—he is even more sociable.

The strong are generous, being rich enough to be generous: the most energetic rebels, the most indomitable enemies of society have always been big-hearted.

Epilogue
May 1968

More than half a century passed between the end of the Bonnot Gang and the final manifestation of the Great Anger in May 1968. In the interim there were moments of rage, such as the anti-military movements of the beginning of World War I, not to mention the actual mutinies in the trenches, but mass working class movements led by the Socialists and Communists ruled the field now. There were still individual voices striving to be heard, some of whom had been in existence during the anarchist movement's heyday, men such as Emile Armand, Manuel Devaldes, and André Lorulot, author of the pamphlet "Men Disgust Me," but they had been almost completely marginalized.

The people's demands were now canalized, and even events such as the strike wave of May-June 1936 were, for all their verve, held in check by the Communists, whose leader Maurice Thorez famously said at the height of the wave: "You have to know when to end a strike." And so it was to continue for the next thirty years—through the Occupation, the post-war reconstruction, the colonial wars in Indochina and Algeria—with popular demands limited or controlled by their leadership.

Until 1968.

The events of May 1968 took the entire organized political class by surprise, though it had been fermenting for some time. The first harbinger of the May events occurred in February of that year, when the Minister of Culture, André Malraux, fired the founder and director of the Cinémathèque Française, Henri Langlois. Petitions, demonstrations, and riots followed, with the entire film world lining up to support Langlois. In films of the demonstrations, alongside filmmakers François Truffaut and Jean-Luc Godard, it is impossible to miss the presence of Daniel Cohn-Bendit, the future Danny the Red, who would come to symbolize May 1968. A month later Cohn-Bendit led the occupation of the university at Nanterre by the

Mouvement du 22 Mars. On May 3, 1968 the explosion occurred, and in the days and weeks that followed, the universities were occupied, factories were closed, barricades went up, a general strike launched, accords were signed and, in the end, Gaullist power was reinforced.

The uprising was unlike anything that had ever occurred. Economic demands were not the fuse, and a simple restructuring of the existing society was not the goal. All of society's relations, from economic to social to educational to sexual had to be changed. The slogans and graffiti of the events said it all: "Be realistic; demand the impossible," "In a society that abolishes adventure, the only adventure possible is the abolition of that society," "Politics happen on the streets," "Religion is the ultimate fraud," "Man's emancipation will be total or it will not be at all," and most poignant, "It is forbidden to forbid." Great anger and great hope illuminated this struggle.

The French left was as unprepared for the events as the rest of the country and did little to help things along. Aside from the Trotskyists of the *Jeunesse Communiste Révolutionnaire*, the Communist, Maoist and the other sections of the Trotskyist left saw May '68 as a spontaneous petit-bourgeois outburst that was unworthy of their support. The only real revolutionary force could be the workers, but when the workers finally joined in, thanks to efforts of the Communist Party the fight turned from one for a new France to one for higher wages. The Grenelle Accords, granting wage hikes, sounded the death knell of the revolution, and thus also of the Great Anger

The spontaneity of the events, the ad hoc nature of the organizations it gave birth to, its failure to overthrow the old order, opened the way for a return to the classical means of struggle. Students going to the countryside or to the factories were hardly examples of the imagination in power. The Great Anger was over. Classical schemas and doctrinal hairsplitting returned in force, and within a couple of years even this marginal movement had petered out. The Mitterand years succeeded in destroying the left as a viable alternative.

But nothing can tarnish the beauty of May '68. And again it is a slogan of the period that speaks most eloquently: *Nous sommes tous des juifs allemands,* "We are all German Jews." Hundreds of thousands of demonstrators marched throughout France chanting this slogan in defense of Daniel Cohn-Bendit, who had been derided by the Communists, among others, as a "German anarchist." Hundreds of thousands of people proclaimed their solidarity with a foreigner, a revolutionary; hundreds of thousands of people proclaimed their status as outsiders to French society. Even more, hundreds of thousands of French men and women proclaimed that they weren't French. For a brief moment, the Great Anger had again triumphed.

It's Only a Beginning
We Continue the Combat*

It's necessary that all those resolved to pursue the combat begun by the workers band together so that real revolutionary unity be brought about, with the goal of overthrowing the current regime, of destroying the current system in order to construct a society from which all forms of oppression will be absent.

WORKERS, CONTINUE TO OCCUPY YOUR WORKPLACES

The fight goes on in you factories. Peacefully hold your bosses hostage. Doing so will mean that many fewer enemies outside; and if it is possible have your company function for you and in relation to the movement so that it can lend it assistance in accordance with your means.

LONG LIVE DIRECT MANAGEMENT, REVOLUTIONARY ARM OF THE WORKERS IN COMBAT.

IT IS NOW THAT WAR MUST BE DECLARED ON THE INSTITUTIONS.

IT IS NOW THAT WE MUST REFUSE EVERY PARLIAMENTARY AND UNION MANEUVER AIMED AT MISREPRESENTING THE STRUGGLE WE ARE CARRYING OUT.

– WORKER-STUDENT ACTION COMMITTEE

---

* From May 1968 Archive, Simon Fraser University.

Address to All Workers[*]

Comrades,

What we have already done in France is haunting Europe and will soon be threatening all the ruling classes of the world, from the bureaucracies of Moscow and Peking to the billionaires of Washington and Tokyo. In the same way that we made Paris dance, the international proletariat will return to the attack on the capitols of all states, on all the citadels of alienation. The occupation of factories and public buildings in all countries has not only blocked the functioning of the economy; even more it has brought in its train a general questioning of society. A profound movement is making almost all sectors of the population to want to change life. What we now have is a revolutionary movement; all that is lacking in order to truly take possession of this revolution is *the consciousness of what it has already done.*

Which forces are going to try to save capitalism? The regime must fall unless it attempts to maintain itself by the threat of having recourse to arms (together with a hypothetical recourse to elections, which can only take place after the capitulation of the movement) or even by immediate armed repression. As for an eventual power on the part of the left, it too will attempt to defend the old world by concessions or by force. The so-called Communist Party, the party of Stalinist bureaucrats, which only began to envision the fall of Gaullism from the moment it saw itself incapable of any longer being its principal protection, will in this case be the best of this "popular government." Such a transitional government will only be a form of "Kerenskyism" if the Stalinists are defeated. This will essentially depend on the consciousness and autonomous organizational capacities of the workers. Those who have already rejected the trivial agreements that filled the union leaderships with joy have yet to discover that they can't "obtain" much more within the framework of the existing economy, but that they can take everything by transforming all its foundations for their own profit. The bosses cannot pay more, but they can disappear.

The current movement has not "politicized" itself by going beyond pitiful union demands on salaries and retirement pensions, abusively

---

[*] From May 1968 Archive, Simon Fraser University; written May 31,1968 signed for the "Comité Enragés-Internationale Situationniste," Paris.

represented as "social questions." It is already beyond *politics:* it poses *the social question* in its starkest form. The revolution in preparation for more than a century is returning to us; it can only assert itself in its own forms. It is already too late for a bureaucratic-revolutionary re-plastering. When an Andre Barjonet*, freshly de-Stalinized, calls for the formation of a common organization that will bring together "all those authentic forces of the revolution who claim to represent Trotsky" we need simply recall that those who claim to represent Trotsky or Mao today, not to mention the pitiful *Federation Anarchiste,* have nothing to do with the current revolution. The bureaucrats can now change their opinion of what they call "authentically revolutionary," but the authentic revolution has no need to change the judgment it passed on bureaucracy.

At the current moment, with the power they hold, and with the parties and unions we know, the workers have no other road than that of directly taking in hand both the economy and all aspects of the reconstruction of social life through unitary base committees, affirming their autonomy *vis-à-vis* any politico-union leadership, ensuring their self-defense, and forming federations at the regional and national levels. In following this road they shall become the sole real power in the country, the power of workers' councils. Failing in this, because it "is revolutionary or it is nothing," the proletariat will again become a passive object. It will return to its place in front of the TV.

What defines the power of the councils? The dissolving of any external power, direct and total democracy, the unification in practice of decisions and execution, the abolition of hierarchy and independent specializations, the conscious management and transformation of all conditions of liberated life, the permanent creative participation of the masses, and internationalist extension and coordination. The demands of the current moment are no less than this. Self-management is nothing less. *Be on guard against the recuperators* of all modernist nuances—even priests—who are starting to talk about self-management, if not of workers' councils, without admitting this *minimum.* They do so because, in fact, they want to save their bureaucratic functions, the privileges of their intellectual specializations, and their future as big shots!

In reality, what is needed now has been needed since the beginning of the proletarian revolutionary project. It is a matter of the autonomy of

---

* Economist for the Communist-led CGT.

the working class. We have fought for the abolition of the wage system, of bourgeois production, the state. It is now a matter of acceding to conscious history, of suppressing all separations and "all that exists independently of individuals." The proletarian revolution has sketched out its proper forms in the councils, in St Petersburg in 1905 as in Turin in 1920, in Catalonia in 1936 as in Budapest in 1956. The maintaining of the old society, or the formation of new exploiting classes, has in every case passed through the suppression of the councils. The working class now knows its enemies and the methods of action that are its own. "The revolutionary organization has had to learn that it can no longer *combat alienation through alienated forms*" (*La Societé du Spectacle*). The workers' councils are manifestly the only solution, since all the others forms of revolutionary struggle have ended in the opposite of what they wanted.

Paris, May 31, 1968
Comité Enragés-Internationale Situationniste
Council for the Maintaining of the Occupations